TRANSPORTATION LABOR ISSUES AND REGULATORY REFORM

RESEARCH IN TRANSPORTATION ECONOMICS

Series Editor: Martin Dresner

Recent Volumes:

Volumes 1–6:	Research in Transportation Economics – Edited by B. Starr McMullen
Volume 7:	Railroad Bankruptcies and Mergers from Chicago West 1975–2001: Financial Analysis and Regulatory Critique – Michael Conant
Volume 8:	Economic Impacts of Intelligent Transportation Systems: Innovations and Case Studies – Evangelos Bekiaris & Yuko Nakanishi
Volume 9:	Road Pricing: Theory and Evidence – Georgina Santos

RESEARCH IN TRANSPORTATION ECONOMICS VOLUME 10

TRANSPORTATION LABOR ISSUES AND REGULATORY REFORM

EDITED BY

JAMES PEOPLES

University of Wisconsin-Milwaukee, USA

WAYNE K. TALLEY

Old Dominion University, Virginia, USA

2004

ELSEVIER

JAI

Amsterdam – Boston – Heidelberg – London – New York – Oxford
Paris – San Diego – San Francisco – Singapore – Sydney – Tokyo

ELSEVIER B.V.
Sara Burgerhartstraat 25
P.O. Box 211
1000 AE Amsterdam
The Netherlands

ELSEVIER Inc.
525 B Street, Suite 1900
San Diego
CA 92101-4495
USA

ELSEVIER Ltd
The Boulevard, Langford
Lane, Kidlington
Oxford OX5 1GB
UK

ELSEVIER Ltd
84 Theobalds Road
London
WC1X 8RR
UK

First edition 2004

Library of Congress Cataloging in Publication Data
A catalog record is available from the Library of Congress.

British Library Cataloguing in Publication Data
A catalogue record is available from the British Library.

ISBN: 0-7623-0891-5
ISSN: 0739-8859 (Series)

♾ The paper used in this publication meets the requirements of ANSI/NISO Z39.48-1992 (Permanence of Paper). Printed in The Netherlands.

CONTENTS

LIST OF CONTRIBUTORS

Jonathan R. Anderson	University of Kentucky, Kentucky, USA
Dale L. Belman	Michigan State University, Michigan, USA
Michael H. Belzer	Wayne State University, Michigan, USA
John D. Bitzan	North Dakota State University, North Dakota, USA
Stephen V. Burks	University of Minnesota-Morris, USA
Frederick Guy	Birkbeck, University of London, UK
Nancy Brown Johnson	University of Kentucky, Kentucky, USA
Benjamin Maxwell	University of Minnesota-Morris, USA
Kristen A. Monaco	California State University, California, USA
James Peoples	University of Wisconsin-Milwaukee, Wisconsin, USA
Daniel P. Rich	Illinois State University, Illinois, USA
Martha Rocha	University of North Carolina, Chapel Hill, North Carolina, USA
Daniel A. Rodríguez	University of North Carolina, Chapel Hill, North Carolina, USA
Ian Savage	Northwestern University, Illinois, USA
Wayne K. Talley	Old Dominion University, Virginia, USA

1. INTRODUCTION AND OVERVIEW

James Peoples and Wayne K. Talley

Strong national economies are heavily dependent on the movement of goods in a timely and efficient fashion. Securing low shipping rates for high quality transportation service contributes to the competitiveness of shippers, which further adds to the growth of economies. Arguably, the significance of transportation service to successful U.S. business operations provided the rationale for regulating transportation industries during the early twentieth century.[1] Entry regulation restricted intra-industry competition in rail, trucking, airlines and maritime shipping, while regulatory agencies set rates along domestic routes. Such economic regulation had the unintended effect of changing labor markets in transportation industries. Artificial barriers to entry created labor markets that were relatively easy to organize. The general ease of passing costs on to shipping customers contributed to industry unions negotiating high wages for transportation workers.

Past research on economic regulation and labor markets in U.S. transportation industries reveal that prior to deregulation rail, trucking, airlines and maritime shipping workforces were heavily unionized and these workers received high wage payments. For instance, unions represented almost all nonmangement workers in the U.S. railroad industry before the easing of rate and entry regulation in this industry (MacDonald & Cavalluzzo, 1996). Rail unions took advantage of work rules defining a work day based on mileage covered as an approach for negotiating high wage levels (Talley & Schwarz-Miller, 1998). Trucking regulation in the U.S. contributed to the International Brotherhood of Teamster organizing 80% of intercity carriage following regulation to an almost complete absence of union drivers prior to the enactment of this policy (Perry, 1986). Union drivers enjoyed wage premiums of over 50% during this period of high membership rates

Transportation Labor Issues and Regulatory Reform
Research in Transportation Economics, Volume 10, 1–9

ISSN: 0739-8859/doi:10.1016/S0739-8859(04)10001-2

(Hirsch, 1988; Rose, 1987). Airline union membership in the U.S. also reached high levels following regulation of this industry in the late 1930s. By 1973, 46% of the industry was organized compared to a 23% unionization rate for the U.S. workforce (Peoples, 1998). Compared to nonairline workers with comparable job responsibilities, airline workers enjoyed industry wage premiums ranging from 20 to 30% during this period of restricted entry and rate regulation (Saunders, 1998). Last, in the U.S. maritime, shipping was heavily organized following economic regulation in the early part of the twentieth century. The International Longshore and Warehouse Union (ILWU), the International Longshoremen's Association and the Teamsters represented the majority of nonmanagement workers in this industry. These unions were generally able to negotiate high wages, although by the late 1960s members were highly susceptible to job displacement from labor-saving technology (Talley, 2002).

Deregulation in the late 1970s and early 1980s vastly transformed the labor market for U.S. transportation workers. Most research in this area focuses on the effect of deregulation on the earnings of nonmanagement company workers in airlines, trucking, rail and maritime shipping. Their findings do not suggest a consistent wage pattern following deregulation. For instance, union rail workers sustained their high wage levels following rail deregulation (Talley & Schwarz-Miller, 1998). Union premiums for truck drivers fell a nontrivial 40% following deregulation in this industry (Rose, 1987). In contrast, airline premiums only fell ten percentage points after airline deregulation (Card, 1998; Hirsch & Macpherson, 2000). Wages of union longshoremen actually increased more than 14% following shipping deregulation.

Deregulation of transportation industries, though, has had a broader effect on workers. Such policy change also influences employees' hours worked per week, working conditions, worker safety, and a host of other labor issues. Deregulation might also influence the earnings of managers and self-employed workers in transportation industries. Examining these issues is valuable in part because such analysis provides a more complete assessment of labor market changes following the shift to a more market-oriented business environment. For instance, while the lack of wage erosion might not suggest reduced labor negotiation strength of rail, airlines and maritime shipping unions, transportation workers might face harsher working conditions and a greater threat of unemployment. Examining earnings of managers and self-employed workers helps reveal if this group of employees also benefited from regulation and if stepped-up competition severely limits their ability to attain high earnings, especially since they are prohibited from benefiting from collective bargaining. Examining earnings of truck owner-operators helps in understanding whether this group of entrepreneurs benefits from a competitive labor market that rewards low cost and efficient service providers.

This volume adds to the debate on deregulation's influence on transportation labor markets in the U.S. by presenting empirical evidence on an array of labor market outcomes in this industry. Contributions to this volume are categorized by their analysis of worker safety, working conditions and employment opportunities, and by their analysis on managerial and self-employed earnings.

WORKER SAFETY, WORKING CONDITIONS AND EMPLOYMENT

Topics on nonwage labor issues are initially presented, beginning with Ian Savage's chapter that examines worker injury rates in transportation industries following deregulation. The significance of his study is highlighted by the heightened attention directed at air transportation service during the beginning of this century. The perception of greater risk associated with this mode of travel also suggests greater risk for aircraft crews, since the primary job duties of these workers require operating the aircraft during flights. Savage indicates that greater financial pressures following deregulation might be a possible source of increased risk. For instance, amid stepped-up competition in this industry, cost saving incentives might influence management's approach toward the frequency with which they fly older aircraft, and the extent to which older craft are maintained. Furthermore, carrier investment in complete insurance coverage might lead to the type of moral hazard problem where fully insured carriers have less incentive to invest in safety enhancing activities. Savage also observes that following airline deregulation technological improvements contributed to safer working conditions.

Safety concerns following deregulation were not limited to airlines as economic deregulation might also have compromised truck driver safety. Following deregulation the employment of hundreds of thousands of truck owner-operators and drivers in small-unregulated carriers made it more difficult to monitor drivers in this sector. In addition, cost-saving pressures present the incentive for drivers to violate safety rules. Savage argues that truck drivers were likely to avoid greater safety risk in part due to improved automotive technology and more stringent safety regulations. He also maintains that government safety regulation and greater expenditure on maintenance created a safer working environment for rail workers following deregulation in the railroad industry.

Savage empirically examines deregulation's effect on worker safety by comparing injury rates among transportation and manufacturing industries. He finds that the post-deregulation renaissance in rail led to a nontrivial improvement in worker injury rates. While raw data suggests an appreciable increase in injury rates in the airlines industry by the late 1990s, Savage reveals that this increase is due almost exclusively to a change in the categorizing of airline injuries to include injuries of 300,000 additional workers who were previously classified as trucking employees. He finds that deregulation is not associated with a change in airline or trucking injury rates when correcting for the industry reclassification of trucking employees. The results from this chapter support the notion that during enhanced competition, safety outcomes have not worsened. Savage shows that improved technology and strict safety regulation have contributed to this safety result. Succeeding chapters in this section build on Savage's findings by examining other determinants and measures of working conditions in the transportation industry.

Following Savage's chapter, the chapter by Daniel A. Rodriguez, Marta Rocha and Michael Belzer examines the effect of trucking carriers' financial performance and worker compensation payments on driver safety. These authors argue that deregulation should have a greater effect on the safety performance of carriers with poor financial performance records. These firms may likely operate using old fleets, paying low wages to workers, and presenting incentives for drivers to work longer hours. Rodriguez, Rocha and Belzer report that such approaches to cost-cutting are associated with poor safety performances. The authors use a negative binomial estimation technique that allows them to take advantage of firm-level data when testing their hypothesis on carrier safety performance. The findings indicate that for small trucking carriers, high liquidity is associated with better safety performance. They also report that small firms that devote a larger share of their revenue to labor expenses tend to have better safety records than small firms providing less lucrative compensation packages to their drivers. Rodriguez, Rocha and Belzer interpret these findings as suggesting that small trucking carriers are particularly sensitive to competition, and that this group of carriers relies on the performance of drivers with relatively high human capital as an approach for addressing safety challenges in this industry.

Chapter 4 by Kristen A. Monaco and Dale L. Belman presents further evidence on the working conditions of truck drivers following deregulation. These authors focus on the influence of information technology on the working lives of truck drivers. This research takes advantage of a unique and richly detailed survey of truck drivers to investigate the relationship between information technologies and the productivity, hours of work and wages of truck drivers. Initially, Monaco and Belman provide an overview of the work and work life of truck drivers. The balance of the chapter presents a cross-sectional study of the effects of technology on earnings, productivity and working conditions. The authors find that although most dash-board truck technologies have little systematic influence on driver earnings or work, satellite communication systems increase drivers' annual earnings through improved efficiency and work intensification.

Analysis of deregulation's influence on airline employment, productivity and working conditions are presented by Nancy Brown-Johnson and Jonathan R. Anderson in Chapter 5. They argue that airline carriers responded to the need to lower costs following deregulation by employing a larger share of part-time workers, increasing the workload of airline employees, and increasing the hours these employees work per week. The authors also suggest that the increased workload pressures that airline employees experienced helps explain why the industry's safety performance did not improve following deregulation. Brown-Johnson and Anderson find that the adoption of the hub and spoke distribution system contributed to increased industry productivity by allowing carriers to increase employment at a slower rate than the increase in airline passengers. Despite the introduction of this labor saving technique, employment still increased by 200,000 workers from the late 1970s to 2002. Flight attendants and pilots experienced significant employment gains. In contrast, Brown-Johnson and Anderson find that the employment of mechanics was largely unaffected by deregulation. They observe that the recent trend toward subcontracting shifted mechanic employment from work performed in-house to work outsourced to other companies. This chapter also reveals that employment of part-time workers contributed significantly to the impressive job growth in this industry. Such an employment pattern is notable, in part, because part-time workers are less likely to receive employee financed health coverage and pensions. Not receiving these types of benefits is even more important to airline employees – given Brown-Johnson and Anderson's findings that enhanced productivity has been achieved at a cost of a less healthy work environment.

Chapters 2–5 reveal the significance of productivity as a determinant of labor market outcomes in transportation industries. In Chapter 6, Daniel P. Rich explains patterns of productivity growth and the sources of technical change in rail, trucking, airlines and water transportation. He notes that deregulation's promotion of market competition has helped create a business environment encouraging technological progress as a means to enhance productivity and lower unit production costs. The introduction of new technologies also influences the labor market by redistributing employment opportunities across occupations. For instance, emerging technologies can lead to job-displacement of workers with substitutable job responsibilities or enhance the opportunity of employment of complements for specific occupations. Hence, as Brown-Johnson and Anderson observed in the previous chapter, the introduction of the hub and spoke system and the adoption of new aircraft technologies possibly have an asymmetric effect on employment across occupations. Rich's chapter presents an additional analysis of technology's uneven employment effects on transportation workers by including an analysis of rail, trucking and water transportation employment patterns.

Previous researchers have observed that the introduction of microwave radio communications eliminated the need for caboose conductors and rear-end brakemen. Computer automation of rail yards changed the industry greatly, reducing the need for traditional types of personnel such as switchtenders, switchmen and yard locomotive engineers (Rich, 1986). In trucking, the use of microwave radio communications by advanced truck load firms (ATLFs) has contributed to a declining demand for owner-operator drivers. In water transportation, containerization of shipping operations dramatically reduced demand for dockworkers. Rich's chapter confirms that deregulation and technological advances have contributed to productivity growth that is nonneutral across occupations. He also observes that the introduction of labor-saving technologies creates a challenge for unions maintaining their membership levels following deregulation.

MANAGERIAL EARNINGS AND EARNINGS OF SELF-EMPLOYED WORKERS

Chapters 7–9 address deregulation's effect on the earnings of managers or the earnings of self-employed workers in transportation industries. These two groups of workers may not have been beneficiaries of regulation in part because they are prohibited from joining unions. Transportation union control over the labor supply prior to deregulation provided the unions with the advantage to negotiate high wages for their members. Compared to nonmanagement company workers, managers and self-employed workers then faced greater challenges sharing regulatory rent. Salary gains of transportation CEOs were possibly limited by political constraints. Self-employed workers, such as owner-operator truck drivers, were generally limited to less lucrative job assignments than those provided to union company drivers.

Chapter 7 by Stephen V. Burks, Frederick Guy, and Benjamin Maxwell examines the effect of deregulation on trucking CEOs. These authors test the predictions on CEO earnings patterns derived from principal-agent theory and the political constraint model. Within the principal-agency framework, owners pay CEOs higher salaries based on the performance of the firm. Salaries should be more sensitive to firm performance following deregulation, given the general removal of rate regulation that limited profitability in trucking. In contrast, the political constraint model suggests that CEO salaries were sensitive to performance prior to deregulation. Within this theoretical framework, CEO salaries were held artificially low due to regulators' response to public discontent over high CEO salaries. CEO salaries, though, can still vary based on firm performance, since performance indicators, such as productivity gains, are viewed as justification for higher salaries. Pay for performance standards would still apply following deregulation. Burks, Guy and Maxwell find evidence consistent with the political constraint model. They report that pay for performance is an important determinant of CEO salary levels, and the returns from enhanced performance did not change significantly, following deregulation. These authors also find that CEOs receive a premium when employed at union firms. CEO pay is also higher when firms switch from a union to nonunion workforce.

Examination of CEO compensation is significant, in part, because CEOs set the agenda for attaining the performance goals of the firm. CEOs, though, represent only a small percentage of managers. Low- to mid-level managers constitute the bulk of employees in this occupation. These managers are generally responsible for making the daily operating decisions that affect the performance of the firm. Despite the significance of low- to mid-level managers in the decision process, there is a dearth of research examining the determinants of pay for this group of transportation employees. John D. Bitzan's chapter contributes to the literature by examining the effect of deregulation on the earnings of low- to mid-level mangers in rail, trucking and airline industries. Bitzan argues that low- to mid-level managers might not have received high pre-deregulation earnings, because regulatory constraints on a firm's financial performance prevent the need for owners to employ high quality managers. Managerial quality, as measured by human capital investment should become a key earnings determinant following deregulation. Bitzan also notes that pay for performance could be a more significant managerial earnings determinant following deregulation, since pay incentives might be needed to compensate managers with unobserved characteristics that command high earnings. Using an Oaxaca decomposition technique, Bitzan finds that managerial quality and the returns to managerial quality generally increase following deregulation in transportation industries. Earnings findings on rail managers reveal higher returns on performance following deregulation.

Beneficiaries of deregulation are not limited to highly qualified managers, as demand for low-cost transportation alternatives should enhance employment opportunities for owner-operator truck drivers. The last chapter in this volume, by James Peoples and Wayne K. Talley, examines this issue by observing the effect of maritime shipping deregulation on the earnings and employment of port-city owner-operators. In this chapter, Peoples and Talley observe that shipping deregulation stimulated container cargo growth at port cities. Owner-operators are especially likely to benefit from ocean transportation deregulation, since these workers depict the low-cost alternative to other types of truck drivers. Economic theory suggests that the market wage rate for owner-operators will increase given the rise in the demand for their services, all else equal. However, earnings gains are not a guarantee given the negotiation advantage of large shipping lines.

Findings from this chapter reveal that the wages of port-city owner-operators have increased relative to other owner-operators following shipping deregulation. These findings are unique to the post-shipping deregulation period as earnings of both port-city and other operators declined for the 1979–1983 period versus those for the regulation period. Employment results support the notion that increased demand for owner-operators at port cities possibly contributed to higher earnings.

ASSESSMENT OF LABOR MARKET CHANGES FOLLOWING TRANSPORTATION DEREGULATION

An assessment of the findings presented in this volume suggests that transportation deregulation has had a profound effect on transportation working conditions by creating a business environment that emphasizes efficiency gains and cost-saving. Enhanced job pressures associated with this new environment challenge the maintenance of safe working conditions. Contributors to this volume reveal that technological advancements and strict safety regulations have helped to avoid an increase in industry injury rates. Safety findings for the trucking industry also identify poorly performing small carriers as the type of firms that safety regulators should identify as safety risks. Hence, policies that promote investment incentives and support continued enforcement of safety regulations are potential approaches for addressing an increasingly important post-deregulation labor issue such as workers' safety.

Findings on compensation of managers and employment of owner-operator truck drivers indicate that these workers are beneficiaries of stepped-up competition following deregulation. The gains experienced by these workers may create greater work pressures for other transportation workers. For instance, the significance of pay for performance for low- to mid-level rail managers could result in these managers demanding enhanced efficiency from workers. Employment gains of owner-operator drivers place downward pressure on the earnings growth of high-wage company drivers. In sum, these insights on labor market outcomes in transportation industries indicate the potential challenges and rewards that workers face in an increasingly competitive business environment.

NOTE

1. Capture theory presents an alternative rationale for regulation. This theory indicates that regulation is a pro-producer policy that is provided in response to industries demand for

such policy change. Alternatively, economic theory of regulation suggests that regulation is not necessarily pro-producer. Rather, powerful interest groups heavily influence which industries receive regulation.

REFERENCES

Card, D. (1998). Deregulation and labor earnings in the airline industry. In: J. Peoples (Ed.), *Regulatory Reform and Labor Markets* (pp. 183–230). Boston, MA: Kluwer Academic Publishers.

Hirsch, B. (1988). Trucking regulation, unionization, and labor earnings: 1973–1985. *Journal of Human Resources*, *23*, 296–319.

Hirsch, B., & Macpherson, D. A. (2000). Earnings, rents, and competition in the airline labor market. *Journal of Labor Economics*, *18*, 125–155.

MacDonald, J., & Cavalluzzo, L. (1996). Railroad deregulation: Pricing behavior, shipper responses and the effects on labor. *Industrial and Labor Relations Review*, *50*, 80–91.

Peoples, J. (1998). Deregulation and the labor market. *Journal of Economic Perspectives*, *12*, 111–130.

Perry, C. (1986). *Deregulation and the decline of the unionized trucking industry.* Philadelphia, PA: Wharton School's Industrial Research Unit.

Rich, S. M. (1986). Changing railway technology in the United States and its impact upon railroad employment since 1945. *Transportation Journal*, *25*, 55–65.

Rose, N. (1987). Labor rent-sharing and regulation: Evidence from the trucking industry. *Journal of Political Economy*, *95*, 1146–1178.

Saunders, L. (1998). Commentary on deregulation and labor earnings in the airline industry. In: J. Peoples (Ed.), *Regulatory Reform and Labor Markets* (pp. 231–248). Boston, MA: Kluwer Academic Publishers.

Talley, W. K. (2002). Dockworker earnings, containerization and shipping deregulation. *Journal of Transport Economics and Policy*, *36*, 447–467.

Talley, W. K., & Schwarz-Miller, A. (1998). Railroad deregulation and union labor earnings. In: J. Peoples (Ed.), *Regulatory Reform and Labor Markets* (pp. 125–154). Boston, MA: Kluwer Academic Publishers.

2. TRENDS IN TRANSPORTATION EMPLOYEE INJURIES SINCE ECONOMIC DEREGULATION

Ian Savage

ABSTRACT

This chapter investigates whether economic deregulation affected the rate of workplace injuries in the railroad, trucking and commercial aviation industries. Bureau of Labor Statistics data for the period 1973–2001 are used to compare these three industries with the trend for comparable occupations in manufacturing. The railroad industry witnessed declining workplace safety in the years prior to deregulation. The subsequent financial renaissance of the industry led to a very notable improvement. In contrast, employee injury rates in trucking and aviation have remained very stable over the past thirty years, and there is no evidence of any effects associated with deregulation.

INTRODUCTION

Most of the research on the linkage between economic deregulation and transportation safety has analyzed changes in the rate of crashes. While employees are killed and injured in these crashes, the vast majority of employee injuries occur in less spectacular circumstances. Government data for the year 2000, shown in Table 1, suggests that fewer than one in nine employee injuries and illnesses in railroads and trucking, and one in 25 in commercial aviation, are due

Transportation Labor Issues and Regulatory Reform
Research in Transportation Economics, Volume 10, 11–33

ISSN: 0739-8859/doi:10.1016/S0739-8859(04)10002-4

Table 1. Causes of Lost Workday Injuries and Illnesses (Year 2000).

	Railroads (%)	Trucking (%)	Aviation (%)	All Private Industry (%)
Over-exertion	18	29	40	27
Contact with object	18	25	22	27
Slips and falls	22	21	16	21
Transportation accidents	12	12	4	4
Exposure to harmful substances	4	2	3	4
Repetitive motion	1	1	2	4
Assaults	1	0	1	1
Other	24	10	12	11

to a crash. Federal Railroad Administration data suggest that 85% of railroad employee injuries do not even involve a moving train. Many injuries occur during maintenance activities. At least a fifth result from slips and falls. In aviation, two fifths of workplace injuries and illnesses are due to overexertion, which includes injuries sustained while lifting objects. Consistent with the leading causal events, the majority of the injuries and illnesses sustained by employees are sprains, strains, cuts and bruises. As shown in Table 2, burns, amputations and trauma represent a very small minority of injuries. Consequently one has to look beyond crash data to determine the effects of deregulation on the safety of employees.

The only previous transportation research that used employee injury data was conducted shortly after deregulation. Viscusi (1987, 1989) analyzed trends for

Table 2. Nature of Lost Workday Injuries and Illnesses (Year 2000).

	Railroads (%)	Trucking (%)	Aviation (%)	All Private Industry (%)
Sprains and strains	57	50	53	44
Bruises	17	10	12	9
Cuts, punctures	7	6	3	9
Fractures	8	8	3	7
Other pain	0	3	9	4
Multiple trauma	0	4	2	4
Back pain	0	3	5	3
Carpal tunnel syndrome	0	1	1	2
Heat burns	0	1	0	1
Tendinitis	0	1	0	1
Amputations	1	0	0	1
Chemical burns	0	0	0	1
Other	10	14	12	16

railroads (reported in the 1987 paper only), aviation and trucking using data from 1972 (when the data was first collected) through 1985. Consequently, he had only a limited amount of data to work with. As deregulation began in 1978 for the airlines and 1980 for railroads and trucking, there was very limited before and after data, and it was not surprising that he did not find any statistically significant relationships.

The availability of 15 years more data permit more reflection on the events since deregulation. Some of the effects of deregulation may not have been apparent when Viscusi conducted his analysis in the mid-1980s. Airline deregulation was phased in over the period from 1978 to 1983; the economic downturn of the early 1980s limited the post-deregulation expansion of all three industries; and the trucking industry at the local "intrastate" level was not fully deregulated until 1995. Yet a time series analysis is still problematic because the pre-deregulation data is limited. In addition, factors unrelated to deregulation, such as changes in technology, attitudes, and public policy, may have altered workplace safety in the past quarter century. Therefore, unlike Viscusi, this paper compares the experiences of the transportation industries with a control group of comparable occupations in manufacturing.

WHY DEREGULATION MIGHT AFFECT WORKPLACE SAFETY

Why might one expect that deregulation would change workplace safety? Economic models explain that a firm's choice of workplace safety is not made in isolation. A profit-maximizing firm has to simultaneously choose product price, the wage rate offered, workplace and product safety, and other quality attributes of its product. Market changes that affect one of these variables will usually have a knock-on effect on all of the other variables. Deregulation was expected to have a major influence on the price and quality of transportation services. Consequently, it would not be surprising if workplace safety was also affected. This would be particularly the case if there is a correlation between the level of safety enjoyed by a firm's employees and the safety of the service which is sold to its customers.

For example, if regulation had limited the supply of low-quality services, then there would be a proliferation of such services after deregulation and a consequent decline in average workplace safety. There was a school of thought that the airlines had over provided quality during the period of regulation when they were constrained from competing on price. Instead, they competed by providing high service frequencies, new equipment, and in-flight frills. After deregulation, average load factors increased and in-flight amenities declined. It would not have been surprising if this decline in quality, either implicitly or explicitly, extended to safety.

Regulation of the trucking industry was marked by restrictions on entry. Moreover, a large proportion of trucking firms had unionized labor. The labor economics literature recognizes that unionization tends to increase workplace safety. Unions represent the infra-marginal worker rather than the tastes of the marginal worker who determines safety in a competitive marketplace. Infra-marginal workers tend to be older and have a lower tolerance for risk. To the extent that customers desiring lower-quality service were not well provided for under regulation, one might expect trucking deregulation to lead to the entry of lower-safety firms, and a consequent diminishing of average workplace safety.

Safety, unlike price, is difficult for consumers to observe. Customers have to form opinions regarding the safety performance of the firms that they use. Firms build a reputation for providing a certain quality of service. In all three industries, regulation limited entry and ensured the continuance of existing firms. These firms had ongoing relationships with their customers and had incentives to consider the effect on their reputation if they shaded on safety. The same is not true in a deregulated environment. Industrial organization economists describe how it is profitable for some firms to "cheat" by posing as high-quality firms and charging a premium price, whereas in reality they are low-quality firms (Klein & Leffler, 1981; Shapiro, 1982). By the time the consumers become aware of the deception, the firms have earned a profit, and can exit the industry before there is a consumer backlash. These types of firms do not worry about their long term reputation. The emergence of such "fly-by-night" firms was feared in both the trucking and airline industries.

Deregulation lowers the barriers to entry, and in all three industries it was feared that some of the new entrants would offer lower levels of safety than the market desires. Some firms would be motivated by avarice, as described in the previous paragraph, but others would suffer from pure inexperience. Safety has the characteristic that the costs, in the form of equipment and training, are incurred up front, yet the "benefits" in the form of a reduced number of crashes occur in a probabilistic fashion over the course of many years. Many new entrants may be very aware of the costs of providing safety, yet are genuinely unaware of the financial implications of crashes. To the extent that their customers cannot observe, at least in the short run, the true level of safety on offer, these firms may provide unjustifiably low safety in their initial period of operation.

Deregulation was expected to shake up the existing market structure, and remove poorly-managed firms. There is a theoretical literature that indicates that firms close to bankruptcy may also be motivated to cheat their customers by reducing safety (Bulow & Shoven, 1978). These firms can reduce expenses by cutting maintenance and training, yet can declare bankruptcy to protect against claims in the event that a major crash occurs.

All in all, every indication was that deregulation would be expected to reduce safety, especially in trucking and aviation. The symptoms were expected to be entry of firms that deliberately and openly provide low safety service, "fly-by-night" cheaters, inexperienced new entrants, and financial distress among some existing firms who are unable to adapt to the new market realities.

EMPIRICAL LITERATURE ON DEREGULATION AND SAFETY

In the mid-1980s there was a fear that the gloomy predictions were coming true. Aviation had one of its worse years for safety in 1985, and Congress had introduced considerable legislation aimed at perceived safety problems in the trucking industry. The concern led to an academic conference in 1987 that looked at many different aspects of safety after deregulation in the aviation and trucking industries (Moses & Savage, 1989). Data on the frequency of crashes was brought up to date in Savage (1999a), who also analyzed the safety performance of the railroad industry. To the extent that crashes do injure employees, and might be symptomatic of workplace safety in general, it is worthwhile to briefly describe the experience in each of the industries.

In the railroad industry, the rate of collisions and derailments started to increase in the 1960s, reversing decades of improvement. In part this was caused by the bankruptcy, or near bankruptcy, of much of the railroad system in the eastern United States which led to disinvestment in the capital stock. Comprehensive safety regulation was introduced with the Federal Railroad Safety Act of 1970 which predated deregulation by ten years. While many new regulations were developed in the early 1970s, it was only later in the decade that the government deployed an inspectorate to enforce the regulations. This coincided with economic regulatory reform. In 1976 the Railroad Revitalization and Regulatory Reform ("4R") Act exempted some commodities from price regulation and started a process by which railroads could abandon unprofitable branch lines. The Staggers Act of 1980 gave railroads greater freedom to negotiate prices with shippers of all commodities and to spin-off poorly-used secondary lines. The financial health of the industry improved considerably, especially after the Staggers Act. The railroads were able to increase maintenance expenditures and rebuild their capital stock. At the same time, more traffic was moving in "unit trains" which do not require switching. This is a safer form of operation as a disproportionate number of collisions and derailments occur during switching operations. The combination of a financial renaissance following deregulation, government safety regulations, and reduced switching led to a dramatic reversal of the upward trend in collisions and derailments. Between 1978 and the mid-1990s, the rate of collisions and derailments fell by 75%. Because these three explanatory factors are highly collinear, there has been considerable disagreement as to their relative contribution to the improvement (Savage, 1998).

The trucking industry has also seen a substantial improvement in safety in the years since the Motor Carrier Act of 1980. The number of fatal crashes involving large trucks, those with a gross vehicle weight greater than 10,000 lbs., has declined somewhat, while truck miles have more than doubled. (Data on crashes that involve only injury or property damage is less reliable, and it is difficult to draw conclusive inferences.) Much of the improvement has occurred because the roads in general are safer. Improved automotive technology, better occupant protection, better emergency medical response and changing attitudes to the use of seat belts and drink-driving have contributed to safer highways. There is evidence that the fatal crash rate for large trucks has declined at a faster rate than the average for all vehicles on the road.

This outcome was not expected at the time of deregulation, when there was a great fear that safety would diminish. There was considerable new entry, especially involving small firms with poorer than average safety records (Corsi & Fanara, 1989). Many middle-sized firms suffered from severe price competition and had to exit the market. The government responded by introducing explicit safety regulations and enhanced enforcement in the Surface Transportation Assistance Act of 1982, the Motor Carrier Safety Act of 1984 and the Commercial Motor Vehicle Safety Act of 1986. These Acts tightened vehicle standards, and introduced a coordinated national Commercial Drivers License. The new license requirements imposed uniform testing across states, and prevented drivers from holding multiple licenses as a way of avoiding the consequences of revocation in one jurisdiction. Many states had to raise driver-testing standards considerably. In addition, federal funding allowed increased enforcement through safety audits of carriers and semi-random inspections at the roadside (Moses & Savage, 1997). Enforcement was further enhanced by the Motor Carrier Safety Improvement Act of 1999 which increased funding and established a separate administration for motor carrier safety within the federal Department of Transportation.

There is evidence that the rate of improvement in safety for mainline ("Part 121") airlines in the 1960s and 1970s did not continue after the Airline Deregulation Act of 1978 (Savage, 1999b). The probable explanation is that the past quarter century has not witnessed the same technological breakthroughs as occurred in the previous quarter century when air traffic control was deployed and second generation jets displaced turboprop aircraft. One segment of the industry that has witnessed substantial improvement in recent times is commuter ("Part 135") operations. This segment expanded rapidly after deregulation as the mainline airlines moved to hub-and-spoke operating strategies. The expansion produced a technology-driven safety improvement, as increased demand led to the deployment of larger and safer aircraft. Piston-engine aircraft with fewer than twenty seats were replaced with larger turboprop aircraft, which were subsequently superceded by 50-seat or larger "regional jets." In 1997, most of this segment of the industry was brought under the same safety regulations as the mainline jet carriers.

Some critics have identified safety problems associated with deregulation. In the mid-1980s, there was concern that competitive pressures had led some airlines to cut safety expenditures, with the finger being pointed at some long-established airlines that had to file for bankruptcy. Academic research, based primarily on *pre*-deregulation data, indicated that there was a positive relationship between financial performance and safety performance for medium and smaller sized carriers (Rose, 1990). The problem with this hypothesis is that, excluding 1985, the early 1980s was also the safest period (in terms of passenger fatalities) in the history of aviation. There was also concern that new entrant carriers might be less safe than those already in the industry. Research concluded that the entrants of the early period of deregulation had similar safety records to established firms (Kanafani & Keeler, 1989). However, the same was not true for the entrants in the early to mid-1990s. The closure of the rapidly-expanding ValuJet in 1996, following a crash near Miami, garnered much publicity. This was due to revelations of significant operating and maintenance problems.

Viscusi's (1987, 1989) analysis of workplace safety looked at all three modes over the period 1972–1985. He used Bureau of Labor Statistics (BLS) data on workplace injuries and illnesses. He ran regressions on the logarithm or log-odds of three different measures of workplace safety: the rate of injuries and illnesses per 100 full-time equivalent (FTE) employees, the rate of injuries and illnesses requiring time way from work or assignment to another job, and the rate of total lost workdays (number of cases multiplied by the length of time away from regular duties). His explanatory variables include the lagged dependent variable, the change in the number of people employed in the industry and deregulation dummy variables. The deregulation variable was not statistically significant in the regressions for any of the risk measures for the airline, trucking or (in the 1987 publication only) railroad industries. The coefficients tended to be negative. Viscusi repeated the analysis, using output rather than a count of workers as the denominator of risk. Again he found no significant relationship with deregulation. Of course, the statistical power of his analysis was hampered by the limited number of observations.

INJURY DATA

The collection of the data used by both Viscusi and this analysis was mandated by the Occupational Safety and Health Act of 1970. The first full-year report was 1972 (U.S. Department of Labor, various years). Data for railroads was not reported until the following year, which will be the first year for this analysis. The most recent data available for this analysis was for 2001. The data is collected by surveys sent to about 175,000 employers under a joint federal and state program. Employers have to report various statistics on the number of occupational injuries and illnesses, and the number of employee hours worked. One of the few exceptions to this process is the railroad industry, where the data is collected by the Federal Railroad Administration, which had already been collecting data of this nature for sixty years. The BLS uses these reports to produce industry-level statistics based on Standard Industrial Classification (SIC) codes at the three- or four-digit level. Data was extracted for three transportation modes and a control group occupation:

Railroads (SIC code 40), which covers "mainline" railroads and excludes mass transit systems other than commuter railroads. The data cover not only the large "class I" railroads but also the smaller "class II" and "class III" railroads.

Trucking and courier services (except air) (SIC code 421), formerly known as "trucking local and long distance." This SIC code only includes the commercial trucking sector. It excludes private trucking. Hours and injuries to trucking workers in these later companies are classified by the SIC code of the firm's principal business activity, such as petroleum refining or grocery store operation. Because the intent of the 1970 Act was to deal with the safety of *employees*, no data is collected on self-employed persons. This does not mean that all "owner-operators" are excluded. Owner-operators who work under long-term lease arrangements with larger trucking firms should, in theory, have their hours of work and injuries reported by the larger firm. This is because the BLS definition of an "employee" includes all those who work under a firm's direction regardless of the remuneration structure. In addition the BLS claims that it makes efforts to survey small firms, which will include those "owner-operators" who employ additional drivers or mechanics.

Air transportation, scheduled and air courier (SIC code 451), formerly known as "certified air carriers." This includes both the mainline and commuter airline industries offering scheduled service under Parts 121 and 135 of the Federal Air Regulations. The haphazard growth of the courier business over the past 30 years, with some major firms developing from an aviation base and some from a trucking base, led to a major continuity break in 1996. In the words of the BLS publication for that year, "air courier operations previously classified in Industry Groups

421, 422, 423, 452, 473 and 478 were reclassified to Industry Group 451." The effect was to transfer 300,000 employees who had been previously classified as working in trucking to scheduled air service. This reduced the number of trucking employees by about a sixth, and boosted aviation employment by about 50%.

The control group occupation was *Manufacturing* (SIC division D). This was chosen for a several reasons. First, manufacturing might be regarded as providing a substitute occupation for the skills of transportation workers. Second, there are similar occupational hazards such as the use of heavy machinery. Third, manufacturing is one of the few industry classifications for which the government collects data on output. Output is used as a denominator of risk for the second part of this analysis.

Other than the reclassification of courier service, data has been collected in a consistent manner over time and reported in a broadly similar format, although the degree of detail expanded significantly after 1992. That said, only one appropriate data series has been reported consistently since the beginning. That is "lost workday injuries per 100 full-time-equivalent (FTE) employees." A lost workday injury means that the employee had to stay at home or, if they remained at work, had restricted activity or had to be transferred to another task. The data used is the number of cases, not the sum total of lost workdays. An FTE employee is defined by dividing the number of hours worked by 2,000 (50 weeks at 40 hours a week). There may be some ambiguity in defining "restricted activity," so some analysts prefer the measure of "injuries with day(s) away from work." These are injuries that require the employee to be absent from the workplace. Unfortunately, this data is only available from 1976, which would further limit the evidence on pre-deregulation trends. Graphical analysis of the two measures for each industry since 1976 indicates that they track each other quite closely.

The analysis is confined to industrial injuries and, unlike Viscusi, excludes illnesses. The primary reason is that, unlike physical injuries, illnesses may only become apparent years after exposure to the unhealthy condition, and possibly after the employee has moved to another occupation. This paper only deals with non-fatal injuries. Comprehensive fatality data only became available in 1992, and suffers from the problem that there is considerable year to year variation. For example, railroad and aviation fatalities have been as low as twenty in some years, and susceptible to variation due to multiple-fatality incidents.

INJURY RATES PER EMPLOYEE

Figure 1 shows a graph of the rates of lost workday injuries per 100 FTE employees for the three transportation modes and manufacturing. Probably the most notable feature is the trend for railroads. Railroad injury rates were the lowest of all of

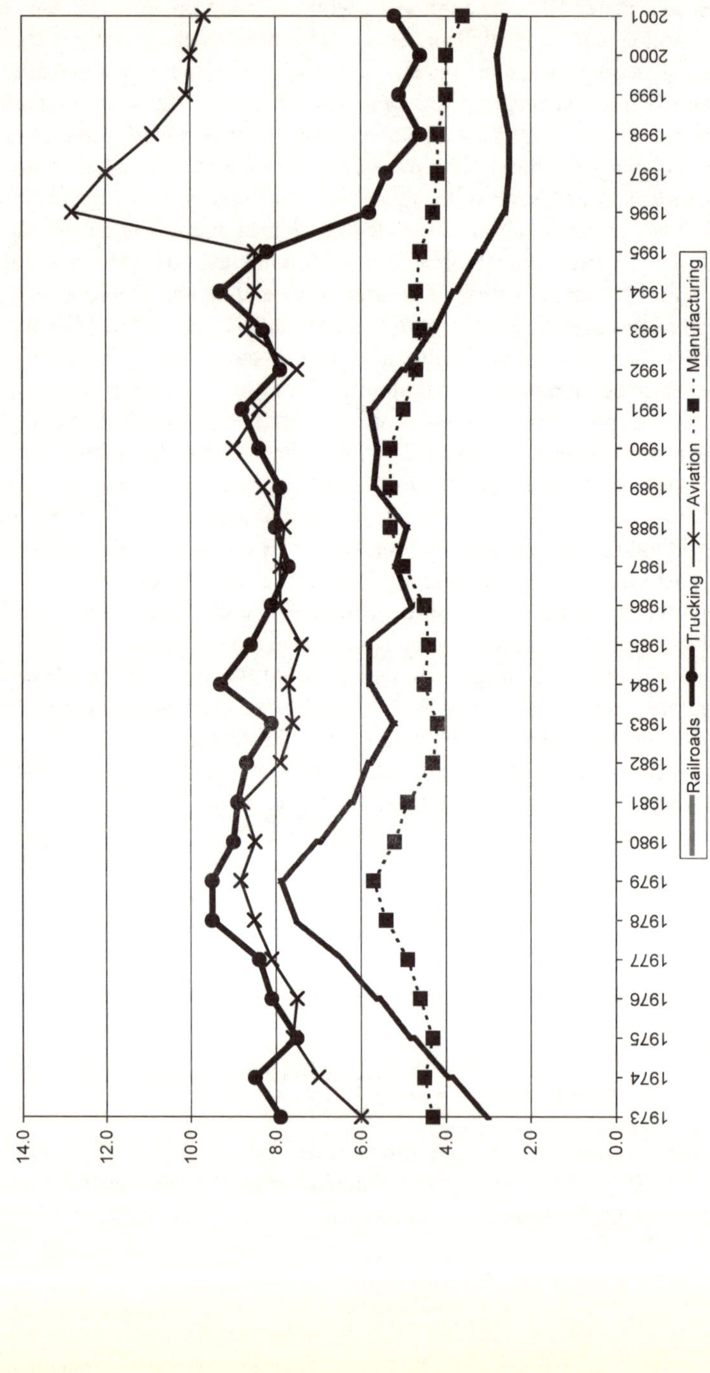

Fig. 1. Lost Workday Injuries per 100 Full Time Equivalent Employees (FTE).

the occupations in 1973, but rapidly deteriorated throughout the 1970s. Then in 1980 the rate started to fall, and by the mid-1990s railroads had once again become the safest of the occupations. This is consistent with the data on collisions and derailments. One does not need to deploy econometric analysis to conclude that deregulation of the railroads coincided with improved workplace safety. The effects in the trucking and aviation industries are less clear. Excepting the discontinuity in 1996, visual inspection suggests that injury rates have been fairly constant, with some cyclical variations. Injury rates in manufacturing started out at about half those in trucking and aviation, and have stayed remarkably constant over the decades.

All of the data series seem to exhibit similar cyclical trends. Injury rates appear to have increased in the late 1970s, declined in the early 1980s, increased again at the end of the 1980s, and fell again in the early 1990s. This phenomenon has been observed by labor economists. These trends coincide with expansion and contraction of economic activity, and in the case of some of the industries an increase and decrease in the numbers employed. The standard argument is that during times of employment growth, less skilled and more accident-prone workers are employed, and during a contraction, these are the first employees to be let go. The exception has been the decline in injury rates during the economic expansion of the mid- to late-1990s. My conversations with BLS staff indicate that the BLS is unsure of the explanation for this change from previous experience.

The formal analysis in this paper uses the ratio of the injury rates in each of the transportation modes to that of manufacturing. The use of this ratio removes the effects of the business cycle, and potentially corrects for other changes in society that have affected the safety of all occupations. Figure 2 shows this relative injury risk ratio for each mode. Econometric techniques are used to analyze the slopes of the data in Fig. 2 in order to tell whether trends after deregulation have differed from those in the 1970s. The regressions use first-difference techniques so as to avoid the usual autocorrelation problems that arise with time-series data. Consequently, the first observation will be for the year 1974, and be the value of the variable in that year less its value in 1973, and so on. Separate regressions will be conducted for each of the three transportation modes.

The following regression is estimated for each mode:

$$\ln\left(\frac{\text{Ratio}_{it}}{\text{Ratio}_{it-1}}\right) = \beta_1 \times 1 + \beta_2 \times 1 \times \text{Dereg}_t + \beta_3 \times \text{Courier}_t + \varepsilon \qquad (1)$$

In the dependent variable, Ratio_{it} is the ratio of injuries per employee in transportation mode i in period t relative to the rate for manufacturing. The subscript $t - 1$ indicates the previous year. The dependent variable, the ratio of risks, is expressed as a logarithm to ensure that the estimated values are positive. It is illogical for an

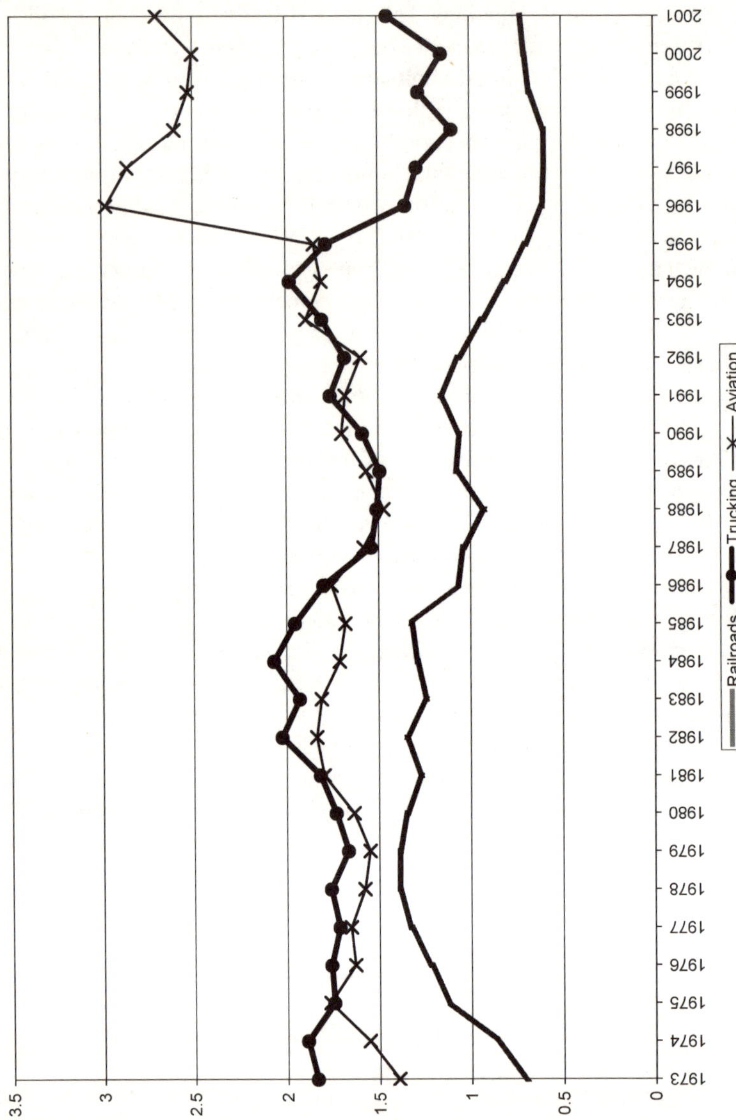

Fig. 2. Lost Workday Injury Cases per 100 Full Time Equivalent Employees (FTE) Relative to Manufacturing.

injury rate to take negative values. Two explanatory time trend variables are used to represent the slopes of the relationships in Fig. 2. The first is an underlying time trend for the entire period. Because the equation is estimated in first differences, this variable will take the value one in each time period. An additional time trend starts in the first full year of deregulation. Aviation deregulation took effect on October 28, 1978, so for this mode Dereg_t is a dummy variable taking the value one in 1979 and later years. Trucking deregulation took effect on July 1, 1980 and the Staggers Act was signed on October 14, 1980. For these two modes, Dereg_t takes the value one in 1981 and later years. The interpretation of the regression is that the trend (slope) of the relative injury risk prior to deregulation is given by β_1, whereas after deregulation it is given by $(\beta_1 + \beta_2)$. Finally, a dummy variable is used in the trucking and aviation regressions to represent the discontinuity in the data due to the redefinition of courier services in 1996. Because the estimated equations are calculated as first-differences, this effect appears as a dummy variable *shift* in the year 1996. Consequently, the variable Courier_t takes the value one in 1996 and zero otherwise.

The results are shown in Table 3. The estimated coefficients confirm the visual impressions from Figs 1 and 2. For the railroads β_1 is statistically significant and positive, and β_2 is negative and statistically significant. Moreover, the absolute value of β_2 is greater than β_1. This means that there was a strong upward (i.e. less safe) trend in relative workplace safety prior to deregulation. However, the magnitude of the (negative) β_2 is so large that it more than canceled out the deteriorating safety trend, and led to safety improvements after deregulation. This produces the inverted V shape of the railroad safety risk shown in Figs 1 and 2.

In contrast, for trucking and aviation, neither β_1 nor β_2 are statistically significant. The magnitudes of the coefficients are much smaller than those for

Table 3. First-Difference Regression Results on the Logarithm of Lost Workday Injury Cases per 100 FTE Employees in Transportation Relative to Manufacturing.

Coefficient (*t* Statistic in Parentheses)	Railroads	Trucking	Aviation
Time trend	0.094	−0.009	0.025
	(2.47)	(0.24)	(0.76)
Deregulation (1981 on for trucking/rail,	−0.124	0.013	−0.022
1979 on for aviation)	(2.81)	(0.32)	(0.62)
Courier redefinition (1996)	–	−0.284	0.474
		(2.93)	(6.44)
R^2	0.233	0.261	0.640
Observations	28	28	28

the railroads, and because β_1 and β_2 have opposite signs, they tend to cancel each other out in the post-deregulation period. In summary, there is no significant underlying time trend, and deregulation does not seem to have altered the situation. Only the redefinition of air couriers has any significant effect.

INJURY RATES PER UNIT OF OUTPUT

The preceding analysis is most appropriate for examining workplace safety from the point of view of employees. It answers the question about the relative risk that employees face in any given year by working in transportation compared with a peer occupation. While society also shares this concern, the metric it uses may be somewhat different. Society may be more interested in the rate of injuries per unit of output. Even if the rate per employee remains constant, improvements in productivity will mean that fewer employees will be injured per unit of output, and hence the industry would in some sense be "safer." This relationship is somewhat controversial. Productivity increases, such as the removal of firemen from diesel railroad locomotives and cabooses from the rear of trains, were argued at the time to lead to a greater safety risk. Yet at the same time, these changes removed staff from very vulnerable positions and probably contributed to overall improved worker safety.

For this analysis, the measure of railroad output is ton-miles of freight moved by all classes of railroads (Eno Transportation Foundation, various years). Because BLS data for trucking injuries is only for the "commercial" segment of the industry, the most appropriate measure of output is a series called domestic inter-city ton-miles for "Interstate Commerce Commission trucks" (Eno Transportation Foundation, various years). For scheduled aviation, the output measure is revenue passenger enplanements on scheduled flights by U.S. flag carriers (Federal Aviation Administration, various years). This type of output measure is commonly used in aviation safety analysis, rather than passenger-miles, because most of the crash risk occurs during the take off and landing stages of flight. In addition, the amount of ground handling, whereby gate agents, ramp employees and maintenance personnel might be injured, will be largely invariant with the length of the flight. Output data for manufacturing is obtained in a monthly survey (Board of Governors of the Federal Reserve System, monthly). This is a measure of physical output, and is shown as an index using a base of 1997 equals 100. For the purposes of this analysis, the base of the index was changed to 1973 equals one.

Figure 3 shows trends in the ratio of total industry employment to output for the three transportation modes and manufacturing. For the sake of easy comparison,

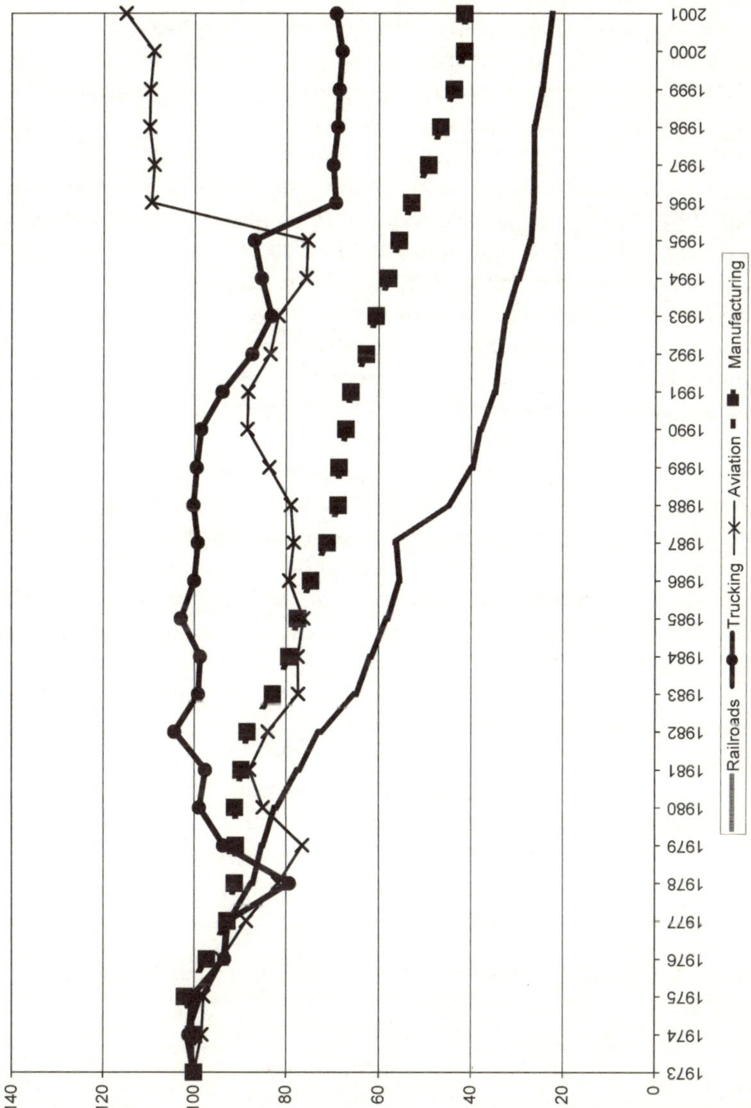

Fig. 3. Index of Employment to Output with 1973 = 100.

the data has been normalized so that the rate in 1973 for each industry is set equal to 100. Railroad productivity has improved continuously and dramatically since the mid-1970s. The ratio of employees to output is now only 27% of the level at the time of deregulation. The railroad productivity improvements have been greater than the remarkable 54% improvement in manufacturing productivity over the same period. In contrast, the trends in trucking and aviation productivity are less clear. There was improved productivity in the 1970s and again in the early 1990s, but constant and perhaps deteriorating trends in other time period. The reclassification of air courier employees in 1996 produces a significant discontinuity in both data series. The implication is that the improved railroad productivity post-deregulation should exacerbate the earlier finding that deregulation was associated with improvements in employee safety, while the effects in the trucking and aviation industries are not readily apparent.

Data is available to directly calculate the rate of total lost workday injuries per unit of output for all years for railroads and manufacturing, and from 1992 onward for trucking and aviation. For earlier years in the latter modes, the total number of injuries can be inferred by multiplying the rate of injuries per 100 FTE employees by an estimate of FTE employees derived from employment data. Details of these calculations are in the Data Appendix. Total injuries are then divided by output to obtain an injury rate. A summary of the denominator of injury rates for the various industries are shown in Table 4. The choice of the orders of magnitude for the various units of output was made so that the injury rates for the various industries were of comparable magnitudes, typically between one and ten per unit of output.

Figure 4 shows the trends in injuries per unit of output for each of the three transportation modes and for manufacturing. For ease of comparison, the data is shown as an index with 1973 set equal to 100. The adverse trend in employee injury rates for the railroads relative to manufacturing prior to deregulation, followed by a distinct subsequent improvement is clearly apparent. The effect is more dramatic than the decline in injuries per employee shown in Fig. 1. The relative injury rates in both trucking and aviation have no discernable trends, but considerable year-to-year variation. The effect of the reclassification of air courier

Table 4. Measures of Industry Output Used to Calculate Injury Rates.

Industry	Output Measure
Railroads	100 Billion ton-miles
Trucking	10 Billion ton-miles
Aviation	10,000 Revenue passengers enplaned
Manufacturing	Index of manufacturing production with 1973 = 1

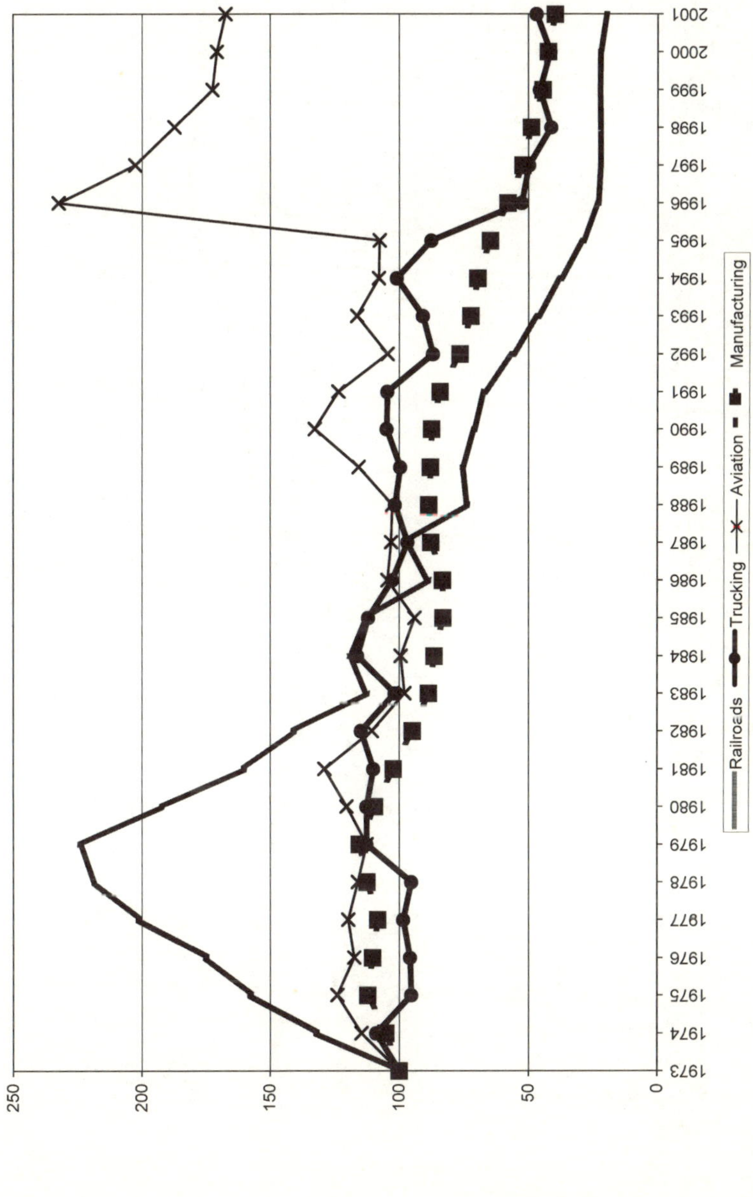

Fig. 4. Index of Lost Workdays per Unit of Output with 1973 = 100.

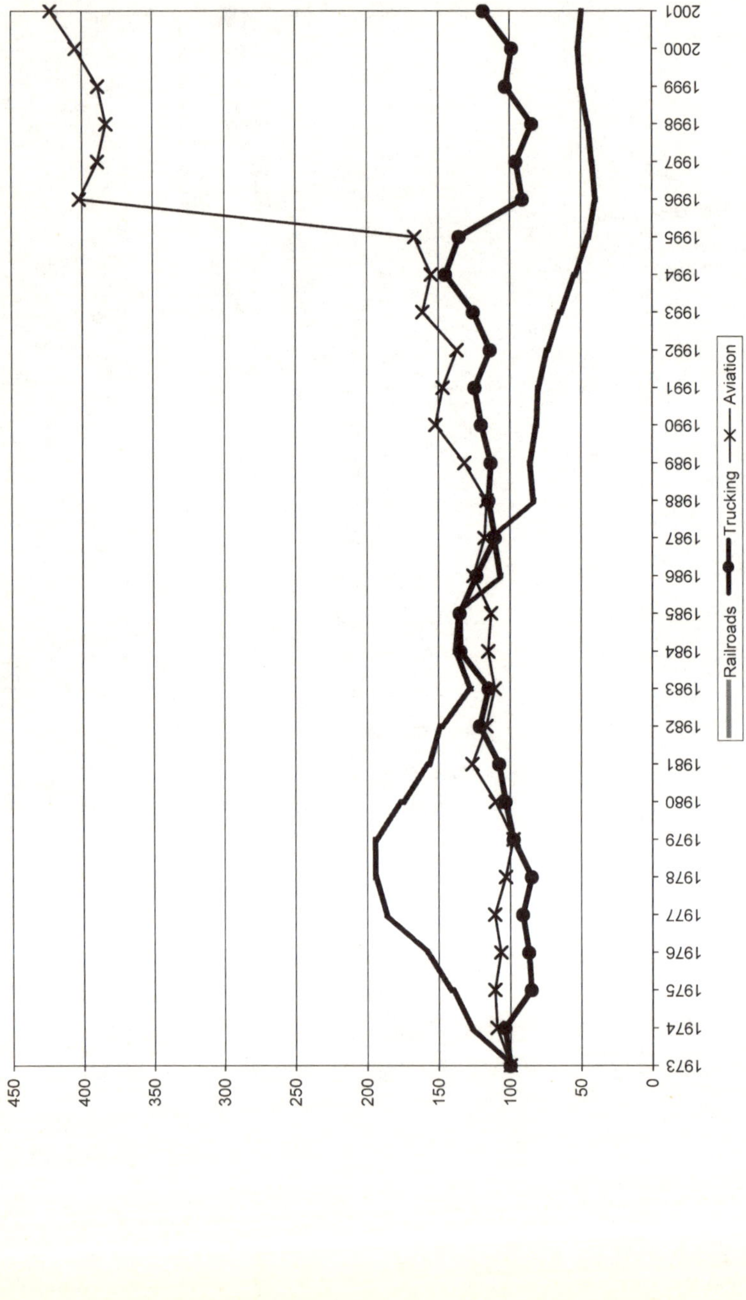

Fig. 5. Index of Lost Workday Injuries per Unit of Output Relative to Manufacturing, with 1973 = 100.

employees in 1996 is very obvious. The stagnation of injury rates in aviation and trucking compares unfavorably with the downward trend in injury rates in manufacturing which started in the late 1970s.

Figure 5 shows an index for each transportation mode of the ratio of the injury rates to that of manufacturing. For comparison purposes, the value of each index series in 1973 is set equal to 100. The slow deterioration in injury rates in aviation and trucking relative to manufacturing is readily apparent. Between the late 1970s and the redefinition of air couriers in 1996, safety per unit of output declined by about 50% compared with manufacturing. For the railroads, the post-deregulation improvement in safety in Fig. 4 is somewhat muted in Fig. 5 because manufacturing has also seen improvements in productivity.

A second group of regressions was conducted on the base data underlying the indices in Fig. 5. As before, the dependent variable is transformed into logarithms to avoid predicting a negative ratio of relative risk. A first difference specification is used to reduce econometric problems. The right-hand side variables are the same as the first group of regressions:

$$\ln\left(\frac{\text{Ratio}_{it}}{\text{Ratio}_{it-1}}\right) = \beta_1 \times 1 + \beta_2 \times 1 \times \text{Dereg}_t + \beta_3 \times \text{Courier}_t + \varepsilon \qquad (2)$$

where Ratio_{it} is the ratio of injuries per unit of output in transportation mode i in period t relative to the rate for manufacturing. The other variables are as defined earlier.

The regression results are shown in Table 5. For the railroads β_1 is almost statistically significant at the 5% level and is positive, and β_2 is negative, highly statistically significant, and 75% larger than β_1. This means that there was an upward (i.e. less safe) trend in relative workplace safety prior to deregulation,

Table 5. First-Difference Regression Results on the Logarithm of Rate of Lost Workday Injury Cases per Unit of Output in Transportation Relative to Manufacturing.

Coefficient (t Statistic in Parentheses)	Railroads	Trucking	Aviation
Time Trend	0.080	0.004	0.006
	(1.92)	(0.11)	(0.18)
Deregulation (1981 on for trucking/rail, 1979 on for aviation)	−0.141	0.027	0.018
	(2.93)	(0.50)	(0.48)
Courier Redefinition (1996)	–	−0.423	0.858
		(4.02)	(11.01)
R^2	0.280	0.395	0.845
Observations	28	28	28

that was more than compensated for in the years after deregulation. As in the earlier analysis with respect to injuries per employee, there is an inverted V shape relationship. For trucking and aviation, both β_1 and β_2 are positive, but small, and not statistically significant. Even when the effects are combined together, one cannot reject the null hypothesis of a zero slope at the 10% level. Contrary to the visual suggestion of Fig. 5, one cannot definitively conclude that relative workplace safety has declined in these industries. Only the redefinition of air couriers has any significant effect in the regressions.

CONCLUSIONS

Only in railroads does there appear to be any linkage between deregulation and workplace safety. There is evidence that safety started to deteriorate in the mid-1960s. The cause was the financial crisis which led to bankruptcies in the eastern United States, and a more general rundown in the infrastructure. The federal government addressed this problem with the introduction of comprehensive safety regulation in 1970. Previously, the industry was largely self-regulated. Specific rules were written and a federal and state inspectorate was hired over the course of the 1970s. Despite this, workplace safety continued to deteriorate throughout the 1970s. Deregulation in 1980 led to a financial renaissance of the industry. Capital expenditures increased significantly. It is obvious from a graphical analysis, and confirmed by regressions, that the previous upward trend in workplace injuries was reversed. By the early 1990s the injury rate was lower than it was in 1973. This improving trend was magnified by increased productivity. The rate of employee injuries per ton mile is now only a quarter of what it was in 1979.

In contrast there has been no statistically-significant trend in the rate of workplace injuries in trucking and scheduled aviation, and no effects of deregulation can be detected. This finding is consistent with aviation crash data which shows a stagnation in crash rates since the mid-1970s, following rapid technology-driven improvements in the 1960s. It would appear that technology and employee safety is also stagnant in other aspects of aviation, such as ramp operations, maintenance and customer service.

In trucking, there is evidence that the rate of fatal crashes on the public highway involving heavy trucks has declined by 50% over the past twenty-five years. However, this is not evident in workplace injury data. There are several explanations for this inconsistency. Much of the reduction in highway crash rates has come from improved occupant protection of passenger vehicles that are in collision with heavy trucks. Occupants of these vehicles, rather than truck drivers, are disproportionately victimized by crashes. Moreover, injuries in traffic crashes only represent a small minority of injuries sustained by trucking employees. It would appear that other injury-producing aspects of the trucking profession, such as loading and unloading, and climbing in and out of cabs, has not changed much in the past thirty years.

REFERENCES

Board of Governors of the Federal Reserve System (monthly). *Industrial production and capacity utilization*. Washington, DC: Board of Governors of the Federal Reserve System.

Bulow, J., & Shoven, J. (1978). The bankruptcy decision. *Bell Journal of Economics*, *9*, 437–456.

Corsi, T. M., & Fanara, P. (1989). Effects of new entrants on motor carrier safety. In: L. N. Moses & I. Savage (Eds), *Transportation Safety in an Age of Deregulation*. New York: Oxford University Press.

Eno Transportation Foundation (various years). *Transportation in America*. Washington, DC: Eno Transportation Foundation.

Federal Aviation Administration (various years). *Air carrier traffic statistics*. Washington, DC: U.S. Government Printing Office. (Prior to 1983 published by the Civil Aeronautics Board.)

Kanafani, A., & Keeler, T. E. (1989). New entrants and safety. In: L. N. Moses & I. Savage (Eds), *Transportation Safety in an Age of Deregulation*. New York: Oxford University Press.

Klein, B., & Leffler, K. E. (1981). The role of market forces in assuring contractual performance. *Journal of Political Economy*, *89*, 615–641.

Moses, L. N., & Savage, I. (1989). *Transportation safety in an age of deregulation*. New York: Oxford University Press.

Moses, L. N., & Savage, I. (1997). A cost-benefit analysis of United States motor carrier safety programs. *Journal of Transport Economics and Policy*, *31*, 51–67.

Rose, N. L. (1990). Profitability and product quality: Economic determinants of airline safety performance. *Journal of Political Economy*, *98*, 944–964.

Savage, I. (1998). *The economics of railroad safety*. Boston, MA: Kluwer.

Savage, I. (1999a). The economics of commercial transportation safety. In: J. Gómez-Ibáñez, W. B. Tye & C. Winston (Eds), *Essays in Transportation Economics and Policy: A Handbook in Honor of John R. Meyer*. Washington, DC: Brookings Institution.

Savage, I. (1999b). Aviation deregulation and safety in the United States: Evidence after twenty years. In: M. Gaudry & R. Mayes (Eds), *Taking Stock of Air Liberalization*. Boston, MA: Kluwer.

Shapiro, C. (1982). Consumer information, product quality and seller reputation. *Bell Journal of Economics*, *13*, 20–35.

United States Department of Labor, Bureau of Labor Statistics (various years). *Occupational injuries and illnesses in the United States by industry*. Washington, DC: U.S. Government Printing Office. (Known as *Occupational injuries and illnesses – counts, rates and characteristics* from 1992.)

Viscusi, W. K. (1987). The effect of transportation deregulation on worker safety. In: *Proceedings of the Transportation Deregulation and Safety Conference*. Evanston, IL: Northwestern University Transportation Center.

Viscusi, W. K. (1989). The effect of transportation deregulation on worker safety. In: L. N. Moses & I. Savage (Eds), *Transportation Safety in an Age of Deregulation*. New York: Oxford University Press.

DATA APPENDIX

This appendix describes the data preparation that was necessary to deal with years for which certain data items were either missing or reported inconsistently. For 1977–1979, the rate of lost workday injuries per 100 FTE employees was not shown at a sufficient level of disaggregation for scheduled aviation. For these years, the reported rate for "Transportation by Air" (SIC code 45) was adjusted using the ratio of the injury rate in SIC 451 to SIC 45 observed in 1976 and 1980.

Injury rates per unit of output are calculated by dividing total lost workday injuries by the measures of output that are described in the text. While information of total injuries is reported each year for railroads and manufacturing, they are only given at a sufficient level of disaggregation for trucking and aviation since 1992. For the earlier years in trucking and aviation, it is necessary to estimate the total number of injuries by multiplying the known rate of injuries per 100 FTE employees by an estimate of the FTE employees in those years. Because FTE data is never shown explicitly in the published data, another BLS database, the "Covered Employment and Wages (CEW) Program," is used as the basis for employment data.

Because the survey methods are different, CEW employment numbers may not accord with the FTE data collected as part of the injury surveys. However, for the years between 1992, when reporting was expanded, and 1996, when courier services were reclassified, it is possible to compare the CEW employment data with an implied value for FTE employees. The latter are calculated by dividing total injuries by the injury rate per 100 FTE employees. For trucking, the FTE employee number appears to be about 0.983 times the CEW employment number. The equivalent number for aviation is lower at 0.874. An estimation of FTE employees for earlier years can be made by multiplying the CEW employment figures by these factors.

CEW employment data was reported for SIC 421 and 451 in 1976, 1983–1984, 1986–1987, and from 1989. For the trucking industry, the missing data was estimated using the ratio to the employment in trucking (SIC 421) to total employment in Trucking and Warehousing (SIC 42) less the reported number of employees in Warehousing (SIC 422) from neighboring years when the full data is known. The numbers are always very close. Missing data for 1973–1975 and 1977–1982 are calculated by using the average ratio of (SIC 42 – SIC 422)/SIC 421 for 1976 and 1983. The 1985 data was estimated by using the average ratio for 1984 and 1986, and the 1988 data was estimated using the average ratio in 1987 and 1989.

Similar calculations were made for aviation. For 1973–1975 and 1977–1982 employment was estimated by using the average ratio of employment in scheduled air transportation (SIC 451) to total aviation (SIC 45) in 1976 and 1983. The 1985 and 1988 data was calculated by using the ratio of employment in SIC 451 to total employment in SIC 45 less employment in "Airports, Flying Fields and Airport Terminal Services" (SIC 458). As with trucking, the 1985 data was estimated by using the average ratio for 1984 and 1986, and the 1988 data was estimated using the average ratio in 1987 and 1989.

Because total injury data is given every year for the railroads, it is not necessary to use employment numbers to estimate these data. However, employment data is used as the numerator of the productivity rates shown in Fig. 3. Railroad employment data from the CEW survey is missing after 1995. Fortunately alternative data is available from the Department of Labor's "Current Employment Survey." These two data series have always been almost identical.

3. THE EFFECTS OF TRUCKING FIRM FINANCIAL PERFORMANCE ON DRIVER SAFETY

Daniel A. Rodríguez, Marta Rocha and Michael H. Belzer

ABSTRACT

This chapter uses trucking firm-level information to address the paucity of multivariate analysis accounting for the safety effect of various types of truck driver compensation and firm financial performance. Using negative binomial regression models, we find that small firms with high liquidity are correlated with better safety performance. Likewise, small firms that devote a higher share of their revenues to labor expenses tend to have better safety outcomes. Although the dataset is limited in many ways, these associations suggest that small firms may be particularly sensitive to the competitive nature of the truckload sector, relying on the human capital of drivers to overcome safety challenges due to their size.

INTRODUCTION

Public policy governing transportation services that places greater emphasis on competition and a growing economy has generated significant demand for low cost freight transportation. Theory suggests that intense competition potentially could

Transportation Labor Issues and Regulatory Reform
Research in Transportation Economics, Volume 10, 35–55

ISSN: 0739-8859/doi:10.1016/S0739-8859(04)10003-6

create a business environment implicitly encouraging trucking firms to engage in risky operations that lower costs, even though costs associated with vehicular accidents are expensive. Past research reports that the public health burden of large truck crashes, as measured by deaths per 100,000 people, has not improved over time (Arnold et al., 1997). In addition, compared with other occupations, truck drivers had the highest number of worker fatalities in 2002, with 80.7% of those deaths occurring in crashes (Lyman & Braver, 2002; U.S. Department of Labor, Bureau of Labor Statistics, 2003). With trucking operations accounting for almost one third of the total ton-miles transported, and such operations expected to grow in the future, trucking safety continues to command heightened attention from researchers and policy-makers.

Several other groups share an interest in improving the safety outcomes of trucking operations. For instance insurance companies may inadvertently subsidize high risk trucking firms by not charging them enough; trucking firms with poor safety performance records face high insurance premiums and costly litigation fees; and shippers face losses from damaged or destroyed products, as well as litigation as an involved party. The trucking companies' challenge to provide safe working conditions for drivers and other motorists, while operating a profitable business, presents researchers with the opportunity to test predictions derived from economic theory. Empirical research on trucking safety performance generally includes variables depicting driver characteristics and behavior, trucking load characteristics, vehicle characteristics and roadway conditions as safety determinants. However, relatively little empirical research has addressed the link between motor carrier financial performance, worker compensation level, and driver selection and training to safety outcomes. Yet these factors have been prominently identified in several studies, including *Gearing Up for Safety* (Office of Technology Assessment, 1988) and in GAO's *Freight Trucking: Promising Approach for Predicting Carriers' Safety Risks* (Office of Technology Assessment, 1991). Empirical studies that do include these factors as safety determinants suggest that trucking firms' financial performance and drivers' human capital investment seem to be significantly associated with crash involvement (Bruning, 1989; Chow et al., 1987; Corsi & Fanara, 1988; Corsi et al., 2002; Hunter & Mangum, 1995; Moses & Savage, 1992).

This study improves on previous research in several ways. First, it employs a more extensive dataset that includes firm financial performance, in addition to specific non-driving compensation policies and benefits. Second, the analysis relies on count models, which capture the non-normal distribution of crash data, which in turn provides theoretical and empirical improvements over past research. Finally, whereas earlier studies predominantly focused on bivariate correlations, count models allow for testing associations between firm performance and safety, while simultaneously controlling for other relevant firm characteristics. Thus, the advantage of the empirical approach used in this study is it allows testing for several hypotheses that have been postulated in the literature. In addition the empirical modeling of trucking safety performance contributes a tool that may be useful for policy makers. As such, the research builds on prior work to extend the trucking safety research literature, while it addresses urgent policy and action-oriented needs.

DETERMINANTS OF DRIVER SAFETY

Human capital theory suggests that variations in human capital across individuals and firms contribute to differences in labor force outcomes, such as productivity and safety (Becker, 1962, 1964). Within this theoretical framework, relatively high worker compensation is required to employ individuals who possess highly valued qualities. In a competitive market, higher pay would allow firms to attract and retain drivers possessing characteristics that are associated with better driver safety records. This association between driver behavior, driver pay, and driver characteristics has been tested empirically in several studies of the trucking industry. For instance, Krass (1993) detects a significant inverse relationship between wages and crash risk for the period after economic deregulation of the trucking industry.[1] The combined findings of Hirsch (1993), Rodríguez et al. (2003) and Monaco and Williams (2000), support the notion that the employment of drivers with skills that command high wages helps explain the association between high wages and strong safety performance. Hirsch (1993) suggests that human capital differences among drivers may explain a substantial fraction of driver wage differences between union and non-union drivers, as the former may have greater human capital than the latter. Monaco and Williams (2000) conclude that trucking industry compensation and human capital characteristics appear to be more significant determinants of safety than are demographic variables. Other studies have also supported a connection between driver safety and human capital characteristics and driver compensation (Beilock, 1994). However, only a few studies have examined this relationship explicitly and none has focused on crash frequency.

In addition to human capital investment, other factors such as occupational demands also influence safety outcomes. Past research has examined the link between occupational factors such as working conditions and driver fatigue. Fatigue arguably is one of the most important risks factor that emerges from analyzing the role of occupational factors in driver safety (Feyer et al., 1993; Shaw et al., 2003). Most studies of fatigue have examined the causes and the extent of fatigue in truck drivers (Hakkanen & Summala, 2000; Lyznicki et al., 1998; McCartt et al., 1997) and the link between fatigue and crash risk (Hensher et al., 1992). McCartt et al. (1997, 2000) find that drivers believe that the scheduling of loads (measured as driving hours and waiting time for loads) contributes significantly to fatigued driving. Similarly, after conducting focus groups to examine the factors related to truck crashes, Chatterjee et al. (1994) conclude that direct pressure from dispatchers forces drivers to work long hours under unsafe conditions. Lin et al. (1993) rely on operational data from another large national less-than-truckload (LTL) carrier to find that total driving time has a greater effect on crash risk than either time of day or driving experience.[2] Hence, even if trucking companies pay high wages to attract and maintain safe drivers, poor working conditions can still lead to poor safety records.

Determinants of driver safety are not limited to driver compensation, driver attributes and occupational demands of drivers. The financial performance of trucking firms also is expected to influence safety outcomes for several reasons. This occurs if, for example, investment decisions of trucking firms were artificially constrained or if there is divergence in private and social incentives to invest in safety. When firms have additional information about their safety levels than other market participants, they may invest too much or too little than what is socially desirable and thus financial conditions would be reflected in safety outcomes. This is because trucking firms can be viewed as choosing a level of safety that balances the cost of additional safety investments with the benefits of reduced crash risk. Likewise, regulatory incentives also influence safety investments. Firms choose to comply with safety regulations based on the incremental cost of doing so, the probability of being caught without complying with the regulations, and the costs related to non-compliance.

Safety investments of a firm can include hiring drivers with higher levels of human capital, maintaining vehicles better, and complying with internal and external safety regulatory incentives. The benefits of lower crash risk for a firm include lower insurance premiums or self-insurance set-asides, higher prices, and higher reputation and quality of service. Shippers have some incentives to monitor firm safety and to penalize those firms that underinvest in safety, because this may lead to negative results for the shipper, such as unreliable delivery times and damaged goods.

The importance of financial performance as a safety determinant has heightened significance in an unregulated economic environment. In the deregulated trucking market, carriers have emphasized efficiency and low shipping costs. Efficiency gains in a labor-intensive industry such as trucking might be achieved through increased work loads. Lower shipping costs might arise from trucking firms lowering the value of worker compensation packages, and pressure to adopt these managerial practices may vary by carrier profitability. Profitable carriers have enough resources to invest in human capital and in maintenance, whereas financially distressed carriers might tend to reduce expenditures on maintenance and in other areas that affect safety, or engage in operating practices that are not conducive to safety.

Indeed, theoretical and empirical models provide further insight into the links between safety investments and firm financial performance. Models of financial constraints (Fazzari & Athey, 1987; Fazzari & Petersen, 1993) and decision-making nearing bankruptcy (Chen et al., 1995; Opler & Titman, 1994) provide theoretical examples of such connections. Empirically, the evidence in trucking shows some support for the notion that profitable carriers have safer working conditions and better safety performance than unprofitable carriers. For instance, findings by Chow et al. show that carriers close to bankruptcy skimp on maintenance, use older equipment, and use owner-operators (Chow et al., 1987).[3] A statistically significant positive association between trucking profitability and safety performance is reported by Corsi and Fanara (1988). They find that such significance occurs when estimating the association between operating ratio (operating expenses divided by operating revenue) and crash rates for Class I and II carriers in 1977 and 1984.[4] However, Blevins and Chow (1988) further studied the profitability-safety relationship during the post-deregulation era using bivariate analyses, finding no statistically significant results.

In summary, there is some evidence suggesting a relationship between firm financial performance and safety. Past research also suggests that occupational demands and human capital characteristics are related to driving behaviors and crash outcomes. Given the apparent link between level of driver pay and driver safety, one expects that firms would raise pay in order to skim the cream of the trucking labor market. Since trucking deregulation, the payment of high wages occurs only in protected sectors (those with barriers to entry) and in unionized firms.[5] Furthermore, on average, earnings of truck drivers and the quality of driving jobs continue to erode, especially among non-union drivers (Belzer, 1995, 2000). Although speculative, two explanations may be possible: either motor carriers' post deregulation financial performance weakened such that they were limited in the pay they could provide workers, or trucking firms perceive that the benefits of higher pay did not justify the high labor costs.

Previous findings may be explained by the fact that distressed carriers can stay in business by cutting costs in motor freight operations, by running old fleets, by paying lower wages, and by requiring or providing incentives for drivers to work longer hours. Each of these approaches to cost-savings can lead to poor safety performance. Limited empirical research on safety performance links driver compensation, driver behavior and trucking firms' economic welfare. This study thus builds on prior research while recognizing that financial performance, firm operations, and human capital can be important determinants of truck driver crash involvement.

FIRM-LEVEL DATASET

Sources

Three predominant data sources reporting firm level information on trucking companies are used to examine the effect of driver compensation, occupational demands, and firm financial performance on safety. The primary data source for the firm level study is "The National Survey of Driver Wages" published by Signpost, Inc. This is a quarterly convenience survey of approximately 200 truckload firms of various sizes. These firms were chosen on the basis of the *Commercial Carrier Journal* list and other sources of top 100, second 100, and other truckload firms. Signpost also includes most of its own subscribers in the data, but there are many firms in the sample who do not subscribe to it. A caveat associated with the Signpost data set is the non-randomness of the sample selection. For instance, small carriers are most likely to be excluded from the sample. Nonetheless, most of the carriers are national, and these national carriers – in combination with some regional firms – reasonably represent the labor market. Although Signpost was unable to provide an assessment of the randomness of the sample, the Signpost data recently were used for a compensation study conducted by the American Trucking Association Foundation[6] and are considered by many in the industry to provide a reasonable approximation of driver pay in truckload. Signpost data were obtained for the fourth quarter of 1998. In the summer of 2000 a supplemental survey of firms identified in the Signpost data was implemented. This was due to concerns with the quality of data on non-driving compensation in the original Signpost dataset.[7]

The second source provides information on crashes, an indicator of carrier safety, reported in the Motor Carrier Management Information System (MCMIS) by the U.S. Department of Transportation (DOT). The data set includes all carriers, but suffers from the limitation of only partial reporting of carrier crashes by responsible state authorities, though incomplete reporting does not seem to vary systematically by state.

The third source of firm-level information is taken from the Motor Carrier Financial and Operating Statistics (F&OS) Program, administered by the U.S. Department of Transportation's Bureau of Labor Statistics (BTS). This information comprises over 200 fields of data collected from Class II (adjusted annual operating revenue from $3 to $10 million) and Class I (larger than $10 million) motor carriers. It includes a variety of financial and operating statistics, originally collected by the Interstate Commerce Commission (ICC).[8] The frequency of missing motor carriers and variables is a shortcoming of this data source, unfortunately. For instance, even though 10,000 firms were listed

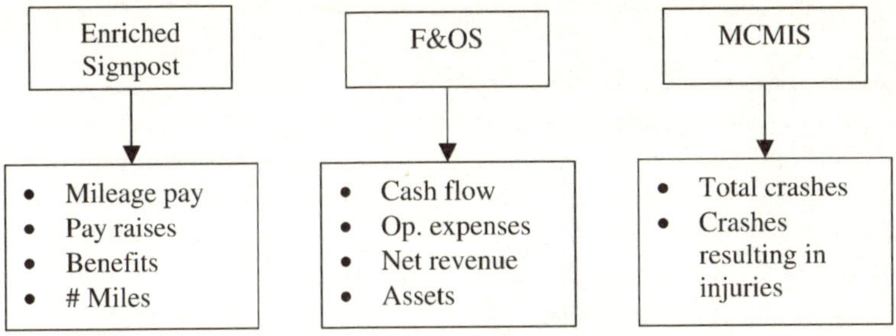

Fig. 1. Primary Data Sources.

in the TTS National Motor Carrier Directory as being Class I or Class II firms with at least $3 million in revenue, both the American Trucking Associations and Transportation Technical Service (TTS) publish F&OS data on approximately 2,000 firms only. A new program by the BTS seeks to remedy this reporting deficiency and resolve the discrepancy between the TTS data and Financial and Operating Statistics obtained by the BTS. Nevertheless, where available, Form M Data have the advantage of providing more accurate and up to date firm-level measures of fleet size, miles of operation, and other variables than is available from other sources.

Data from the enriched Signpost data, MCMIS, and from the DOT's F&OS were merged by matching carriers listed in each survey. Additional information on the number of power units per firm for 1997 was obtained from the 1999 National Motor Carrier Directory.[9] Taken together, the resultant dataset provides a rich set of information in part because it contains financial indicators, firm characteristics, operations, and safety data. One major shortcoming of merging these datasets, however, comes from the reduced sample size obtained, which varies from approximately 60 to 102 truckload motor carriers, depending on the variables selected. Figure 1 lists the variables taken from the sources to examine truck driver safety performance.

Variables Observed

The sample used in the analysis consists of firms with mileage-paid employee drivers responding to our supplementary survey of Signpost respondent firms. Of 178 firms that paid their employee drivers by the mile, we received valid responses from 102 firms, representing a response rate of 57%. Of those, we were able to successfully match 62 firms with F&OS data for 1997. When a firm did not match the F&OS, the 1998 data were used. Additionally, two firms were removed from the dataset because they were not for-hire firms, leaving a total of 60 firms in our dataset.

The dependent variable for our analysis is a firm's safety performance (CRASH), which is represented by the number of the Department of Transportation-reported crashes during 1998 for each firm. Descriptive statistics for the 60 firms listed in the merged dataset show that they had an average of 74.7 crashes (Table 1). These crashes resulted in an average of 2.4 fatalities and 35.9 injuries per firm in the observation year. Explanatory variables presented in Table 1, other than firm financial performance variables, include measures of compensation for driving (PAY), which can be viewed as proxies for unobserved human capital characteristics, uncompensated non-driving time (UNPAID), safety and

Table 1. Summary Statistics at the Firm-Level.

Variable Label	Explanation	Mean	Std. Dev.	Min	Max
CRASH	Number of DOT reportable crashes per firm	74.65	121.31	5.00	660.00
FATALS	Number of crash-related fatalities per firm	2.35	4.35	0	23.00
INJURIES	Number of crash-related injuries per firm	35.90	57.82	1	332
PAY	$/Mile for drivers with 3 years experience	0.29	0.02	0.24	0.37
UNPAID	Number of hours of unpaid time per mile driven in a typical run	0.0043	0.0034	0.0001	0.0151
PAIDVAC	Total vacation, holiday and sick pay	757.68	306.02	350.00	2000.00
RAISE	Average yearly increase in mileage pay	0.0064	0.0035	0.00	0.02
SAFEBON	1 if firm offers a safety bonus, zero otherwise	0.57	0.50	0.00	1.00
HEALTH	Contribution of driver to health plan	160.72	67.22	0.00	368.33
LIFEINS	Amortized value of company paid life insurance	15,858.33	10,700.11	0.00	50,000.00
MILES	Miles driven by a firm in the previous year (millions)	98.30	180.40	1.50	1106.30
P. UNITS	Number of power units owned and leased by the firm	829.43	1267.99	66.00	7193.00
CF_RATIO	Cash flow ratio	0.68	1.30	−7.12	3.62
OP_RATIO	Operation ratio	0.95	0.06	0.83	1.21
LABPREV	Labor expenses per revenue ratio	0.35	0.11	0.07	0.58

compensation incentives (RAISE, SAFEBON), benefits (PAIDVAC, HEALTH, LIFEINS), exposure (MILES) and firm size (POWER UNITS).[10]

The analysis of financial effects on safety performance focuses on three different indicators used to measure the financial welfare of the firm. Two of these ratios – operating ratio and labor cost per revenue – measure profitability. Operating ratio (OP_RATIO) is calculated as a carrier's operating expenses divided by its operating revenue. The average operating ratio of the sample of firms used in the study is 0.95, which according to Corsi et al. (2002) is indicative of a poor financial performance, but is representative of the competitive conditions of the truckload industry sector. The labor cost per revenue ratio (LABPREV) measures the proportion of net revenue paid out in salaries and wages, which in this sample is 35%. Based on human capital theory (Becker, 1964), we hypothesize that the higher the labor cost per revenue ratio, the better the firm safety performance, ceteris paribus.

The third financial welfare measure reported in the data set is cash flow ratio (CF_RATIO). Defined as the cash flow from operations divided by current liabilities, the cash flow ratio is used to determine whether a firm is generating enough cash flow to cover its current liabilities. Arguably, this measure is more reliable than related liquidity measures, such as current ratio, because it accounts for changes in both the income statement and the balance sheet while eliminating the impact of accounting conventions. Firms with higher cash flow ratios to current liabilities have greater cash resources to meet their financial obligations. Conversely, low liquidity indicators represent risk of bankruptcy due to an inability to pay the current debts. Findings in Table 1 suggest that the minimum value of cash flow ratio is −7.12, the maximum is 3.62, and the average is 0.68. The low negative value is from a firm with few liabilities and a negative cash flow. This variation in liquidity in the sample suggests that the firms examined include those facing a high risk of bankruptcy as well as trucking firms with enough liquidity to meet their financial obligations.

SPECIFICATION OF SAFETY MODEL

A model testing structural relationships of safety investment decisions could be estimated if enough data on investments are available. Given the lack of such data and the constraints in quantifying the safety inputs of a trucking firm, we develop a reduced-form model of safety performance. Following Rose (1990), we assume that financial performance is exogenous to safety outcomes. Our measure of safety outcome is the total number of crashes per firm (Table 1). A second measure also examined is total injuries resulting from crashes for each firm, but all results were virtually identical to those using crashes. Thus, we focus solely on crashes here.

The Poisson family of probability distributions provides a useful stochastic specification for examining firm crash counts. Such models have been applied to safety research for airlines (Rose, 1990), automobiles (Dionne & Vanasse, 1992), and more recently to trucking (Moses & Savage, 1996; Rodríguez et al., 2003). If we assume that each mile of activity carries some probability of resulting in a crash, then the expected number of crashes for firm i, n_i, can be modeled as a function of the crash rate per unit of exposure (million miles), λ_i, and the number of miles (in millions). We parameterize the crash rate as an exponential function of firms' characteristics to ensure that the crash rates are nonnegative. If independent variables are denoted by the vector X_i, the crash rate will be given by $\lambda_i = \exp(X_i\beta + \varepsilon_i)$, where $\exp(\varepsilon_i)$ is a Gamma-distributed error term that is a function of $X_i\beta$ for the ith observation,[11] and the expected number of crashes is:

$$E(n_i) = \mathrm{MILES}_i^{\beta_0} \cdot \exp(X_i\beta + \varepsilon_i) \tag{1}$$

where β_0 is the estimated elasticity of crashes with respect to exposure. The coefficient β_0 will determine if the crash rate increases with miles ($\beta_0 > 1$), decreases ($\beta_0 < 1$) or does not change ($\beta_0 = 1$).

The gamma-distributed error term allows the variance to differ from the conditional mean of the distribution and thus is a more general expression of the Poisson regression model. If crashes are distributed as Poisson random variables with conditional mean given by (1), the model corresponds to the negative binomial model and the parameters can be estimated directly using maximum likelihood methods.

SAFETY ESTIMATION RESULTS

We begin our analysis by estimating a reduced-form model, with exposure, firm size, and our three financial indicators as independent variables. Due to the relatively low number of firms in the dataset, the three financial variables are included independently in separate models. The first set of results contains estimates using operating ratio. The second and third sets of results contain estimates from models using cash flow and labor expense per revenue ratios as the financial performance variables. Estimates of elasticities at variables' means are also provided for each of the models.[12] To determine the best-fitting model we first estimate a Poisson model, which we use as a baseline against which the more general negative binomial models can be tested. Likelihood ratio tests allow for identifying the preferred specification between the Poisson and the negative binomial model. Results for the preferred models are provided in Table 2.

Table 2. Total Crashes and Firm Financial Performance, Negative Binomial Regression.

	Operating Ratio Model			Cash Flow Ratio Model			Labor Costs Per Revenue Ratio Model		
	Coef.	*t*	Elast	Coef.	*t*	Elast	Coef.	*t*	Elast
LOGMILES	0.075	1.32	0.29	0.075	1.31	0.29	0.070	1.22	0.27
P. UNITS	0.002***	9.29	1.33	0.002***	9.01	1.31	0.002***	9.47	1.35
P. UNITS^2	−1.6E-07***	−6.82	−0.37	−1.6E-07***	−6.62	−0.36	−1.6E-07***	−6.91	−0.37
OP_RATIO	−0.963	−0.86	−0.91						
CF_RATIO				0.061	1.08	0.04			
LABPREV							−0.269	−0.46	−0.09
CONSTANT	3.430***	3.20		2.492***	11.72		2.620***	8.74	
ALPHA	0.178***			0.177***			0.179***		
Log-lik. at intercept		−318.87			−318.87			−318.87	
Log-lik. at convergence		−260.28			−260.08			−260.54	
Pseudo R^2		0.17			0.17			0.18	
LR of alpha = 0		392.51			377.39			386.46	

*** Significant at a 99% confidence level.

Consistent with expectations of overdispersion because the variance of crashes exceeded the mean, results suggest that the negative binomial model was the preferred model. The overdispersion parameters in the negative binomial specification always are significantly different from zero at high levels of confidence. The overall fit of the models seem adequate, with all of them explaining between 16.5 and 18.3% of the log-likelihood of a constant-only model. Adjusting for the degrees of freedom, the models explain between 16.4 and 16.6% of the log likelihood of a constant-only model.

Estimated Influence of Financial Performance on Crash Frequency

None of the financial coefficients of interest are statistically significant. Across equations, other coefficients have consistent signs and levels of significance. The coefficient for power units and its square term suggest that the larger the firm, the higher the crash frequency but at a decreasing rate. By contrast, the coefficient for the log of miles traveled is not statistically significant, suggesting that the crash rate decreases with miles and is independent of the size of the firm, as measured by the number of power units. A model constraining the coefficient for the log of miles to one (not shown), which is equivalent to modeling crash rate (crashes per million miles) instead of the crash frequency, produced similar results.

Even though we found no systematic differences in crash rates based on financial performance, it is possible that these effects are significant depending on the size of firm. Smaller firms, for example, have a limited ability to institutionalize safety practices and thus may rely more on the human capital of their drivers for safe driving. Likewise, in the highly competitive truckload sector, smaller trucking firms may be more vulnerable to sudden shifts in market demand than larger firms. Similarly, larger firms may provide additional institutional means for safe driving such as stronger maintenance programs and institutionalized safety departments (including trained safety directors), as well as the resources allowing the firms to participate in safety contests and other performance-enhancing learning activities. To examine this hypothesis, we grouped firms into three categories – small, medium, and large – according to the number of power units owned or leased by the carrier. Firms with fewer than 100 power units were classified as small, whereas firms with more than 1000 power units were classified as large. An interaction term between the financial performance measure and firm size is used to test our hypothesis which results in three variables for operating ratio (OR_SMALL, OR_MEDIUM, OR_LARGE), cash flow ratio (CF_SMALL, CF_MEDIUM, CF_LARGE) and labor expense per revenue ratio (LR_SMALL, LR_MEDIUM, LR_LARGE). Table 3 shows results following a similar format as before.

Table 3. Total Crashes and Financial Performance by Firm Size, Negative Binomial Regression.

	Operating Ratio Model			Cash Flow Ratio Model			Labor Costs Per Revenue Ratio Model		
	Coef.	*t*	Elast	Coef.	*t*	Elast	Coef.	*t*	Elast
LOGMILES	0.056	1.00	0.22	0.070	1.28	0.27	0.058	1.03	0.22
P. UNITS	0.001**	6.32	1.24	0.002**	8.21	1.33	0.002**	6.61	1.32
P. UNITS^2	−1.5E-07**	−4.99	−0.34	−1.6E-07**	−6.28	−0.36	−1.6E-07**	−5.29	−0.36
OR_SMALL	−1.245	−1.14	−0.08						
OR_MEDIUM	−0.582	−0.53	−0.40						
OR_LARGE	−0.534	−0.48	−0.11						
CFR_SMALL				−0.984*	−2.25	−0.03			
CFR_MEDIUM				0.093	1.58	0.04			
CFR_LARGE				−0.010	−0.1	0.00			
LR_SMALL							−1.263*	−2.25	−0.04
LR_MEDIUM							0.104	0.19	0.03
LR_LARGE							−0.095	−0.14	−0.01
CONSTANT	3.222**	3.06		2.518**	11.93		2.595**	9.33	
ALPHA	0.162**			0.159**			0.159**		
Log-lik. at intercept		−318.87			−318.87			−318.87	
Log-lik. at convergence		−257.00			−256.79			−257.83	
Pseudo R^2		0.19			0.20			0.19	
LR of alpha = 0		341.45			347.71			331.67	

* Significant at a 95% confidence level.

** Significant at a 99% confidence level.

The results for operating ratio suggest that there is no detectable difference in the relationship between operating ratio and safety outcomes by firm size. However, the results for the cash-flow ratio model show a statistically significant relationship between safety and small-firm liquidity. Higher liquidity in small firms is related to a lower expected number of crashes. The elasticity estimate suggests that 10% greater liquidity among small firms yields a 0.3% lower crash frequency. A similar finding is reproduced for the labor costs per revenue ratio model, which suggests that small firms with higher labor expenses relative to their revenue have better safety outcomes. This is consistent with our hypothesis that small firms rely more on labor market selection to improve safety outcomes than larger firms.

These results suggest that efficiency wages appear to play a significant role in a labor-intensive industry like trucking, especially among smaller firms less able to manage and monitor drivers. Smaller firms have a greater need to align the incentives of drivers with firm incentives. While the size of the effect is small, these results suggest that it is important for public policy to encourage small firms to rely on higher driver compensation in place of the kind of driver monitoring, training, and supervision that larger firms can provide. The results also suggest that small firms are likely to suffer the most in times of tight labor markets, partly because their safety investments come from hiring better prepared drivers. Likewise, policy makers should consider whether small firms could be encouraged or required to maintain greater liquidity and driver compensation as a safety measure. This consideration could be undertaken either within the formal regulatory framework (regulation) or the informal regulatory framework (insurance pricing and monitoring).

Influence of Compensation Factors on Crash Frequency

While the primary interest of our study is on the relationship between firm financial performance and driver safety outcomes, we take advantage of the richness of the data to examine whether driver compensation policy is related to driver safety outcomes. To reiterate, empirical evidence (e.g. Belzer et al., 2002; Hirsch, 1993; Monaco & Williams, 2000; Rodríguez et al., 2003) provides support for the idea that compensation helps to explain firm safety outcomes. In the context of our study, driver compensation is an explicit measure of firms' safety investments. Of course, firms can make investments in other safety areas not observed here, such as improved vehicle maintenance, or in technology. Nonetheless, we consider it important to include explicit measures of safety investments, while using firm financial performance and driver compensation to account for unobserved investments. Furthermore, this differs from previous analyses in that our measurement of compensation goes well beyond per mile rates to include pay raises (RAISE), uncompensated non-driving time (UNPAID), safety incentives, (SAFEBON), and benefits (PAIDVAC, HEALTH, LIFEINS).

All the compensation variables were introduced simultaneously as a block to a regression equation that included each of the financial performance measures by firm size. Results for the model including compensation variables are provided in Table 4. A test of the hypothesis that the compensation coefficients are simultaneously equal to zero can be rejected at a 89% level of confidence, at a 95% level of confidence, and at a 93% level of confidence for the operating ratio, cash flow, and labor cost per revenue ratio models, respectively. From a statistical standpoint, this suggests that inclusion of the compensation variables, as a block, appears warranted. Most models explain around 21% of the log-likelihood of a constant-only equation. As in the previous equations, alpha is greater than zero, indicating that the negative binomial specification is preferred to a Poisson specification. The coefficients and elasticities for the firm financial performance variables remain similar to those obtained in Table 3, with one exception. The liquidity measure for the medium-sized firms (cash flow ratio model) becomes marginally significant at 90% level of confidence.

Throughout the three models, two compensation variables emerge as consistently related to crash outcomes: UNPAID and HEALTH. The former measures the number of hours of unpaid time per mile driven in a typical run, and the coefficient is positive, as expected. The greater the number of unpaid work hours per mile driven, the higher the number of crashes in the firm. HEALTH measures the driver's monthly contribution to a health plan. A higher number represents a reduction in compensation, offsetting higher wage rates. Unexpectedly, the coefficient for this variable is negative, indicating that the higher the average driver contribution, the lower the crash frequency. Although explanations for this result are possible, the quality of the health plan available to drivers should be observed before speculating about the meaning of this result. For example, it is possible that employees pay more for better quality health plans (access to any private health facility vs. an HMO). Thus, risk averse employees are likely to subscribe to the more expensive plan and such risk aversion may transfer to work habits, as they may be more likely to be safer employees.

Finally, no other compensation variables are statistically significant at standard levels of confidence. Although this may be more a result of the small sample size than of the relationship between individual variables and crashes, it is surprising to find that PAY and PAIDVAC and SAFEBON are not statistically significant. In addition to sample size, other factors may contribute to improving the explanatory power of the model, such as additional driver-level factors (e.g. driving ability and

Table 4. Total Crashes, Financial Performance by Firm Size, and Compensation Variables Negative Binomial Regression.

	Operating Ratio Model			Cash Flow Ratio Model			Labor Costs Per Revenue Ratio Model		
	Coef.	*t*	Elast	Coef.	*t*	Elast	Coef.	*t*	Elast
PAY	−2.129	−0.81	−0.62	−0.996	−0.39	−0.29	−1.185	−0.42	−0.34
UNPAID	43.662**	2.49	0.19	44.942**	2.59	0.19	53.998***	3.09	0.23
PAIDVAC	3.5E-04	−1.48	−0.27	3.4E-04	−1.48	−0.26	3.3E-04	−1.35	−0.25
RAISE	−12.296	−0.65	−0.08	−6.776	−0.36	−0.04	7.197	0.37	0.05
SAFEBON	−0.097	−0.85	−0.05	−0.117	−1.01	−0.07	−0.094	−0.84	−0.05
HEALTH	−0.003***	−2.76	−0.45	−0.003***	−3.12	−0.51	−0.003***	−2.95	−0.49
LIFEINS	−4.0E-06	−0.8	−0.06	−4.0E-06	−0.81	−0.06	−4.0E-06	−0.88	−0.07
LOGMILES	0.038	0.69	0.15	0.035	0.67	0.14	0.023	0.43	0.09
P. UNITS	0.001***	6.21	1.17	0.002***	8.80	1.29	0.001***	6.09	1.23
P. UNITS^2	−1.4E-07***	−4.75	−0.31	−2E-07***	−6.56	−0.35	−1E-07***	−4.69	−0.33
OR_SMALL	−1.670	−1.58	−0.11						
OR_MEDIUM	−1.054	−0.98	−0.72						
OR_LARGE	−0.849	−0.79	−0.17						
CFR_SMALL				−1.165**	−2.59	−0.03			
CFR_MEDIUM				0.091*	1.65	0.04			
CFR_LARGE				0.038	0.37	0.01			
LR_SMALL							−1.798***	−3.05	−0.06
LR_MEDIUM							−0.205	−0.37	−0.05
LR_LARGE							0.048	0.06	0.00
CONSTANT	5.080***	3.62		3.672***	4.82		3.775***	4.21	
ALPHA	0.127***			0.121***			0.120***		
Log-lik. at intercept		−318.87			−318.87			−318.87	
Log-lik. at convergence		−252.10			−250.24			−250.06	
Pseudo R^2		0.21			0.22			0.22	
LR of alpha = 0		187.30			206.19			185.33	

*Significant at a 90% confidence level.
**Significant at a 95% confidence level.
***Significant at a 99% confidence level.

ability to tolerate fatigue), vehicle factors (vehicle condition), other occupational factors (time spent waiting for loads, or loading and unloading, regularity of schedule, and hours worked/awake), and environmental factors (weather and quality of roads).

CONCLUSIONS

Recent research has shown that financial performance measures, firm characteristics, operation characteristics, and human capital factors have an important influence on crash involvement. Using a distinct methodological approach and a unique dataset, this research provides evidence showing that such factors tend to be important predictors of frequency of crash involvement. In particular, this study finds that low liquidity and low labor expenses per revenue of trucking firms with fewer than 100 power units are correlated with high crash frequencies. This supports our hypothesis that small trucking firms can invest in safety by devoting more resources to driver compensation, thereby improving safety outcomes. In contrast, a firm's operating ratio was not significantly related to crash frequency.

In a second model specification we also test the hypothesis, from conventional economic theory, that firms paying higher compensation to workers should have better quality workers and have fewer crashes. Compensation variables examined include direct compensation, safety, vacation and health benefits. As expected, we find some evidence showing that firms offering greater compensation experienced a lower crash frequency, controlling for financial measures. However, the coefficients for the direct compensation variable, pay rate, were not statistically significant. One explanation for this could be that pay is an endogenous variable that has been treated as exogenous in a model designed to capture financial effects.

A limitation of this study is the small number of firms available in the dataset. Although there is a strong potential for continued research relying on the merger of two or more trucking industry and federal/state data sources, the process of merging data may propagate the shortcomings of various sources. The Signpost dataset includes most of the larger carriers and excludes thousands of smaller carriers. This bias toward the bigger carriers shrinks the sample size and excludes thousands of small carriers, which our models suggest may have the biggest safety problems in combination with low liquidity and driver compensation. On the other hand, Financial and Operating Statistics data cover only large firms in interstate commerce, and despite the obligation to file this form, only a relatively small fraction of firms do so. It also is plagued by missing values in a number of data elements. Despite this, the empirical findings suggest it is important to account for carrier economic condition and for the level of investment in human capital in the study of truck safety. The effort demonstrated in this study provides a basis for future research on firm financial factors affecting truck driver safety.

NOTES

1. "Deregulation" in this paper refers to "economic deregulation." Belzer (2000) argues that a distinction must be made between economic and social regulation. Although the latter – including hours-of-service and other safety regulations – have an economic impact, they are not designed primarily to regulate the economic environment but rather regulate the social consequences of economic competition.

2. Not surprisingly, occupational factors also have been associated with illegal substance use (Hensher & Battelino, 1990; Hensher et al., 1992) and a higher propensity to speed (Hensher et al., 1991).

3. Owner-operators are considered low cost alternatives to for-hire carriers.

4. Further research on the profitability-safety performance association for trucking firms is reported by Bruning (1989), Moses and Savage (1992, 1996), Hunter and Mangum (1995), Wilde (1995) and Corsi, Barnard and Gibney (2002).

5. Past findings by Hirsch (1988) and Rose (1987) show declining for-hire wage rates following deregulation.

6. The American Trucking Association Foundation is now known as the American Transportation Research Institute.

7. The information on compensation for non-driving work in Signpost suggests a wide degree of payment methods difficult to compress into a single measure. The original Signpost data on pay for loading and unloading is presented as either a flat rate, or an amount per hour, or one of several other modes. This data does not permit development of a more finely tuned scale of pay for loading and unloading.

8. See http://www.bts.gov/mcs/desc.html.

9. Signpost only provides categorical data regarding the number of power units.

10. Information in Table 1 indicates significant variation in driver compensation across trucking firms. For instance, the average starting rate of pay for a driver with three years experience was 29 cents per mile, with a minimum of 24 cents and a maximum of 37 cents per mile (PAY). The variable UNPAID, measuring the number of hours of unpaid time per mile driven, measures the amount of uncompensated time relative the paid time. The mean amount of unpaid time is 0.004 hours per mile driven. Since an average trip in this data set is about 890 miles, on average drivers worked 3.56 hours of unpaid time per trip. PAIDVAC measures the value of the sum of pay for vacation, holiday and sick time. The average firm offers about $757.7 worth of paid time off per year, with a minimum of $350 and a maximum of $2,000. More than half of the firms provide a safety bonus (SAFEBON). The average driver contribution to the health plan (HEALTH) is about $160 per year with a minimum of zero and a maximum of $368, while the amortized value of company-paid life insurance is $15,858 (LIFEINS).

11. For details, see Cameron and Trivedi (1998, pp. 70–77). Using Cameron and Trivedi's terminology, this is known as the NB2 parameterization.

12. For a given independent variable X_j, the elasticity is evaluated numerically as $\partial \log E(n_i)/\partial \log(X_{ji})$ at the means of the independent variables (see Table 1).

REFERENCES

Arnold, P. K., Hartley, L. R., Corry, A., Hochstadt, D., Penna, F., & Feyer, A. M. (1997). Hours of work and perceptions of fatigue among truck drivers. *Accident Analysis and Prevention, 29*, 471–477.

Becker, G. (1962). Investment in human capital: A theoretical analysis. *Journal of Political Economy, 70*(Suppl.), 9–44.

Becker, G. (1964). *Human capital: A theoretical and empirical analysis*, with Special Reference to Education. New York: Columbia University Press.

Beilock, R. (1994). Schedule tightness and work hours of long-distance tractor trailer drivers in the United States. Presented at Canadian Transportation Research Forum, Victoria (BC).

Belzer, M. H. (1995). Collective bargaining after deregulation: Do the teamsters still count? *Industrial and Labor Relations Review, 48*, 636–655.

Belzer, M. H. (2000). *Sweatshops on wheels: Winners and losers in trucking deregulation*. London: Oxford University Press.

Belzer, M. H., Rodriguez, D., & Sedo, S. (2002). *Paying for safety: An economic analysis of the effect of compensation on truck driver safety*. Report to the Federal Motor Carrier Safety Administration, Prime Contract Number DTFH 61-98-C-0061.

Blevins, M., & Chow, G. (1988). Truck safety and financial distress: A preliminary analysis. *Journal of the Transportation Research Forum, 29*, 18–23.

Bruning, E. R. (1989). The relationship between profitability and safety performance in trucking firms. *Transportation Journal, 28*, 40–49.

Cameron, A. C., & Trivedi, P. K. (1998). *Regression analysis of count data*. Cambridge: Cambridge University Press.

Chatterjee, A., Cadotte, E., Sink, H., Venigalla, M., & Gaides, G. (1994). *Driver-related factors involved with truck accidents*. Raleigh, NC: Institute for Transportation Research and Education.

Chen, Y. N., Weston, J. F., & Altman, E. I. (1995). Financial distress and restructuring models. *Financial Management, 24*, 57–75.

Chow, G., Vasina, M., Gritta, R., & Adrangi, B. (1987). Definition and measurement of financial fitness in the trucking industry. *Journal of the Transportation Forum, 28*, 319–324.

Corsi, T. M., Barnard, R., & Gibney, J. (2002). *Motor carrier industry profile: Linkages between financial and safety performances among carriers in major industry segments*. Prepared for U.S. Department of Transportation, Federal Highway Administration and the Federal Motor Carrier Safety Administration. Available at the FMCSA-Volpe web site February 2004. http://ai.volpe.dot.gov/carrierresearchresults/pdfs/financialsafety_mcips.pdf.

Corsi, T. M., & Fanara, P., Jr. (1988). Driver management policies and motor carrier safety. *Logistics and Transportation Review, 24*, 153–163.

Dionne, G., & Vanasse, C. (1992). Automobile insurance ratemaking in the presence of asymmetrical information. *Journal of Applied Econometrics, 7*, 149–165.

Fazzari, S. M., & Athey, M. J. (1987). Asymmetric information, financing constraints, and investment. *Review of Economics and Statistics, 69*, 481–487.

Fazzari, S. M., & Petersen, B. C. (1993). Working capital and fixed investment – new evidence on financing constraints. *Rand Journal of Economics, 24*, 328–342.

Feyer, A. M., Williamson, A. M., Jenkin, R., & Higgins, T. (1993). *Strategies to combat fatigue in the long distance road transport industry – bus and coach perspective*. Sydney, Canberra: CR 122. Australian National Occupational Health and Safety Commission.

Hakkanen, H., & Summala, H. (2000). Sleepiness at work among commercial truck drivers. *Sleep*, *23*, 49–57.

Hensher, D., & Battelino, H. C. (1990). Long-distance trucking: Why do truckers speed? Presented at Australasian transport research forum.

Hensher, D., Battellino, H. C., Gee, J. L., & Daniels, R. F. (1991). *Long distance truck drivers on-road performance and economic reward*. Sydney: Sydney University, Australia, Institute of Transport Studies.

Hensher, D., Daniels, R., & Battellino, H. (1992). Safety and productivity in the long distance trucking industry. Presented at the 16th Australian Research Board Conference, Perth.

Hirsch, B. T. (1988). Trucking regulation, unionization and labor earnings: 1973–1985. *Journal of Human Resources*, *23*, 296–319.

Hirsch, B. T. (1993). Trucking deregulation and labor earnings: Is the union premium a compensating differential. *Journal of Labor Economics*, *11*, 279–301.

Hunter, N., & Mangum, S. (1995). Economic regulation, employment relations, and accident rates in the U.S. motor carrier industry. *Labor Studies Journal*, 48–63.

Krass, A. (1993). The impact of the U.S. motor carrier act of 1980 on road safety in California: An econometric policy evaluation. *Logistics and Transportation Review*, *29*, 179–192.

Lin, T. D., Jovanis, P., & Yang, C. Z. (1993). Modeling the safety of truck driver service hours using time-dependent logistic regression. *Transportation Research Record*, *1407*, 1–10.

Lyman, S., & Braver, E. R. (2002). Occupant deaths in large truck crashes in the United States: 25 years of experience. *Accident Analysis and Prevention* (in press).

Lyznicki, J., Doege, T., Davis, R., & Williams, M. (1998). Sleepiness, driving and motor vehicle crashes. *Journal of the American Medical Association*, *279*, 1908–1913.

McCartt, A., Hammer, M. C., & Fuller, S. F. (1997). Understanding and managing fatigued driving: Study of long-distance truck drivers in New York State. Presented at International Large Truck Safety Symposium, Knoxville, Tennessee.

McCartt, A., Rohrbaugh, J. W., Hammer, M. C., & Fuller, S. Z. (2000). Factors associated with falling asleep at the wheel among long-distance truck drivers. *Accident Analysis and Prevention*, *32*, 493–504.

Monaco, K., & Williams, E. (2000). Assessing the determinants of safety in the trucking industry. *Journal of Transportation and Statistics*, *3*, 69–80.

Moses, L. N., & Savage, I. (1992). The effectiveness of motor carrier safety audits. *Accident Analysis and Prevention*, *24*, 479–496.

Moses, L. N., & Savage, I. (1996). Identifying dangerous trucking firms. *Risk Analysis*, *16*, 359–366.

Office of Technology Assessment (1988). *Gearing up for safety: Summary and report*. Washington, DC: Office of Technology Assessment, Congress of the United States.

Office of Technology Assessment (1991). *Freight trucking: Promising approach for predicting carriers' safety risks*. Washington, DC: Office of Technology Assessment, Congress of the United States.

Opler, T. C., & Titman, S. (1994). Financial distress and corporate performance. *Journal of Finance*, *49*, 1015–1040.

Rodríguez, D. A., Rocha, M., Khattak, A., & Belzer, M. H. (2003). The effects of truck driver wages and working conditions on highway safety: A case study. *Transportation Research Record*, *1883*, 95–102.

Rose, N. (1990). Profitability and product quality: Economic determinants of airline safety performance. *Journal of Political Economy*, *98*, 944–964.

Rose, N. L. (1987). Labor rent sharing and regulation: Evidence from the trucking industry. *Journal of Political Economy*, *95*, 1146–1178.

Shaw, J. D., Nina, G., & Delery, J. E. (2003). Voluntary turnover, work force performance, and financial performance. *Academy of Management Journal* (under review).

Wilde, G. (1995). *Improving trucking safety and profitability through safety incentive schemes.* Australia: Queen's University.

4. AN ECONOMETRIC ANALYSIS OF THE IMPACT OF TECHNOLOGY ON THE WORK LIVES OF TRUCK DRIVERS

Kristen A. Monaco and Dale L. Belman

ABSTRACT

We investigate the relationship between technology and drivers' work using data from the Sloan Trucking Industry Driver Survey. We find that the largest firms are most likely to equip their trucks with satellite based systems (SBS), providing some evidence of scale effects of this technology. Drivers who use satellite systems may be paid less per mile, however, receive 17.6% higher annual earnings, due to the increased mileage, about 22,000 additional miles per year. Part of this mileage gain is explained by efficiencies provided by these systems, but drivers with satellites also work 14% more hours weekly.

INTRODUCTION

Although the effect of technology on productivity, employment and conditions of work has long been a topic of research in the social science community, the IT revolution of the last two decades has spurred new interest. Current research has been particularly concerned with the effect of technological change on income distribution and the employment opportunity for less skilled workers.

Transportation Labor Issues and Regulatory Reform
Research in Transportation Economics, Volume 10, 57–78

ISSN: 0739-8859/doi:10.1016/S0739-8859(04)10004-8

This research takes advantage of a unique and richly detailed survey of truck drivers to investigate the relationship between IT and the productivity, hours of work and wages of truck drivers. The occupational focus of this research is unique in the technology literature but is required to understand the linkages between technology and outcomes such as productivity, earnings and work effort. Although improved communications and monitoring technologies are being implemented throughout the U.S. economy, the implementation for truck drivers is very different from that of other settings such as retail trade and manufacturing. Differences in employment structures among occupations causes technologies with similar purposes to elicit different responses from employees and results in different outcomes. Occupational studies provide deeper insights into the operation of technology, at the cost of applying to a narrower range of employees. This said, truck drivers are among the largest occupations in the United States with the 2,840,900 employees and self-employed workers in truck driving in 1995 comprising 2.4% of the employed labor force. Truck driving is also among the fastest growing major occupations with employment rising by 75% between 1973 and 1995.

This paper is divided into three parts. The first provides an overview of the work and work life of truck drivers. The second examines which types of drivers have access to and use technology. The balance of the paper is given over to a cross sectional study of the effects of technology on earnings, productivity, and working conditions. The cross sectional study builds on a unique data set of 573 structured interviews with truck drivers to investigate how technology has affected drivers' earnings, productivity, and working conditions. We find that, although most truck board technologies have little systematic influence on driver earnings or work, satellite communication systems, a recently implemented communications and location technology, increase drivers' annual earnings through improved efficiency and work intensification.

THE WORK LIFE OF AN OVER-THE-ROAD DRIVER

Long Haul truck drivers' work life, represented in word, song and film as that of a cowboy with an eighteen wheel horse, is distinct from that of most employees. Drivers work longer hours than the typical full-time employee, spend extended periods away from home, are often not directly compensated for time spent working, receive few benefits relative to their age and work experience, and suffer high levels of turnover. Their work life reflects the particular needs and competitive pressures of the motor freight industry as well as the regulatory framework which controls drivers' work. Truck drivers are exempt from the Fair Labor Standards Act requirements for overtime pay and pay for time worked. Instead, they are subject to the hours of service (HOS) regulations of the Department of Transportation. These rules limit drivers to sixty hours of work time in seven days, and require an eight-hour break after ten hours of driving and fifteen hours of total work time.[1] Drivers, rather than employers, are liable for violations of the HOS regulations. The working conditions for truck drivers, particularly the long hours of work and accompanying problems with chronic sleep deprivation and drowsiness, have been a source of concern as they are perceived to affect public safety. These concerns are motivating research on truck drivers' sleep patterns (Atkinson, 1999; Lyznicki, Doege et al., 1998) as well as the first substantial revision of the hours of service rules since 1937 (Federal Motor Carrier Safety Administration, 2000).[2]

Our description draws extensively on a survey of full-time over-the-road and local drivers in the motor freight industry conducted by the Sloan Foundation Trucking Industry Program (TIP) and the Institute for Social Research in the summer and fall of 1997.[3] The survey, which includes data from 573 drivers, collected a range of data including respondents' work history; the characteristics of their current work; the structure of compensation; time spent working, waiting, and resting; and use of technology. As it was focused on over-the-road (OTR) drivers and conducted in truck stops, the survey under-sampled metropolitan area drivers, who are less likely to use truck stops than OTR drivers, and it may have under-sampled organized drivers.[4,5] It has advantages over the more commonly used Current Population Survey (CPS) in collecting a richer body of information, eliciting more accurate responses about compensation and hours of work, collecting economic data on owner-operators as well as employees, and avoiding some matters of representativeness.[6] A description of the survey methodology and summary of results may be found in Belman, Monaco, and Brooks (BMB, forthcoming).[7]

What does this survey tell us about the work life of truck drivers? Drivers are, in many respects, typical blue-collar workers. They are somewhat older than a national sample of blue-collar workers, a result of the 21 year legal minimum age for obtaining a Commercial Drivers License (Table 1a). Consistent with their greater age, drivers are also more likely to be married and have children than other blue-collar males. Although few women are employed as drivers, the racial and ethnic composition of the driver labor force is comparable to that of other blue-collar workers. The educational attainment of drivers is also similar to that of other blue-collar workers: 43.6% of drivers have a high school degree, 21.8% have some college courses, and 4.5% have a college degree. Judged by their annual income, motor freight drivers are solidly middle class (Table 1b). The median annual income of drivers in 1996 was $35,000, slightly above the $34,522

Table 1a. Characteristics of Driver Survey and National Blue Collar Samples.

Characteristic	TIP Driver Survey (%)	National Blue Collar Sample (%)
Age		
Gender		
Male	97.2	60.2
Race		
White	85.3	83.1
African-American	8.9	12.8
Other	4.1	3.3
Ethnicity		
Hispanic	2	8.5
Marital status		
Never married	12.8	26.4
Married	63.6	54.5
Widowed	2.6	3.2
Divorced/separated	11.1	15.9
Education		
Less than high school	2.3	6.8
Some high school	18.3	14.0
High school diploma	43.6	48.9
Vocational degree	4.4	4.8
Some college	22.7	18.6
Associate degree	3.9	4.8
College degree or more	4.8	5.2

Note: Data on truck drivers from the TIP driver survey. National blue collar sample taken from 1997 CPS. Except for data on gender, CPS data is limited to male blue collar workers age 18 and older.

median family income for families with a wife who is not in the paid labor force (Mishel, Bernstein & Schmidt, 1999, Table 1.5).[8]

Drivers appear less middle-class when hours of work, rates of pay, benefits, and working conditions are considered. 90% of drivers work under compensation schemes that link pay to mileage (BMB, p. 44). To earn a middle-class income, the median respondent needed to drive 110,000 miles a year and work approximately 3,000 hours (BMB, pp. 40, 44 & 50). Respondents averaged 11.4 hours of work in the prior 24 hours; 8.5 hours were spent driving while 3.1 hours were spent on other duties and waiting (Table 1c). Although most drivers worked five or fewer days in the last seven, 20% reported working six days and an additional 19% reported working all seven (BMB, p. 95). Using data on the last seven calendar

Table 1b. 1996 Annual Incomes of Truck Drivers and the National Male Labor Force.

	1996 Income
Truck drivers	
Mean	$35,985
10th percentile	$15,000
25th percentile	$26,000
Median	$35,000
75th percentile	$45,000
90th percentile	$53,000
National labor force	
Family income, wife not in labor force	
Median	$34,522
Earnings of year-round full-time male workers with high school diploma	
Mean	$32,521

Note: Family Income and Earnings of Year Round Full-Time Male Workers from *State of Working America: 1998–1999.*

days, the median driver reported working exactly 60 hours, but 25% reported working at least 70 hours and 10% reported working at least 90 hours (BMB, p. 95). Based on data on the last pay period, we found the median respondent worked 62 hours in seven days; mean work time was 65.7 hours (BMB, p. 99). Drivers also take little time off work. The median driver took five days of vacation, four holiday days, and no sick leave in 1996 (BMB, p. 66). Assembling these elements, the typical driver works approximately 3,000 hours annually, earning their way into the middle-class income by working 1.5 full time jobs.[9] The median driver would earn only a modest $23,340 for a standard 2,000 hour year.

Table 1c. Mileage and Hours of Work of Truck Drivers.

	Miles Driven			Hours Worked	
	Last 24 Hours	Last 7 Days	Last Year	Last 24 Hours	Last 7 Days
Mean	439.7	2126	109,965	11.4	63.2
10th percentile	130	700	50,000	5.8	38
25th percentile	268	1500	82,000	8.2	50
Median	400	2186	110,000	11.0	60
75th percentile	583	2800	130,000	14.0	75
90th percentile	750	3500	160,000	18.0	90

Note: Data from TIP Driver Survey.

How much do drivers earn per hour? While only 10% of drivers are paid by the hour, an hourly rate, inclusive of all earnings including bonuses, can be constructed as the ratio of reported annual income to estimated annual hours of work. The average hourly wage of drivers was $11.67, 76% of the $15.45 average hourly earnings of the employed force (Mishel, Bernstein & Schmidt, 1999, p. 123). Union drivers earned the top rate of $14.68 per hour, while non-union drivers averaged $10.75 and non-union owner-operators earned $12.03. Benefit coverage and levels are also relatively low. Conventional pension plans are rare; only 26.6% of drivers participated in such plans and most of these were union members. Deferred compensation plans such as a 401(K) are more common; 46.6% participated in such plans, but the median driver had less than $5,000 in his or her account (BMB, p. 59). Medical insurance is more common among employees; 100% of union members and 87.4% of non-union employees reported some form of medical insurance, but only 66% of owner-operators carried such plans. Over half of these plans were contributory. Only 27.4% were fully funded by the employer, most of these were found in the organized sector (BMB, p. 59).

The dynamics of the occupation, in which drivers compensate for low rates through long hours of work, leads to frequent violations of the hours of service rules, inadequate rest, and drowsiness while driving. Responses to questions on working time over the last seven days and the last pay period suggest that working up to and beyond the legal hours of work is ubiquitous. Consistent with anecdotal evidence of drivers' gaming of the hours of service rules (DiSalvatore, 1988), only 16.1% of respondents to the TIP survey believed that logbooks accurately reflected drivers' hours of work. 56% reported that they had worked more than they had logged in the last 30 days, and 55% reported that they had driven more than ten hours without an eight hour break in the last 30 days. Problems of dozing and lack of sleep while driving are common; 35% of drivers reported dozing while driving at least once in the last 30 days, and 15% reported dozing at least three times over that period (BMB, p. 161). While most drivers reported at least six hours of sleep in the last twenty-four hours, 5.4% reported two or fewer hours of sleep and 15% of drivers reported not sleeping in the 24 hours before returning home (BMB, p. 86).

Turnover and quit rates are high. Although the median driver had worked in his or her occupation for 12 years, median service with the current employer was 18 months (BMB, p. 107). Only 21% of non-union employees had been with their employer for four years or more. One quarter of non-union employees reported quitting a driving job in the last year, and the same proportion of non-union owner-operators reported terminating a lease or otherwise breaking a long-term relationship with an employing firm (BMB, p. 107). High turnover results from drivers seeking better employment, but respondents suggested that some companies force out drivers who would otherwise qualify for the higher rates that come with longer service.

There is considerable inequality among drivers with regard to wages, hours of work, and working conditions. The most obvious division is between organized employees, non-union employees, and owner-operators.[10] The median union member earned $44,000 annually, 26% more than non-member employees' median earnings of $35,000 and 33% more than non-union owner operators. The median non-union owner-operator's earnings after truck expenses were 6% less than those of non-union employees. The pattern of inequality for hours is different. Owner-operators worked the shortest hours: 56 hours per week with 11 days off annually for an annual work year of 2824 hours at the median. Union employees worked 60 hours per week, took 15 days off for an annual work year of 2940 hours (BMB, p. 74). Non-union employees worked the longest hours: 65 hours per week, eight days off and an annual work year of 3306 hours. These differences in annual hours result in a pattern of hourly rates that diverges from that of annual earnings. Union employees had the highest hourly rates, earning 37% more than non-union employees, while owner-operators earned 12% more per hour than non-union employees (BMB, p. 74).

Non-wage benefits were also unequally distributed. Union members were more likely to participate in pension plans (77%) and medical insurance plans (100%) than were non-union employees (21.4 and 87.4%) or owner-operators (15.4 and 66.2%) and were only slightly less likely to participate in deferred compensation plans and IRAs (44.0 and 29.4%) than were non-union employees (59.8 and 12.8%) or owner-operators (15.3 and 33.3%) (BMB, p. 59). Organized drivers' ability to maintain considerably better wages and benefits may rest, in part, on the union's retreat into segments of the industry which have barriers to entry (such as less than truckload freight), which are more concerned with the quality of work than the price (such as new auto haul), or local markets which are highly organized.

There were also considerable differences in earnings within each of these groups. Among non-union employees, the driver at the 25th percentile earned 23% less than the median driver, while the driver at the 75th percentile earned 28% more than the median driver. The dispersion of earnings is more marked at the 10th and 90th percentile, with the former earning 52% less than the median, and the latter earning 48% more. The dispersion of earnings is smaller among organized drivers, but substantially larger among owner-operators. The narrower spread in earnings of union employees is consistent with the literature that finds that unions reduce wage variance through rate standardization; the larger dispersion of owner-operators' earnings may be due to the greater risk assumed by owner-operators.

WHO USES TECHNOLOGY?

The most recent technologies adopted by the industry, communications and location technologies, routing technologies, and computing technologies, are used directly by drivers. The Driver Survey indicates that faxes are the most commonly used technology (32.3% report using a fax), but satellite-based communication and location systems (29.5%) are almost as common, as are beepers (28.5%) and cell phones (31.1%) (Table 2). In contrast, relatively few drivers use e-mail

Table 2. The TIP Driver Survey Sample: Descriptive Statistics.

Communications technologies	
Fax	32.3%
Beeper	28.5%
Two way radio	6.8%
Cellular phone	31.1%
E-mail	2.3%
Satellite based system	29.5%
Computing technologies	
Laptop computer	5.1%
Routing technologies	
Dispatcher	32.6%
Cb radio	64.7%
On-board computer with maps	8.1%
Laptop with maps	3.9%
Collective bargaining	
Union member	12.3%
Human capital	
Age	42.0 years
Occupational experience	15.0 years
Less than high school education	20.2%
High school diploma	43.8%
Vocational or technical degree	4.5%
Some college	21.8%
Associate of arts	4.4%
College degree or higher	4.5%
Other characteristics	
Local driver	12.5%
Owner operator	24.8%
Private carriage	17.4%
Paid by the hour	15.5%
Paid percent of revenue	36.0%

(2.3%), and a modest number use two-way radios (6.8%). The most common routing technology is CB radio (64.7%); the second is use of a dispatcher (32.6%). Computer mapping technologies, such as on-board computer maps (8.1%) and laptops with maps (3.9%), are relatively uncommon. Despite news stories about the use of laptop computers by drivers (Kopytoff, 1999), only 5.1% of drivers have such equipment in their trucks. With certain exceptions, notably fax machines, few drivers report using multiple technologies.

Although influenced by customers and employees, firms control the adoption of technology. Given the cost of technology to firms, there must be a profit incentive for firms to implement new technologies such as Satellite Based Systems (SBS). Breshnahan et al. (2002) propose that technology will be adopted if it improves firm performance by improving service to customers or aligning the incentives of firms and workers. This finding is echoed by Hubbard (2000). Acemoglu (2000) echoes this importance of workers in successful implementation of technology; firms will receive no returns to technology if the technology is not "complementary" to worker skills.

Using firm data collected by the American Trucking Association and the Department of Transportation, Chakraborty and Kazarosian (1999) assess technology's impact on trucking firms. They find that the adoption depends upon the segment of the market served by the firm. Heavier loads, longer trips, and time sensitivity increase the likelihood that the firm will adopt technologies such as SBS (including Automatic Vehicle Location – AVL) and on-board computers.

As a survey of drivers, rather than firms, the TIP Driver Survey provides a different perspective on the adoption of technology. In addition to the extensive information collected about drivers, the survey included questions on presence and use of technology (gadgets in the parlance of the survey) as well as on the characteristics of the employing firm. This allows further testing of the hypotheses about forces driving the adoption of technology.

We begin with some descriptive statistics, dividing workers by the operating characteristics of their firm and examine the prevalence of the most common technologies within these subgroups (Table 3).

Not surprisingly, over-the-road drivers are more likely than local drivers to use SBS (32.1% vs. 15.6%) and less likely to use two-way radios (5.2% vs. 17.8%) or cell phones (28.5% vs. 48.9%) in their work. SBS is also more common among for-hire drivers than private carriage (34.6% vs. 5.3%). Drivers in private carriage are more likely to use cell phones (44.6% vs. 28.3%). The usage of SBS between owner operators and employee drivers is close (25.9% vs. 30.4%), however owner operators are more likely to use beepers (52% vs. 20.6%) and cell phones (38.6% vs. 28.6%).

Table 3. Technology Adoption: Descriptive Statistics.

	Local (%)	Over-The Road (%)	Private Carriage (%)	For Hire (%)	Drybox (%)	Other Trailer (%)	Owner Operator (%)	Employee Driver (%)	Union (%)	Nonunion (%)
Pay phone	79.8	92.3	90.1	90.8	88.3	93.0	90.0	91.0	91.3	90.6
SBS	15.6	32.1	5.2	35.3	42.3	18.1	25.9	31.4	11.1	32.7
Fax	12.3	35.3	24.2	34.1	33.7	31.1	43.3	28.7	22.7	33.6
Beeper	37.0	27.2	26.8	28.8	20.4	36.4	52.0	20.6	16.8	30.0
Radio	17.8	5.2	1.0	6.2	6.1	7.6	5.4	7.3	2.3	07.4
Cell phone	48.9	28.5	44.6	28.3	30.8	31.5	38.6	28.6	44.9	29.3
N	50	422	88	385	234	238	126	346	46	426

There is a marked difference in SBS adoption between union and nonunion drivers (11.1% vs. 32.7%). Union drivers are more likely to use cell phones (44.9% vs. 29.3%) and less likely to use beepers (16.8% vs. 30%) than nonunion drivers. While the lower utilization of SBS may be associated with unionism *per se*, it is more likely explained by the concentration of union drivers in the LTL and local delivery sectors of the industry.[11] As LTL firms tend to run regular routes with little discretion in driver's scheduling, the gains from accurate tracking and real time communications would be small. Similarly, local cartage is not characterized by the communications problems of companies with large OTR divisions. Finally, comparing drivers by type of trailer hauled, drivers with dryboxes are more likely to have SBS in their trucks than those hauling other trailer types (42.3% vs. 18.1%).

To examine the use of technology in more detail, we focus on one technology, Satellite Based Systems. It is becoming the dominant truck specific technology and that with the most potential to align the incentives of firms and drivers. We estimate a probit model of the use of this technology. The dependent variable takes a value of one if the driver has SBS in his/her truck, zero otherwise. As the focus is on the types of firms that are more likely to adopt this technology, the first model includes only firm characteristics as explanatory variables. These controls include dummy variables for local, private carriage, union, owner operator, drybox, pay method, and firm size. Dummy variables are included for pay as percent of revenue, or by the hour, with pay by the mile taken as the common omitted pay system. Satellite systems are characterized by returns to scale as firms have to purchase equipment and man a central operation that can handle a large number of trucks. We control for scale effects with dummy variables for firm size. Firms with fewer than 25 drivers are the base group and dummies are includes for 25–99 drivers (F25), 100–249 drivers (F249), 250–499 drivers (F250), 500–999 drivers (F500), 1000–4999 drivers (F1000), and 5000 or more drivers (F5000). Results of this estimation are presented in column 1 of Table 4.

We present the partial derivatives of the probit evaluated at the means, the counterpart of the coefficients obtained from linear models. The coefficients may be interpreted as the percentage change in the likelihood of observing a satellite system for a unit change in the explanatory variable. The results are consistent with the descriptive statistics. Drivers in private carriage are 21% less likely than for-hire drivers to have SBS in their trucks. Union drivers are 20.4% less likely to use SBS in their work than nonunion drivers. Pay method matters as well. Drivers paid percent of revenue or by the hour are 16.3 and 14.6% less likely to use SBS than driver paid by the mile. The estimates also indicate that satellite-based systems are characterized by scale effects and that these systems are not economically useful to firms with fewer than 250 drivers. The coefficients on the largest firm sizes are positive and significant. Firms with more than

Table 4. Adoption of Satellite Based Systems: Probit Estimation.

	DF/dx	DF/dx
Local	−0.0681 (−0.82)	−0.0348 (−0.40)
Private carriage	−0.2107*** (−3.33)	−0.2171*** (−3.45)
Owner operator	0.0642 (1.13)	0.0626 (1.06)
Union	−0.2042*** (−3.62)	−0.1968*** (−3.39)
Drybox	0.1586*** (3.45)	0.1428*** (2.97)
%	−0.1634*** (−3.36)	−0.1582*** (−3.17)
Hourly	−0.146** (−2.13)	−0.1425** (−2.11)
F25	−0.0173 (−0.24)	−0.0125 (−0.16)
F100	0.1189 (1.47)	0.1012 (1.20)
F250	0.4639*** (4.79)	0.4838*** (4.76)
F500	0.5218*** (5.19)	0.4989*** (4.65)
F1000	0.4471*** (5.01)	0.4472*** (4.73)
F5000	0.6180*** (4.17)	0.6143*** (3.93)
Less than high school		−0.0430 (−0.72)
Vocational/technical		−0.0982 (−0.99)
Some college		−0.0335 (−0.58)
Associate		−0.0353 (−0.34)
College graduate		0.7570 (0.65)
Age		0.0440** (2.09)
Age-squared		−0.0005** (−1.96)
Occupational experience		−0.0193** (−2.10)
Occ exp-squared		0.0003 (1.34)
Black		0.1688** (2.04)
Hispanic		0.0736 (0.41)
Native American		0.0821 (0.55)
Veteran		−0.0130 (−0.27)
Female		0.1569* (1.65)
Married		0.0190 (0.24)
Separated, divorced, widowed		0.0246 (0.29)
N	440	439
Likelihood ratio	172.07	193.72
Pseudo *R*-squared	0.3229	0.3641

Note: The derivatives of the likelihood function, the marginal effect of the explanatory variable on the likelihood of observing a driver using a satellite system, is evaluated at the mean of the explanatory variables. The marginal effect of indicator variables are estimated by comparing the predicted probabilities when the indicator takes on the values of 0 and 1 with all other variables held at their mean value.

250 drivers are between 44 and 62% more likely to use SBS than firms with less than 25 drivers.

We next extend the model to incorporate personal characteristics. The decision by firms to adopt technology may be influenced by the types of drivers in their labor force, not just by the segment of the market they serve. For example, firms may adopt SBS in order to enable them to hire and easily monitor less experienced (and thus less costly) drivers. A probit model is estimated with the same controls as the first model, plus controls for education, age, experience, race/ethnicity, veteran status, gender, and marital status. The results are presented in column 2 of Table 4.

The inclusion of individual characteristics does not significantly affect the prior results. No firm characteristics gain or lose statistical significance and the magnitudes of the coefficients do not change appreciably. The statistically significant personal characteristics include age, experience, gender and race. Age has a non-linear relationship to use of SBS technologies. Younger drivers are more likely to use these technologies but, because of the negative quadratic term, older drivers are indicated to be less likely to be in SBS-equipped trucks. The coefficient on occupational experience (years as a driver) is negative and significant, suggesting technology may be used as a substitute for experience. Education is unrelated to use of SBS systems. This is not entirely surprising since, although the base units require considerable technical knowledge to operate, the truck borne units require only basic literacy to read and type responses. Finally, the coefficients on Black and Female are positive and significant. Women typically have considerably less experience in truck driving than men and this may explain the positive relationship to use of SBS systems. The racial effect is not as readily explained.

TECHNOLOGY AND DRIVER WORKLIFE

We next use data from the TIP Driver Survey to examine the relationship between technology and annual earnings and rates of pay. We further examine the causal mechanisms underlying earnings outcomes by considering the effects of technology on driver output, as measured by annual mileage, on work intensity as measured by hours of work, and on HOS violations.

Though fundamental aspects of drivers' work have proven immune to technological change – the driver still moves the truck from the shipper to the receiver – the industry has undergone a technological transformation. Logistics software has taken over the work of the dispatcher, providing better coordination of trips and higher load factors. Improved drive train technologies have extended the life of equipment, reducing capital costs. Changes in regulations have permitted longer, heavier trailers, increasing drivers' productivity.

Communications technologies, such as satellite systems, beepers, cell phones, and two-way radios, locate trucks in real time and permit communication between the firm and driver without requiring the driver to stop. These systems offer firms the capacity to reroute as information becomes available while reducing time spent on pay phones. E-mail may be more helpful to owner-operators who use it to find loads and as a rapid, dependable communication. Such technologies should make drivers more productive by better coordinating their activities and reducing non-productive, non-remunerative time. To the degree that communications technologies allow drivers to use their time more efficiently, it would be expected that they would be associated with improved mileage and earnings but would not affect other dimensions of drivers' work.[12] If, in addition, firms use these technologies to monitor drivers and keep them from taking unauthorized breaks, income and mileage would increase but time spent working might also rise.

The gains from new routing technologies, such as maps on PCs and on-board computers, are less obvious. These technologies can provide information on current conditions, but the information is unlikely to be more current than that from road atlases supplemented by CB radio. Computing technologies, such as laptop PCs, should help drivers, particularly owner-operators, to run their businesses in an efficient manner and facilitate the use of communication technologies such as e-mail. If computing and routing technologies affect drivers' work, they might reduce work time, as they reduce unproductive time. Driver earnings should increase as paid work time would rise as a proportion of all work time and as owner-operators use their computing facilities to choose loads that pay more or are better coordinated with other loads on the trip.

There is limited evidence that technology has improved driver productivity. Data on trucks from the TIUS, suggest that driver monitors, such as vehicle locators, are associated with incentive gains to firms (Hubbard, 2000). Both incentive and efficiency gains are captured by firms through communications technology such as electronic vehicle management systems (Hubbard, 2000). Schneider National, an early adopter of satellite based systems, which is also among the nation's largest TL firms, reported that these systems reduced their total driver hours by nearly one million annually (Davis, 1999). Giant Foods estimated that truck borne communications technologies resulted in 1200 fewer phone calls between drivers and dispatchers per day (Schulman, 1999). Contrary evidence tends to be more anecdotal, with some trucking firms indicating that satellite technologies do not benefit their operations but are adopted because customers believe that they are important.

In the remainder of this paper, we consider the effects of technology on rates of pay and annual income. We take advantage of the depth of information in the driver survey to further examine whether these effects are underlain by an effect on annual mileage, productivity, and the intensity of work (hours worked in the last seven days and the number of violations of the ten-hour limit in the last thirty days). In combination, these results provide a comprehensive view of the consequences of these factors for drivers' work lives. The models include controls for respondents' race, ethnicity, gender, and marital status; human capital; union status; for the industry segment; the region of domicile; whether the respondent is an owner-operator, a local driver, or employed in private carriage; the method of pay; and the number of drivers working for the employing firm.[13] We employ a parallel specification across the models. The model for violations of the ten-hour limit includes controls for 1996 annual miles and income.[14] With the exception of the equation for violations of the ten-hour rule, we estimate the equations allowing for simultaneity in the error terms between matched observations, a SUR estimate, to improve the efficiency of the estimates. Results are in Table 5.

Annual Earnings

The dependent variable in the annual earnings equation is the log of annual earnings from driving for employee drivers. Owner-operators reported net earnings after truck expenses but before taxes. Mean earnings were $33,300.

Most communications, routing, or computing technologies do not affect drivers' annual earnings. Satellite systems have a strong positive effect, raising earnings by 17.6%. The effect of satellite systems on drivers' earnings is notable both in magnitude and in the number of drivers (28.6%) who receive this advantage. Drivers with beepers earn 10.3% more annually, while drivers who use a two-way radio or route using PC maps earn 18 and 21% less annually, respectively.

Given that some technologies have a favorable effect on annual earnings, what might be the source of this favorable effect? Firms may have to pay higher *rates* to obtain the more skilled and committed workers needed to operate the technology. Technology may also improve earnings by reducing unproductive time and so increasing mileage or by intensifying work through closer monitoring of driver activities. Technology need not have a singular effect; it may increase rates and mileage and the intensity of work. We investigate these possibilities by examining the relationship between these factors and effective mileage rates, annual miles, and apropos of work intensification, hours worked per week and violations of the hours of service regulations.

Mileage Rates

We turn first to the mileage rate equation. We use "effective" mileage rates, the ratio of annual earnings to annual miles, so that drivers who are paid under other systems are included in the estimates and so that bonuses, payments for on-duty, non-driving time, and other forms of monetary compensation are incorporated. The mean rate for the sample is 38.9¢ per mile.

Table 5. Effects of Technology on Truck Drivers: Regression Estimation.

Variable	Annual Earnings	Mileage Rates	Annual Mileage (1996)	Hours Worked in Last 7 Days	Violations of 10 Hour Rule
Communications technology					
Fax	0.0079 (0.10)	−0.0614 (1.17)	3338.73 (0.50)	3.2892 (0.74)	0.4928 (0.35)
Beeper	0.0980* (1.65)	0.1055** (2.81)	74.3651 (0.02)	3.7387 (1.17)	0.1586 (0.15)
Radio	−0.2039** (2.10)	0.1224** (1.99)	−23972.35** (3.08)	−5.3188 (1.02)	−2.7071 (1.56)
Cell phone	0.0557 (1.01)	0.0596* (1.71)	−512.549 (0.12)	1.4139 (0.48)	−0.6850 (0.71)
E-mail	−0.0049 (0.05)	−0.0091 (0.15)	4764.044 (0.64)	−2.6177 (0.53)	−0.0812 (0.05)
Satellite based system	0.1622** (2.41)	−0.0586 (1.37)	21716.98** (4.02)	6.5767* (1.82)	−1.5072 (1.25)
Computing technology					
Laptop computer	0.1025 (0.87)	−0.0150 (0.20)	11534.29 (1.22)	−1.9963 (0.32)	0.7529 (0.37)
Routing technology					
Use dispatcher	−0.4951 (0.93)	0.0540 (1.60)	−5528.186 (1.29)	2.7855 (0.97)	1.2236 (1.29)
cb radio	−0.3532 (0.67)	−0.0404 (1.22)	7912.266* (1.88)	−0.7006 (0.25)	2.7838** (3.00)
On-board computer w/maps	0.0022 (0.02)	−0.0212 (0.34)	−4985.488 (0.64)	−5.4687 (1.04)	0.1318 (0.08)
Laptop with maps	−0.2339* (1.93)	−0.0963 (1.23)	7797.63 (0.78)	−7.7456 (1.16)	−1.0640 (0.48)
Collective bargaining					
Union member	0.1350* (1.66)	0.0385 (0.75)	−1504.706 (0.23)	−0.3571 (0.08)	0.4493 (0.31)
Human capital					
Age	−0.0348* (1.76)	−0.0343** (2.74)	−2464.61 (1.56)	−1.1087 (1.05)	−0.4755 (1.37)
Age^2	0.0004* (1.70)	0.0004** (2.81)	22.72 (1.25)	0.0072 (0.59)	0.0035 (0.88)
Occup. exp	0.0311** (3.42)	−0.0004 (0.07)	983.95 (1.35)	−0.4845 (0.99)	−0.0043 (0.03)
Occup. exp^2	−0.0007** (3.23)	−0.00006 (0.42)	−19.649 (1.06)	0.0187 (1.51)	−0.0001 (0.31)
Less than HS	−0.0632 (0.97)	−0.0718* (1.74)	7317.651 (1.40)	0.9887 (0.28)	−0.7058 (0.62)
Vocational deg.	0.0021 (0.02)	0.2022** (2.61)	−3855.575 (0.39)	15.1960** (2.31)	6.1176** (2.85)
Some college	−0.0441 (0.55)	0.02984 (0.73)	−9125.581* (1.77)	0.2071 (0.06)	1.0595 (0.93)

Associate of arts	0.0729 (0.55)	−0.0123 (0.15)	315.4873 (0.03)	3.1040 (0.44)	−0.1132 (0.05)
College or more	−0.1937* (1.65)	−0.0247 (0.333)	−9297.122 (0.99)	14.7174** (2.33)	4.2706** (2.08)
Characteristics of work					
Owner-operator	−0.1051 (1.62)	0.0344 (0.83)	−11131.95** (2.13)	−12.9922** (3.72)	1.3799 (1.21)
Local driver	−0.0012 (0.02)	0.2543** (4.84)	−22796.93** (3.43)	2.5704 (0.58)	0.5150 (0.35)
Private carriage	0.1556** (2.37)	0.0410 (0.99)	7441.995 (1.42)	−0.3571 (0.08)	−1.7256 (1.48)
Paid by hour	−0.0421 (0.55)	0.0695 (1.42)	−14210.47** (2.30)	−4.2461 (1.02)	−0.3566 (0.26)
Paid% of revenue	0.0258 (0.45)	0.1530 (0.42)	3901.628 (0.84)	1.2789 (0.41)	1.3478 (1.32)
Additional controls					
Annual miles	No	No	No	No	0.000047** (4.25)
Annual wage	No	No	No	No	−0.000017 (0.53)
Race/ethnicity/gender/marital status	Yes	Yes	Yes	Yes	Yes
Region	Yes	Yes	Yes	Yes	Yes
Industry segment	Yes	Yes	Yes	Yes	Yes
Firm size	Yes	Yes	Yes	Yes	Yes
Diagnostics					
N	395	395	395	395	395
RMSE	0.4273	0.2709	34285.22	22.9965	7.6538
χ^2	135.2545	191.7986	189.8318	151.4758	168.9935

*Significant at 10%.

**Significant at 5%.

The relationship of technology to mileage rates is more varied than the relationship to annual earnings. Drivers using satellite systems are paid 5.9¢ per mile *less* than drivers without satellite systems, but the relationship is only significant in an 18% test. In contrast, two-way radios, beepers, and cell phones, communications technologies typically used within a local area are associated with rates that are between 6 and 12.2¢ more per mile. The negative effect of satellite systems would be consistent with firms engaging in productivity-sharing with their labor force, with the lower rates compensating the firm for the expense of the system. Alternatively, the close communication between drivers and firms afforded by satellite systems may substitute for over-the-road experience and allow firms to employ less experienced drivers at lower wages. This is consistent with the coincident use of satellites and extensive recruitment of new drivers by Schneider and Hunt, the largest non-union TL firms. Driver survey data indicates that, while 28% drivers with at least four years in the occupation are in satellite-equipped trucks, 35% of drivers with less than four years of experience are in such vehicles. The higher mileage rates found for short-range communications systems may result from lower annual mileage, because of lower speeds and additional time spent loading by pick up and delivery drivers.

Mileage

Mileage is an essential element of driver productivity and is central to driver earnings. Mileage varies with the type of work. Local pick up and delivery workers drive fewer miles annually than over-the-road drivers. Allowing for differences in types of work, employees with higher mileage provide additional deliveries, earn more revenue for their firm, and increase their earnings. Drivers in the sample averaged 124,865 miles in 1996.

Mileage is influenced by some technologies. Drivers with satellites on their trucks drove an additional 21,717 miles, 17.4% more miles than the mean. The use of CB radio for routing was associated with an additional 7912 miles. In contrast, the use of a two-way radio for communication was associated 23,972 fewer miles driven in 1996. The longer mileage associated with use of CB radios likely reflects both the effects of obtaining up-to-date information as well as the type of driver who uses CBs. Two-way radios have limited range, and their use suggests a driver who makes short trips with more frequent pick-ups and deliveries.

Hours Worked and Violations of Hours of Service Violations

We discuss the final outcome measures, hours of work in the last seven days and the number of times a driver has driven more than ten hours without a break, together.

The hours of service equation includes two additional explanatory variables, 1996 mileage and 1996 income, to control for factors related to excessive hours (Monaco & Williams, 2000). Our data indicate that the typical driver worked 65.4 hours in the previous week and violated the ten-hour rule six times.

Most technologies are unrelated to hours of work or violations of the ten-hour rule. Use of satellite systems increases both the hours of work and the probability of driving beyond the ten-hour limit. Drivers with such systems are estimated to work an additional 6.6 hours of work per week, 14% more hours than the base group. Satellite systems do not directly increase the number of violations of the ten-hour rule, but the increase in mileage associated with such systems would lead to one additional violation each thirty days.[15] Use of a CB radio is associated with an additional 2.8 violations in the last thirty days. The effect of CB radios on violations of the ten-hour rule may be attributable to drivers' ability to track and avoid police and DOT inspectors. The result for hours of work is consistent with the effect of CB radios found in the mileage equation.

CONCLUSION

We investigate the relationship between technology and drivers' worklives using data from the TIP Driver Survey. Focusing first on which types of drivers are more likely to use satellite technology, we find that drivers in private carriage, union drivers, and those paid by the hour or as percent of revenue are least likely to drive trucks equipped with SBS. The largest firms are most likely to equip their trucks with SBS, providing some evidence of scale effects of this technology. There is also evidence that SBS technology is used as a substitute for experience.

Research on the effects of technology on labor markets finds that current technologies are most useful to better-educated workers, are skill-biased, and that they act to reduce the earnings of less educated workers. Examining the impact of satellite technology on worker outcomes, we find that SBS does more than simply lower drivers' pay. Consistent with the skill-bias hypothesis, drivers who use satellite systems may be paid less per mile. This effect is, however, statistically weak and would account for a modest reduction in earnings throughout trucking. In contrast, drivers on satellite-equipped trucks realize 17.6% higher annual earnings. The higher earnings are due to the increased mileage of such drivers, about 22,000 additional miles per year. Part of this mileage gain is explained by efficiencies provided by these systems, but drivers with satellites also work 14% more hours weekly. The increased hours would account for approximately 60% of the increase in mileage; the remaining 40% is associated with improved productivity and is captured entirely by firm. The overall finding, that technology improves productivity and earnings but intensifies and lengthens the work day, is consistent with sociological studies of technology (Graham, 1995).

Given the apparent benefits of satellite technology to both firms and workers, it is interesting to gauge the feelings of drivers towards technology. The TIP Driver Survey questioned the drivers on their likes and dislikes of the technology they used.[16] We focus on these responses for those drivers who used SBS. Ten percent of drivers stated that there was nothing they liked about SBS. The vast majority indicated that they liked the increased efficiency and convenience provided by the SBS. 32% liked that they did not need to stop to contact their dispatcher, 39% liked that they did not have to use a truckstop pay phone, 17% liked that they could get information directly from the company without stopping the truck, and 18% indicated that they felt SBS allowed them to save time and improve their efficiency.

Not surprising, the biggest complaint about SBS was that drivers felt monitored (24%). Other dislikes include being bothered or too easy to reach (11%) and technical problems with the systems (9%). It is notable; however, that 37% of the drivers reported that there was nothing they disliked about the satellite systems.

NOTES

1. These regulations went into effect on January 4, 2004. Drivers are now required to take a ten-hour break after 11 hours driving and 14 hours of work.

2. Historic concern about the risk to the public posed by overtired transportation workers is reflected in limits on the hours of railway operative employees in the 1890s (Commons, Leschoier & Brandeis, 1935).

3. The survey was funded by the Alfred P. Sloan foundation.

4. Twelve percent of survey drivers reported union membership, about half the rate indicated by the Current Population Survey (Hirsch & Macpherson, 1998, p. 78). This reflects the under-sampling of drivers who work within metropolitan areas as well as the strength of unionism in segments of motor freight industry, such as parcel express, whose drivers drive short routes under tight deadlines and are less likely to use truck stops for fueling or breaks.

5. The data in the TIP survey does compare favorably to the data found in other data sets of truck drivers. Annual mileage reported in the Driver Survey is similar to that of tractor-trailers used for trips of more than 200 miles as reported in the 1997 Vehicle Inventory and Use Survey. The age, gender, and education of Driver Survey respondents are similar to those of truck drivers in the Current Population Survey (Belzer, Burks, Fulton, Grimes, Swan & Sedo, 2001).

6. The TIP driver survey is more accurate on issues of compensation and hours of work, the two central work related items collected by the CPS, because the TIP questions are structured for the compensation systems used in trucking and are not asked by government employees. As will be discussed, drivers often violate federal and state hours of service restrictions and deceive local, state, and federal employees about their hours of work. This appears to carry over to their attitudes to all government employees, including CPS surveyors. In contrast, the TIP survey was structured to reassure drivers about anonymity:

the surveyors were not government employees, and they elicited information on actual rather than legally permissible time. Finally, CPS' use of proxy respondents and the failure to collect working hours information on drivers who report variable hours results in under-representation of OTR drivers for key economic data as well as adds inaccuracy to reported pay and hours.

7. The survey utilized a two stage sampling design. In the first stage, truck stops were chosen randomly within state/size categories. In the second stage, interview approaches were randomized by time of day as well as by the individual entering the truck stop or fuel line. Only drivers holding a class C Commercial Drivers License who were currently employed as drivers and were driving a truck at the time of the interview were eligible for the survey. Surveys were conducted on weekdays with the exception of follow up telephone interviews, which collected information on the last full day of work (potentially a weekend).

8. Drivers' mean income, $35,985, was slightly above their median earnings.

9. See Belman, Monaco and Brooks (forthcoming) for details on the construction of annual hours of work.

10. As there were only two union owner-operators in the sample, we do not provide separate descriptive statistics on this group.

11. It is possible that union drivers are in a better position than nonunion drivers to prevent SBS adoption due to privacy concerns.

12. There is little reason to believe that the new communications technologies would change rates of pay as they do not require substantial training to master. The reduction in unremunerated time would increase the effective wage rate of drivers, and this could affect their hours of work. The direction of the effect would depend on whether drivers had a dominant income or substitution effect and whether they were close to their hours of service limits.

13. The driver survey estimates suffer the usual limitations of cross section estimates. We are only able to evaluate how technology, human capital, and union membership affect wages at a point in time, not across time. For example, we do not know how much wages fell because of de-unionization, only the current union premium.

14. The models are estimated using survey weights and allowing for clustering of characteristics by truck stop. Most are estimated with 395 observations. Fifty-one employee drivers were excluded as they were not working as drivers in 1996 and did not report 1996 income, or because they reported a 1996 income from driving of less than $5000 or more than $100,000. 27 owner-operators were eliminated because their reported earnings net of truck expenses were extremely low, under $2,800, or extremely high, over $100,000. We excluded 17 drivers because they did not report their industry segment. 11 were excluded because of the lack of information on firm size.

15. An additional 10,000 annual miles of driving is associated with 0.47 violations of the ten-hour rule every 30 days.

16. Each respondent was allowed to give up to three responses to the questions, "What do you like about your gadget?" and "What do you dislike about your gadget?"

REFERENCES

Acemoglu, D. (2000). Labor- and capital-augmenting technical change. NBER Working Paper 7544.

Atkinson, W. (1999). Driver HOS: How long is too long? *Logistics and Management Distribution Report*, *38*, 73–75.

Belman, D., Monaco, K. A., & Brooks, T. J. (forthcoming). *Sailors of the concrete sea: A portrait of truck drivers' work and worklives.* East Lansing: Michigan State University Press.

Belzer, M., Burks, S. V., Fulton, G., Grimes, D., Sedo, S., & Swan, P. (2001). Reply to Thomas Hubbard-American Trucking Association Critique of University of Michigan Trucking Industry Program Driver Survey Data, press release, Wayne State University.

Brandeis, E., Commons, J. R., & Lescohier, D. D. (1935). *The history of labor in the United States, 1896–1932* (Vol. III). New York: Macmillan.

Breshnahan, T., Brynjolfsson, E., & Hitt, L. (2002). Information technology, workplace organization, and the demand for skilled labor: Firm-level evidence. *Quarterly Journal of Economics, 117*, 339–376.

Chakraborty, A., & Kazarosian, M. (1999). Product differentiation and the use of information technology: Evidence from the trucking industry. NBER Working Paper 7222.

Davis, C. (1999). Rolling down the highway. *Satellite Communications, 23*, 38–42.

DiSalvatore (1988). Large cars. *The New Yorker*, 12 September, 39–77; 19 September, 63–84.

Federal Motor Carrier Safety Administration, U.S. Department of Transportation (2000). *Notice of proposed rule making, hours of service for drivers, driver rest and sleep for safe operation.* 49 CFR parts 350, 390, 394, 395, 398, Docket Number FMCSA 97–2350.

Graham, L. (1995). *On the line with Subaru-Isuzu.* Ithaca: Cornell University Press.

Hirsch, B., & Macpherson, D. A. (1998). Earnings and employment in trucking: Deregulating a naturally competitive industry. In: J. Peoples (Ed.), *Regulatory Reform and Labor Markets.* Boston, MA: Kluwer Academic Publishers.

Hubbard, T. (2000). The demand for monitoring technologies: The case for trucking. *Quarterly Journal of Economics*, 533–560.

Lyznicki, J. M., Doege, T. C. et al. (1998). Sleepiness, driving, and motor vehicle crashes. *Journal of the American Medical Association, 279*, 1908–1914.

Mishel, L., Bernstein, J., & Schmidt, J. J. (1999). *The state of working America.* Ithaca: Cornell University Press.

Monaco, K., & Williams, E. E. (2000). Assessing the determinants of safety in the trucking industry. *Journal of Transportation and Statistics, 3*, 69–79.

Schulman, R. (1999). Trucking in real time. *Supermarket Business, 54*, 14–22.

5. AIRLINE EMPLOYMENT, PRODUCTIVITY, AND WORKING CONDITIONS FOLLOWING DEREGULATION

Nancy Brown Johnson and Jonathan R. Anderson

ABSTRACT

Despite predictions that the Airline Deregulation Act of 1978 would lower wage levels for airline workers, evidence of significant wage declines did not appear until the 1990s. The lagged wage effects suggest that airlines used alternative employment strategies to adjust to the new competitive environment. This chapter examines whether and the extent that deregulation had an effect on non-wage employment factors including employment, productivity, and working conditions. Employment has expanded but with periods of significant economic downturns, part-time workers are increasingly used, and industry productivity has also advanced but at a rate concomitant with the manufacturing sector. Some evidence of deteriorating working conditions exists including increased fatigue among pilots and flight attendants, customer abuse, and continuing high levels of injuries.

There are no signposts in the sky to show a man has passed that way before. There are no channels marked. The flier breaks each second into new uncharted seas.

Anne Morrow Lindbergh

Transportation Labor Issues and Regulatory Reform
Research in Transportation Economics, Volume 10, 79–108

ISSN: 0739-8859/doi:10.1016/S0739-8859(04)10005-X

INTRODUCTION

As we celebrate the centennial of the first flight, American commercial aviation has grown from a fledgling industry in the 1930s to a dominant form of transport today. The industry has evolved from the early days of aviation when each flight was fraught with frequent perils to the 1960s when flying was a luxury and was sold as an experience. Today, the uncharted seas referred to above are no longer the pathways through the sky but the economic challenges of navigating airlines through the post regulatory era characterized by uncertainty and financial vulnerability. Airline employees are along for the ride – it has not always been a pleasant journey.

The Airline Deregulation Act (ADA) of 1978 stripped much of the industry of its allure by bringing commercial air travel within the financial means of many more people who were not previously served due to financial restraints. To accommodate greater passenger accessibility the industry's capacity tripled following deregulation. Concomitantly, airline deregulation removed economic protections explicitly designed to protect the industry from cutthroat competition leaving airlines far more vulnerable to economic swings than when they enjoyed financial insulation of regulation. Consistent profitability has been elusive for many carriers and bankruptcies, virtually nonexistent under regulation, have become commonplace under deregulation. The precarious financial status of many carriers affects employees and their working conditions in the industry.

Although past research on the effects of deregulation on workers focused almost exclusively on wage effects, these effects were slow to manifest. The early 1990s was the first time that economists found evidence that deregulation had significant consequences for airline worker's wages – more than twelve years after deregulation (Johnson, 2002). These lagged wage effects suggest that airlines met the increased competitive environment instead by availing themselves through other employment-related strategies targeted to reduce labor costs including employment adjustments, using part-time workers, increasing productivity, and changing working conditions. This chapter explores the extent that air carriers exercised these employment strategies in order to adapt to the deregulated environment. Specifically, we proceed by first providing an overview of the effect of deregulation on the industry and second investigating the effects of deregulation on employment, productivity, and working conditions.

AIRLINE DEREGULATION AND INDUSTRY PERFORMANCE

Early in the evolution of commercial aviation, the Civil Aeronautics Act of 1938 established the Civil Aeronautics Board (CAB) to assign airline routes, regulate fairs, control inter-airline agreements, and promote air safety. Government regulation was justified based upon the fear of vigorous competition for routes such that one airline industry lobbyist was quoted as saying, "There is nothing to prevent the entire air-carrier system from crashing to the earth under the impact of cutthroat and destructive practices" (Petzinger, 1995, p. 14). Under these protections, airlines were left to compete solely on service as pricing and routes were no longer choices afforded to airline managers. The industry, although not terribly profitable, was stable. For the most part, existing airlines neither had to worry about new entrants or their own failure.

The Airline Deregulation Act of 1978 opened the skies to unfettered competition and some might contend, brought about the return of the destructive competition presaged in the 1930s. Deregulation eased government control over routes and pricing – airlines could freely enter and exit the market, set fares without government intervention, merge, create alliances with other carriers, and fail. Deregulation also encouraged a wave of new entrants that used price as the basis for competition and threatened the established carriers' viability. Some analysts have argued that competition will drive fares down to levels equaling marginal costs but that fail to cover average costs because airlines' short-run marginal costs are lower than average costs (see Morrison & Winston, 1995 for a discussion). This analysis has served to fuel concerns about post-deregulation destructive competition. Some economists challenge this analysis by citing evidence that indicates that the airlines have enjoyed periodic profitability and that their unprofitable periods track with business cycle downturns as illustrated in Table 1 (Morrison & Winston, 1995). These authors contend that unprofitable periods arise in part from overcapacity stemming from poor economic forecasts and management (Meyer, Oster & Strong, 1987; Morrison & Winston, 1995). As the lead time to build aircraft is substantial, airlines must make capacity decisions years in advance of the anticipated passenger demand and these decisions cannot be easily reversed when forecasts prove inaccurate. Further, Morrison and Winston (1995) empirically demonstrated the relative importance of airline management as contrasted with input costs, operating characteristics, and reservation systems, as a key factor in distinguishing between the more profitable carriers and the less profitable carriers. These authors surmise that on average carriers have experienced more profitability under deregulation than they did under regulation (Morrison & Winston, 1995).

Even though there is disagreement over deregulation's influence on airline profits, economists generally agree that average air fares declined from 10 to 30% since deregulation (Goetz, 2002; Morrison & Winston, 1995). Such fare reductions are not uniform throughout the industry and vary based upon region, degree of airport and city-pair competition, and the passenger's elasticity of demand for a particular flight among other factors. As such, some passengers such as business

Table 1. Airline Profitability.

Year	Annual Operating Revenues ($000)	Annual Operating Profit/Loss ($000)	Net Profit/Loss ($000)	Cumulative Operating Profit/Loss ($000)[a]	Cumulative Net Profit/Loss ($000)
1970	9,289,658	43,031	−200,503	5,439,165	2,226,533
1971	10,045,577	328,475	28,007	5,767,640	2,254,540
1972	11,163,271	584,470	214,851	6,352,110	2,469,391
1973	12,418,777	585,266	226,693	6,937,376	2,696,084
1974	14,699,125	725,740	321,641	7,663,116	3,017,725
1975	15,355,921	127,879	−84,204	7,790,995	2,933,521
1976	17,501,215	721,933	563,354	8,512,928	3,496,875
1977	19,924,800	908,040	752,536	9,420,968	4,249,411
1978	22,883,955	1,364,863	1,196,537	10,785,831	5,445,948
1979	27,226,665	199,055	346,845	10,984,886	5,792,793
1980	33,727,806	−221,615	17,414	10,763,271	5,810,207
1981	36,662,555	−454,770	−300,826	10,308,501	5,509,381
1982	36,407,635	−733,435	−915,814	9,575,066	4,593,567
1983	38,953,672	310,410	−188,051	9,885,476	4,405,516
1984	43,825,047	2,151,511	824,668	12,036,987	5,230,184
1985	46,664,414	1,426,264	862,715	13,463,251	6,092,899
1986	50,524,933	1,323,101	−234,909	14,786,352	5,857,990
1987	56,985,709	2,468,889	593,398	17,255,241	6,451,388
1988	63,748,886	3,436,503	1,685,599	20,691,744	8,136,987
1989	69,315,854	1,811,267	127,902	22,503,011	8,264,889
1990	76,141,739	−1,912,335	−3,921,002	20,590,676	4,343,887
1991	75,234,234	−1,784,741	−1,940,157	18,805,935	2,403,730
1992	78,357,040	−2,444,460	−4,791,284	16,361,475	−2,387,554
1993[a]	85,298,379	1,438,172	−2,135,626	17,799,647	−4,523,180
1994	89,036,582	2,713,455	−344,115	20,513,102	−4,867,295
1995	95,117,473	5,859,518	2,313,591	26,372,620	−2,553,704
1996	102,443,738	6,209,069	2,803,915	32,581,689	250,211
1997	109,917,304	8,586,794	5,167,657	41,168,483	5,417,868
1998	113,810,206	9,327,810	4,903,203	50,496,293	10,321,071
1999	119,455,126	8,403,305	5,360,252	58,899,598	15,681,323
2000	130,838,619	6,998,931	2,486,298	65,898,529	18,167,621
2001[b]	115,526,896	−10,325,852	−8,274,866	55,572,677	9,892,755
2002[b]	106,881,130	−8,568,855	−11,295,141	47,003,713	−1,402,331

Source: Air Transport Association. http://www.airlines.org/econ/d.aspx?nid=1034.

[a] Cumulative profit and loss data is the sum of the annual profits from 1938 to the reported year.

[b] Excludes fresh-start accounting extraordinary gains of Continental and Trans World.

travelers or those from less competitive markets face relatively higher fares (Goetz, 2002; Morrison & Winston, 1995). Nonetheless, lower post deregulation fares are associated with increased demand for airline travel as illustrated in Table 2 (Morrison & Winston, 1995; Robson, 1998). For instance, information presented in this table indicates that between 1970 and 2002, enplanements have increased more than three and a half times on average from a 170 to 612 million, revenue passenger miles (RPMs) – the miles flown by paying passengers – have increased more than four-fold from 132 to 640 billion, and available seat miles – an indicator of capacity – has more than tripled from 265 to 893 billion. Thus, there are more people boarding more flights and flying more miles than ever before.

Following deregulation, many airlines moved from a point-to-point to a hub-and-spoke basis for operation to efficiently address the increased demand arising from lower prices. Hub-and-spoke networks fly passengers to a central locale and then disperse them from this central locale to their destination. These networks contribute to economies-of-scope in that the cost of adding a spoke is less than the cost of adding a separate point-to-point route (Goetz, 2002). Economies-of-scope are defined as the forces that result in unit cost decreases as the scope of the firm's activities increase (Goetz, 2002; Holloway, 1997).[1] Evidence of these economies generated from the move to a hub-and-spoke network is found in Table 2 which illustrates that the number of departures have risen only 76% from slightly over 5,000 to over 9,000 between 1970 and 2002 in contrast to the growth in RPMs of over 400% for this same period. Thus, airlines have become more effective at using their capacity as indicated by load factors, the percent of the plane filled with revenue generating passengers. Over the last five years planes, on average, have operated at over 70% of capacity – a rate much higher than in the regulatory years when planes were typically operating half full.

Despite the increased average profitability and the increased efficiencies that arose from the move to hub-and-spoke networks, many airlines have performed poorly. Table 3 lists an unofficial compilation of airline bankruptcies occurring since the late 1970s. With the exception of the few intrastate carriers, regulatory era airlines did not file bankruptcy as the CAB arranged mergers so that unprofitable carriers could continue operating (Air Transport Association, 2004). This is not the case in the deregulatory era. Fully 153 bankruptcies have occurred since deregulation. Of these bankruptcies, many, but not all, have failed. Although many of the troubled carriers have been quite small, the bankrupt large regional or major carriers (highlighted in bold) were of consequence and include some former trunk carriers such as Braniff, Eastern, Pan Am, and TWA.

In sum, the airline industry has grown significantly following deregulation. Industry performance, though, is cyclical and highly dependent upon the strength of the economy. While the deregulated industry has been more profitable on

Table 2. Airline Industry Indicators.

Year	Departures (000)	Enplanements (000)			Revenue Passenger Miles (Millions)			Available Seat Miles (Millions)			Passenger Load Factor (%)		
	System	Domestic	International	System	Domestic	International	System	Domestic	International	System	Domestic	International	System
1970	5,120	153,662	16,260	169,922	104,147	27,563	131,710	213,160	51,960	265,120	48.9	53.0	49.7
1971	4,999	156,195	17,474	173,669	106,438	29,219	135,658	221,503	58,320	279,823	48.1	50.1	48.5
1972	5,046	172,452	18,897	191,349	118,138	34,268	152,406	226,614	60,797	287,411	52.1	56.4	53.0
1973	5,135	183,272	18,936	202,208	126,317	35,640	161,957	244,699	65,898	310,597	51.6	54.1	52.1
1974	4,726	189,733	17,725	207,458	129,732	33,186	162,919	233,880	63,126	297,006	55.5	52.6	54.9
1975	4,705	188,746	16,316	205,062	131,728	31,082	162,810	241,282	61,724	303,006	54.6	50.4	53.7
1976	4,833	206,279	17,039	223,318	145,271	33,717	178,988	261,248	61,574	322,822	55.6	54.8	55.4
1977	4,937	222,283	18,043	240,326	156,609	36,610	193,219	280,619	64,947	345,566	55.8	56.4	55.9
1978	5,016	253,957	20,759	274,716	182,669	44,112	226,781	299,542	69,209	368,751	61.0	63.7	61.5
1979	5,400	292,700	24,163	316,863	208,891	53,132	262,023	332,796	83,330	416,126	62.8	63.8	63.0
1980	5,353	272,829	24,074	296,903	200,829	54,363	255,192	346,028	86,507	432,535	58.0	62.8	59.0
1981	5,212	265,304	20,672	285,976	198,715	50,173	248,888	346,172	78,725	424,897	57.4	63.7	58.6
1982	4,964	274,342	19,760	294,102	210,149	49,495	259,644	359,528	80,591	440,119	58.5	61.4	59.0
1983	5,034	296,721	21,917	318,638	226,909	54,920	281,829	379,150	85,388	464,538	59.8	64.3	60.7
1984	5,448	321,047	23,636	344,683	243,692	61,424	305,116	422,507	92,817	515,323	57.7	66.2	59.2
1985	5,835	357,109	24,913	382,022	270,584	65,819	336,403	445,826	101,963	547,788	60.7	64.6	61.4
1986	6,427	393,864	25,082	418,946	302,090	64,456	366,546	497,991	109,445	607,436	60.7	58.9	60.3
1987	6,581	416,831	30,847	447,678	324,637	79,834	404,471	526,958	121,763	648,721	61.6	65.6	62.3
1988	6,700	419,210	35,404	454,614	329,309	93,992	423,302	536,663	140,140	676,802	61.4	67.1	62.5
1989	6,622	416,331	37,361	453,692	329,975	102,739	432,714	530,079	154,297	684,376	62.3	66.6	63.2
1990	6,924	423,565	41,995	465,560	340,231	117,695	457,926	563,065	170,310	733,375	60.4	69.1	62.4
1991	6,783	412,360	39,941	452,301	332,566	115,389	447,955	543,638	171,561	715,199	61.2	67.3	62.6
1992	7,051	431,693	43,415	475,108	347,931	130,622	478,554	557,989	194,784	752,772	62.4	67.1	63.6
1993	7,245	443,172	45,348	488,520	354,177	135,508	489,684	571,489	200,151	771,641	62.0	67.7	63.5
1994	7,531	481,755	47,093	528,848	378,990	140,391	519,382	585,438	198,893	784,331	64.7	70.6	66.2
1995	8,062	499,000	48,773	547,773	394,708	145,948	540,656	603,917	203,160	807,078	65.4	71.8	67.0
1996	8,230	530,708	50,526	581,234	425,596	153,067	578,663	626,389	208,682	835,071	67.9	73.3	69.3
1997	8,127	542,001	52,724	594,725	442,640	160,779	603,419	640,319	216,913	857,232	69.1	74.1	70.4
1998	8,292	559,653	53,232	612,885	454,430	163,656	618,087	649,362	224,728	874,089	70.0	72.8	70.7
1999	8,627	582,880	53,079	635,959	480,134	171,913	652,047	687,502	230,917	918,419	69.8	74.4	71.0
2000	9,035	610,600	55,550	666,150	508,403	184,354	692,757	714,454	242,496	956,950	71.2	76.0	72.4
2001	8,788	570,126	52,003	622,129	480,348	171,352	651,700	695,200	235,311	930,511	69.1	72.8	70.0
2002	9,029	558,850	52,807	611,657	475,975	163,613	639,587	676,768	215,977	892,745	70.3	75.8	71.6

Source: Air Transport Association http://www.airlines.org/econ/d.aspx?nid=1032.

Table 3. Airline Bankruptcies.

Date	Carrier
5/18/79	New York Airways
11/19/79	Aeroamerica
1/24/80	Florida Airlines
3/3/80	Indiana Airlines
12/15/80	Air Bahia
12/31/80	Tejas Airlines
3/6/81	Mountain West
3/16/81	LANICA
7/13/81	Coral Air
9/11/81	Pacific Coast
9/18/81	Swift Air Line
10/9/81	Golden Gate
1/26/82	Pinehurst Airlines
3/3/82	Silver State Airlines
3/26/82	Air Pennsylvania
4/2/82	Air South
4/16/82	Cochise Airlines
5/13/82	Braniff International
7/8/82	Astec Air East
8/19/82	Will's Air
10/5/82	Aero Sun International
10/19/82	Aero Virgin Islands
11/9/82	Altair
12/9/82	North American
2/1/83	Inland Empire
2/14/83	State Airlines
4/22/83	Golden West
9/24/83	**Continental Airlines**
12/2/83	National Florida
1/30/84	Air Vermont
2/2/84	Pacific Express
2/8/84	Dolphin
4/9/84	Combs Airways
7/3/84	**Air Florida**
7/17/84	Excellair
7/19/84	American International
8/21/84	Emerald
8/29/84	Hammonds Commuter
9/4/84	Air North
9/27/84	Wright Air Lines
10/2/84	Oceanaire Lines
10/10/84	Atlantic Gulf
10/10/84	Connectaire
10/26/84	Air One

Table 3. (*Continued*)

Date	Carrier
11/23/84	Capitol Air
11/28/84	Wren Air Alaska
1/8/85	**Northeastern**
1/22/85	Pompano Airways
2/22/85	Far West Airlines
3/8/85	American Central
3/13/85	Provincetown Boston
3/19/85	Sun West Airlines
5/1/85	Wise Airlines
8/19/85	Cascade Airways
10/7/85	Wheeler Airlines
12/2/85	Pride Air
1/21/86	Southern Express
1/30/86	Imperial Airlines
2/11/86	Arrow Airways
4/9/86	Sea Airmotive
8/19/86	Trans Air
8/28/86	Frontier Airlines
2/19/87	Chicago Airlines
2/23/87	McClain Airlines
2/27/87	Rio Airways
3/6/87	Air Puerto Rico
3/10/87	Gull Air
3/12/87	Royal West Airlines
4/3/87	Air Atlanta
6/17/87	Air South
9/9/87	Royale Airlines
1/5/88	Sun Coast Airlines
1/14/88	Air New Orleans
1/15/88	Air Virginia
1/20/88	Mid Pacific Airlines
3/4/88	Exec Express
5/6/88	Caribbean Express
5/25/88	Pocono Airlines
6/20/88	Virgin Island Seaplane
8/11/88	Princeton Air Link
9/14/88	Qwest Air
9/27/88	Southern Jersey Airways
3/9/89	Eastern Air Lines
3/14/89	Big Sky Airlines
7/19/89	Air Kentucky
9/28/89	**Braniff International**
10/26/89	Presidential Airways
11/12/89	Resorts International

Table 3. (*Continued*)

Date	Carrier
11/17/89	Resort Commuter
1/23/90	Pocono Airlines
5/10/90	SMB Stage Lines
7/5/90	CCAir
12/3/90	**Continental Airlines**
12/3/90	Britt Airways
12/3/90	Rocky Mountain Airways
1/8/91	**Pan Am World Airways**
1/8/91	Pan Am Express
1/9/91	L'Express
1/18/91	**Eastern Air Lines**
1/20/91	Bar Harbor Airlines
1/22/91	Virgin Island Seaplane
1/29/91	Northcoast Executive
3/25/91	**Midway Airlines**
3/26/91	Grand Airways
4/1/91	Metro Airlines
5/20/91	Jet Express
5/30/91	Metro Airlines Northeast
6/27/91	**America West Airlines**
8/12/91	Mohawk Airlines
11/27/91	**Midway Airlines**
12/31/91	Flagship Express
1/31/92	**Trans World Airlines**
2/28/92	L'Express
6/8/92	Markair
12/15/92	States West Airlines
9/20/93	Evergreen International Aviation
9/21/93	Hawaiian Airlines
6/15/05	Key Airlines
3/21/94	Resorts International
10/11/94	Florida West Airlines
2/3/95	Crescent Airways
4/14/95	Markair
6/30/95	**Trans World Airlines**
12/15/95	The Krystal Company
11/28/95	Grand Airways
1/10/96	GP Express
1/22/96	Business Express
1/23/96	Conquest Airlines
9/30/96	Kiwi International Airlines
7/25/97	Mahalo
8/28/97	Air South
10/5/97	Western Pacific Airlines

Table 3. (*Continued*)

Date	Carrier
11/6/97	Mountain Air Express
2/26/98	Pan American World Airways
7/29/98	Euram Flight Centre
3/23/99	Kiwi International Airlines
6/25/99	Sunjet International/Myrtle Beach Jet Express
9/30/99	Eastwind Airlines
11/29/99	Access Air
2/29/00	**Tower Air**
5/1/00	Kitty Hawk
9/19/00	Pro Air
9/27/00	Fine Air Services
12/3/00	Legend Airlines
12/6/00	National Airlines
1/10/01	**Trans World Airlines**
8/13/01	**Midway Airlines**
1/2/02	Sun Country Airlines
7/30/02	Vanguard Airlines
8/11/02	**US Airways**
12/9/02	**United Airlines**
3/21/03	Hawaiian Airlines
10/30/03	Midway Airlines

Note: This table is a loose, unofficial compilation of research conducted by various individuals. Neither DOT nor ATA maintains official records of air carrier bankruptcy filings.

Source: ATA Unofficial Compilation. http://www.airlines.org/econ/d.aspx?nid=6207.

average than the regulated one, bankruptcies have been frequent as small inaccurate demand forecasts can lead to significant overcapacity problems during a recession. The overall industry growth patterns in combination with bankruptcies foreshadow industry employment trends.

AIRLINE EMPLOYMENT TRENDS

Economic theory is equivocal in its predicted effects of deregulation on employment. On one hand, theory suggests that lower airfares should lead to greater passenger demand. Large enough increases in market demand require greater airline employment. However, economies of scale and scope exist in the industry such that employment would not necessarily rise in direct proportion to the increased demand. As the airlines moved to hub-and-spoke networks the additional feeder routes lead to returns from increased traffic density and marketing.

Labor represents one area where these economies are realized as hub-and-spoke networks can increase the cross-utilization of ticket agents and baggage handlers at the hub networks. Other factors limiting employment growth result from the potential for predatory pricing by larger airlines and concerns of industry consolidation that may hinder the long-term growth of smaller competitors that may not have fully realized scale advantages (Goetz, 2002; Kim & Singal, 1993; Wilkey & MacCartney, 2001). The employment effect of deregulation thus remains an empirical question.

In general we find that as airlines moved from the regulatory period into deregulation they increased employment to keep up with the increased demand for service as indicated in Table 4. Immediately preceding deregulation industry employment levels remained relatively constant at around 300,000 employees. By the mid- to late-1980s employment began growing relatively precipitously and that growth continued virtually unabated until 2000. Employment has more than doubled from 299,870 employees in 1970 to 642,797 in 2002. These totals, however, include individuals working for Federal Express who are reported as airline employees despite the fact that most of these workers' jobs involve ground-related operations (e.g. sorters and drivers).[2] The substantial employment of ground-related occupations is due to Federal Express's status as an air freight carrier. Total airline industry employment figures that include Federal Express workers then overstate industry growth for traditional passenger service occupations. Findings in Table 4 reveal an industry employment growth rate from 1970 to 2002 that is a more modest – albeit large – 68% based upon 1970 employment of almost 300,000 employees rising to slightly over 500,000 employees in 2002 when excluding Federal Express employees from employment calculations.

Table 4 also indicates that the employment growth of part-time employees contributes significantly to total employment growth in the airline industry.[3] In the mid-1970s, part-time employees represented only about 3% of total airline employment but part-time employment increased to over 100,000 employees – almost one fifth of total industry employment – by 2002 including Federal Express. There are only 57,000 part-time workers 11% of total employment (503,455) when excluding Federal Express workers from the industry employment calculations.[4] Part-time employment growth still outpaced that of total employment rising almost 500% between 1977 and 2002 even when excluding Federal Express employees from the employment calculations.

Whether or not information on Federal Express employment is included in the calculation of airline employment, industry employment growth has been steady with only a few notable economic downturns that generally coincide with the national unemployment rate. The relatively high correlation between airline employment and the national unemployment rate ($r = -0.55$) suggests

Table 4. Industry Employment by Year.

Year	Full-time	Part-time[a]	Total	Total Without FedEx
1970	299,870	–	299,870	299,870
1971	291,809	–	291,809	291,809
1972	301,593	–	301,593	301,593
1973	317,222	–	317,222	317,222
1974	311,688	–	311,688	311,688
1975	296,613	–	296,613	296,613
1976	305,446	–	305,446	305,446
1977	307,606	10,892	318,498	318,498
1978	324,211	14,050	338,261	338,261
1979	343,126	14,847	357,973	357,973
1980	340,406	13,858	354,264	354,264
1981	331,671	13,907	345,578	345,578
1982	313,012	16,047	329,059	329,059
1983	305,047	17,523	322,570	322,570
1984	322,583	24,614	347,197	347,197
1985	344,164	32,069	376,233	376,233
1986	392,537	43,335	435,872	389,403
1987	431,732	51,385	483,117	429,829
1988	455,355	58,783	514,138	450,657
1989	488,379	67,335	555,714	470,946
1990	521,597	67,329	588,926	496,482
1991	499,794	67,788	567,582	472,705
1992	494,809	74,196	569,005	475,125
1993	495,615	82,146	577,761	477,425
1994	485,361	100,066	585,427	477,651
1995	500,711	109,652	610,363	491,953
1996	517,007	117,859	634,866	507,080
1997	530,840	125,403	656,243	516,414
1998	566,092	130,316	696,408	551,360
1999	596,349	132,146	728,495	580,225
2000	603,507	128,542	732,049	585,605
2001	545,574	107,914	653,488	512,460
2002	538,761	104,036	642,797	503,455

Source: Department of Transportation, Office of Airline Statistics.
[a] Less than 40 hours per week.

a relatively strong airline employment and business cycle association. This association is depicted in Table 4 as the findings in the fourth column reveal that during the late regulatory period (1974–1975) airline employment declined for two consecutive years in the mid-1970s. The early deregulatory period ushered in the largest period of decline with a total loss of 32,000 jobs between 1980 and 1983. These periods of industry employment declines occur in lock-step with recessionary periods in the U.S. Some of the industry employment decline was likely due to airlines adjusting to the new competitive landscape of deregulation. Notably, the combined effect of these airline job losses during recessionary periods was slightly more than a 9% industry employment reduction.

Between 1990 and 1991 total employment declined by 5% – over 20,000 jobs – and as before, the decline also corresponded with a recessionary downturn. The largest decline, however, was more than 14% and represented the loss of more than 80,000 positions between 2000 and 2002 excluding Federal Express. There is little doubt that the terrorist attacks of September 11 played a momentous role in affecting employment, however, recessionary pressures magnified the employment effects as the airlines were bracing for a recession prior to the attacks. The attacks made the anticipated economic downturn precipitous and dramatic.

Some airline occupations are more susceptible to business cycles than others. Differences in employment patterns should even arise for the three primary industry occupations consisting of pilots, flight attendants, and mechanics. The differing demand elasticities for these three occupational groups should contribute to differing employment patterns. Pilots are likely to have the most inelastic demand as they have the highest skill levels and are difficult to replace. Yet, pilots have few job opportunities outside of the industry and extremely steep pay scales that increase their dependence on their employer. By contrast, flight attendants require less training, making their replacement relatively easy. Although flight attendants have few opportunities outside of the industry, they can leave the industry and pursue alternative careers. Both pilots and flight attendants have minimum staffing levels dictated by the Federal Aviation Administration (FAA), and their unions often bargain to further restrict staffing levels. Pilot and flight attendant demand thus corresponds to the number of flights with some variation based upon the capacity of the aircraft in use. Most aircraft require only two pilots, although a third pilot may be used for longer flights. Flight attendant staffing varies by type of aircraft with commuter planes requiring only a single flight attendant and a DC-10 requiring at least six or seven attendants. Hence, flight attendant employment growth will exceed that of pilots when larger aircraft are employed and this pattern is reversed when carriers shift towards smaller aircraft. Goetz (2002) argues that the move to the hub-and-spoke systems requires larger aircraft suggesting greater employment growth for flight attendants than for pilots at the major carriers.

In contrast, mechanic employment likely has more elasticity than that of either pilots or flight attendants. Although they are skilled, their skill transferability means they can easily work outside of the industry. Carriers, though, can subcontract much of their work increasing demand elasticity of mechanics. Their work volume will typically vary in relative proportion to the number and distance of the flights as routine maintenance schedules are based upon mileage flown.

Employment information on the three major airline employee occupations is presented in Fig. 1. This information indicates that on average pilot employment remained fairly flat throughout the regulatory period (1972–1978), declined modestly in the early regulatory period (1979–1984), and then began to steadily rise throughout the late deregulatory period (1985 to the present). Pilot employment dipped in the mid-1990s – lagging the recession at the beginning of the decade – but this drop was followed by increased employment at the decade's end. Overall the trend in pilot employment at the majors is positive as found in an employment regression with a time trend that indicates an average of 105 jobs created per carrier annually that was significant at the 0.001 level.[5]

Consistent with employment findings on pilots, employment growth for flight attendants has been positive following deregulation with inflections generally occurring for the same years as for pilots. Flight attendant employment oscillated in the late regulatory years (1972–1979) but remained fairly flat throughout the early deregulatory period (1979–1984) with a steady climb until the mid-1990s when employment dropped somewhat following the recession at the beginning of the 1990s. Regressing a time trend on employment suggests that 185 jobs have been created per major carrier per year. This trend variable was significant at the 0.001 level. Thus, flight attendants experienced greater job growth than pilots. Although, this growth may in part have arisen from carriers' fleet composition (larger versus smaller aircraft), it is important to note that flight attendants experienced larger deregulatory wage declines than did pilots. Estimates of flight attendant deregulatory real wage declines have been between 11 and 39%, whereas pilot declines were estimated to be between 3 and 22% (Card, 1998; Crémieux, 1996). Consequently, this data suggests that flight attendants demand curves are more elastic than pilots in that their greater job growth corresponded with larger decreases in real pay.

Findings in Fig. 1 also indicate that on average mechanic employment for the majors followed a very different path from pilots and flight attendants. While mechanics' employment growth remained fairly flat in the regulatory era (1972–1978), it demonstrated severe instability in the early deregulatory period. By the early 1990s, employment had stabilized and has remained relatively constant. Overall, the time trend was insignificant when regressed on mechanic employment which indicates that mechanic employment has not varied significantly over time.

In contrast to pilots and flight attendants' employment, a great deal of maintenance work can be outsourced. Most of the variability in employment arises from the ability of airlines to subcontract out mechanic work as indicated in Table 5. Although these carriers do not represent a complete list of scheduled airlines, they illustrate a definitive trend. On average, maintenance dollars spent on contracting has risen by ten percentage points over this 12-year period. The trend towards using

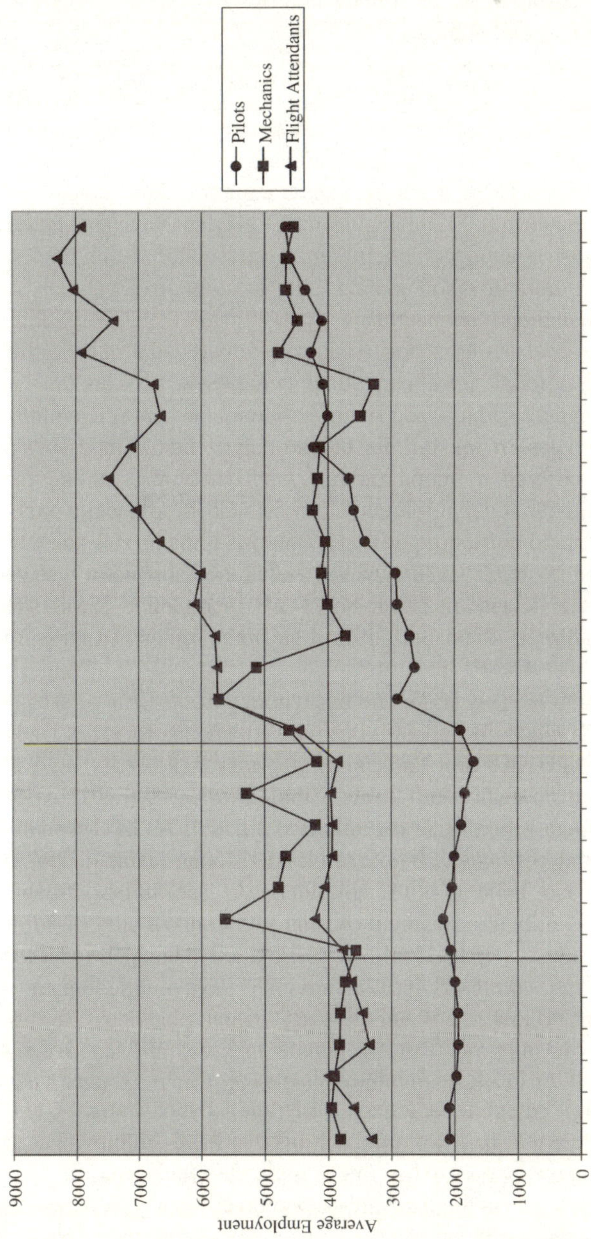

Fig. 1. Average Occupational Employment at the Major Airlines. *Source:* International Civil Aviation Organization: Digest of Statistics: Fleet-Personnel. ICAO: Montreal.

Table 5. Maintenance Contracting.

	Percent of Total Maintenance Dollars Paid to Contractors	
	1990 (%)	2002 (%)
AirTran	na	52
Alaska	71	78
America West	68	77
American	30	41
ATA Airlines	27	16
Continental	44	65
Delta	18	33
Frontier	na	69
Jet Blue	na	45
Northwest	20	45
Southwest	72	72
United	21	33
U.S. Airways	50	50

Source: Back Aviation Solutions report to the Department of Transportation.

contractors began with new entrants that leased aircraft and did not have the funds to invest in maintenance hangers, and as a result used third-parties to perform maintenance work (Alexander, Reed & Mellnik, 2003). The findings in Table 5 suggest that several years after deregulation, more regulatory-era carriers have shifted their work to outside contractors to reduce maintenance costs. Outside contractors have lower cost structures than the carriers resulting from the hiring of mechanics with less training and experience at a lower wage (Alexander, Reed & Mellnik, 2003). Table 5 indicates that in general large, previously regulated carriers (American, Continental, Delta, Northwest, and United) experienced the greatest percentage point gains in subcontracting but they subcontract a much lower percentage of their work. Lower levels of subcontracting may result from being relative latecomers to the subcontracting business and given time these carriers will catch up with the newer entrants, or it may be that these network carriers (hub-and-spoke) may prefer to retain a fair amount of control over maintenance operations as service disruptions in a spoke can reverberate throughout the system. According to the Bureau of Labor Statistics (BLS), approximately 50,000 of the 125,000 aircraft mechanics are working today in scheduled air transport (40%) leaving the remaining 60% to a pool of potential contractors (Bureau of Labor Statistics, 2002).

In sum, deregulation has not affected occupational employment equally. Mechanics, on average, appear to be largely unaffected (either positively or negatively) thus far but the recent trend towards subcontracting may shift mechanic employment from carriers to subcontractors. This shift may erode mechanic wages and working conditions as contractors tend to pay less than do the carriers (Alexander, Reed & Mellnik, 2003). Flight attendants, have experienced the greatest job growth but at the greatest cost to their wages. Pilots have also had significant job growth but have also experienced more moderate wage declines than flight attendants.

AIRLINE PRODUCTIVITY

Deregulation, as previously noted, increased competitive pressures and the need to reduce costs, and become more efficient. Carriers have employed several strategies to increase efficiency. Large network carriers have used hub-and-spoke systems to increase load factors and productivity; whereas, new entrants have tended to make use of point-to-point systems on high density routes. These systems have been combined with discriminatory pricing systems that set fares based upon traveler flexibility such that customers with elastic demand (tourists) pay less than those with less elastic demand structures (business travelers). These strategies all contribute to filling planes with more passengers as the largest operating aircraft costs remain fixed.[6] As such, these strategies also increase labor productivity of those employees involved in flight operations.

Employment changes have not kept pace with the increasing passenger volume suggesting rises in employee productivity. Labor productivity in the airlines industry is often measured by Revenue Passenger Miles (RPM) per employee – a measure of the number of miles flown by revenue generating passengers divided by the number of employees (Hirsch & Macpherson, 2000). However, Gittell, Nordenflycht and Kochan (2004) suggest that more appropriate activity measures for pilots are flight miles, and for mechanics, departures. Multiple measures of productivity help paint a more complete picture regarding where the productivity gains have been achieved.

Figure 2 presents airline productivity information using RPMs and Available Seat Miles (ASMs) – an indicator of capacity (seating capacity × miles flown). These findings on ASMS and RPMs per employee both indicate a steady productivity increase starting in 1970 and continuing until 2002. This increase in productivity, however, is consistent with the general rise in productivity in the economy as a whole as indicated by the trend in non-farm business productivity. The correlation between RPMs per employee and non-farm output per hour approaches one ($r = 0.96$) and the correlation between ASMs and non-farm output per person is also quite large ($r = 0.90$). Airline productivity was relatively low in the regulatory era but quickly matched non-farm productivity following deregulation. Productivity growth has not occurred through the number of departures, as the insert of Fig. 2 indicates, departures per employee actually

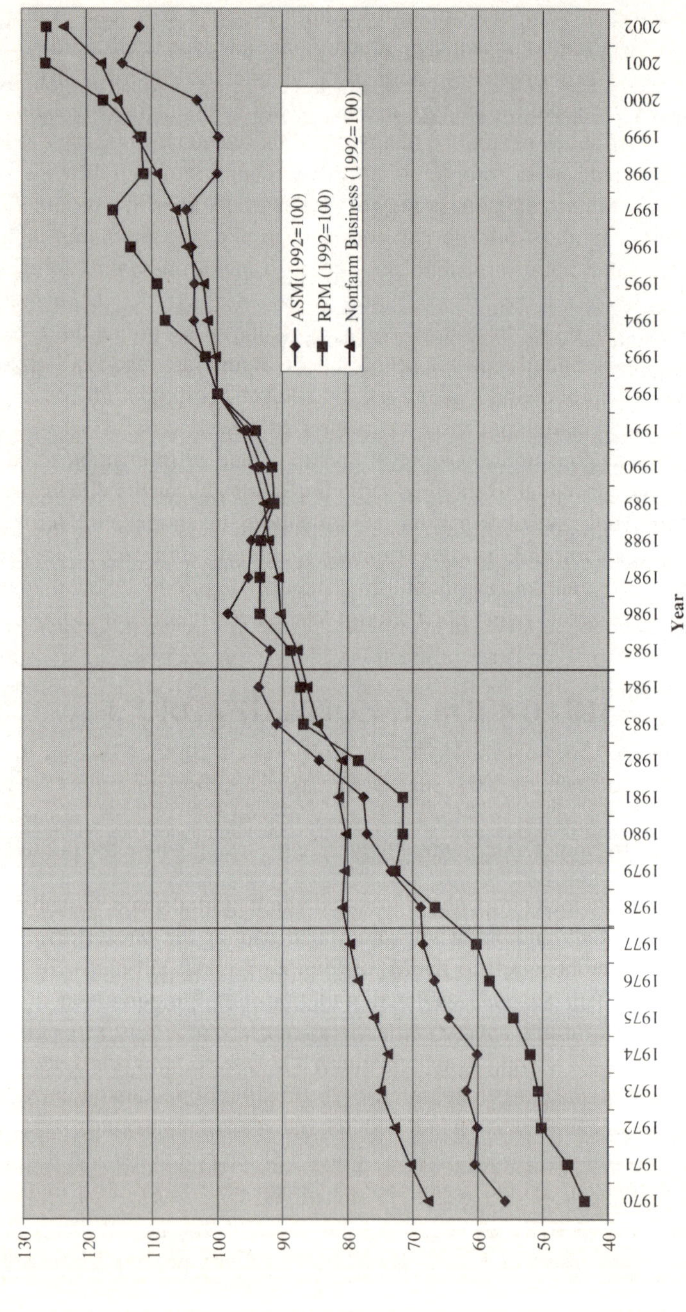

Fig. 2. Labor Productivity. *Source:* Derived from Air Transportation Association and Department of Transportation data.

have only recently exceeded their early 1970s levels.[7] In sum, although airline productivity increased, its growth mirrored the trends in the economy as a whole.

Airline labor productivity depends on a number of factors. First, the FAA establishes minimum staffing levels and hours of work that can be, and often is, limited further by the collective bargaining agreement. Operational factors that affect productivity include average aircraft size, length of haul, flight frequency, and services provided during a flight (Doganis, 2001; Gittell, 2003). Generally, long haul flights with larger aircraft have higher productivity levels relative to shorter hauls using smaller aircraft. This is caused by many flight-related activities such as check-in and baggage handling that does not rise proportionally with aircraft size (Doganis, 2001). Because the bulk of the productivity growth has occurred in the RPMs and ASMs and not through departures, much of productivity growth has likely arisen through employees that interact with passengers (flight attendants, passenger service, and reservation agents) and not through mechanics whose productivity is associated with departures.

WORKING CONDITIONS

Expanding productivity suggests the nature of work has changed for employees throughout the industry. The sources of the productivity gains, however, vary across occupations and have different implications for the working conditions of each occupation. For pilots, the increased productivity tends to arise through increased hours worked but for flight attendants productivity gains have arisen from both increased hours worked and through passenger interactions as indicated by the rising load factors. Although there is not strong evidence of rising productivity for mechanics, there is evidence that they are facing more dangerous working conditions. This section examines the changing nature of work, which will be explored for pilots, flight attendants, and mechanic occupations.

Pilots

Government safety regulation affects the work environment of airline pilots. For instance, limitations on pilot hours of work are governed by complex regulations set by the FAA as Fig. 3 illustrates. The collective bargaining agreement may further limit hours of work over and above the FAA regulations. These rules are undoubtedly an intricate set of guidelines as they govern how many hours a pilot can fly for a given time period, the rest requirements between and during flights, adjustments for weather delays, and restrictions on monthly and annual hours.

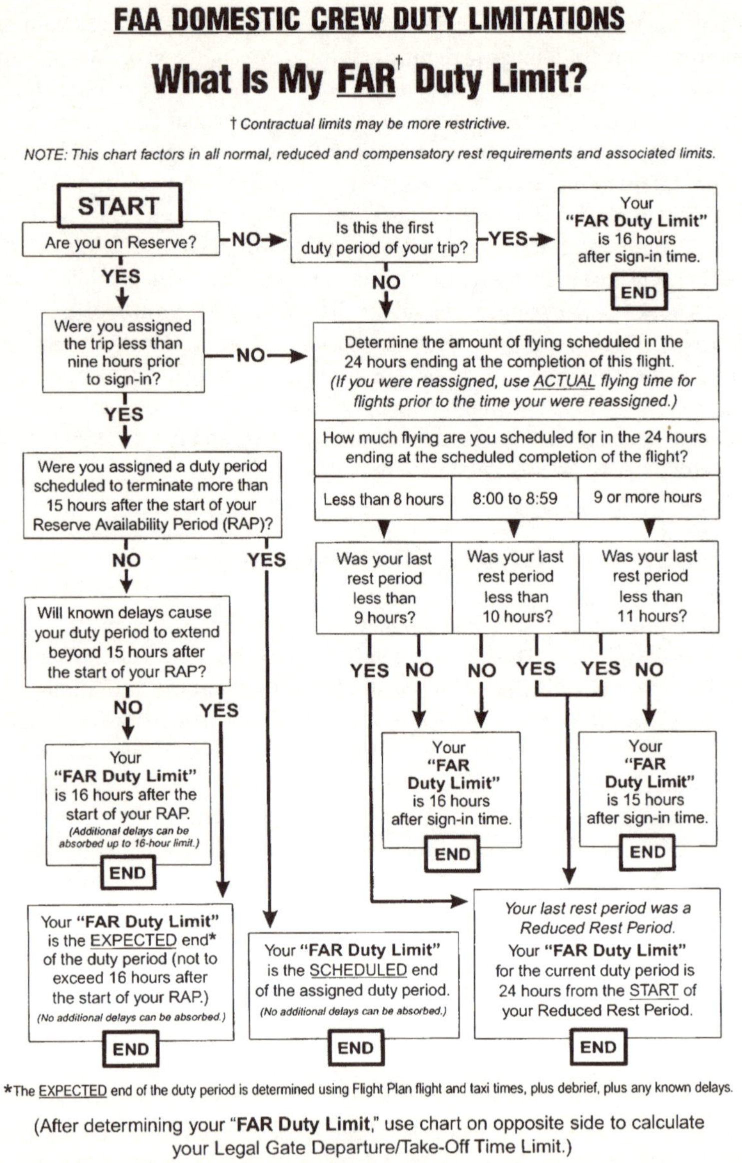

Fig. 3. FAA Rules on Pilot Flight Time. *Source:* Allied Pilots Association. http://www.alliedpilots.org/Public/archive/presskit/rest.20010530.html.

Additionally, these restrictions may vary by reserve status (whether a pilot is waiting to be called) and by how many pilots and flight engineers staff flights.

For over 30 years, government regulations governing hours of service have remained virtually unchanged. However, in 1983, the regulators undertook efforts to simplify thousand of pages of regulations that were easily misinterpreted (Department of Transportation, 1995). Further, the regulations lacked flexibility for adapting to weather conditions and changing flight patterns that emerged from new entrants to the industry – especially the commuter airlines. In 1983, the FAA convened a group of interested parties to engage in a concept of "regulatory negotiation" where all interested parties discussed relevant regulatory issues (Department of Transportation, 1995). An advisory committee was established that created final rules effective in 1985. These final rules were somewhat limited in scope and still considered overly complex, thus the FAA sought to amend these rules in the early 1990s. In the interim, the National Aeronautic and Space Administration (NASA) conducted a series of studies examining the impact of fatigue on pilot performance (cf. Samel, Wegmann, Vejovda, Drescher, Gundel, Manzey & Wenzel, 1997; Sexton, Helmreich & Thomas, 2000). They found that sleep, awake time off, and recovery are primary considerations for remaining alert. These considerations were used to develop effective safety rules (Department of Transportation, 1995). Thus, new rules were implemented in 1996 that address features such as rest, recovery, and weather delays and which superceded the 1985 requirements.[8]

Despite changes in rules and regulations, pilots' self-reports of weekly hours worked have been steadily climbing throughout the entire period as shown in Table 6. This data, compiled from the Current Population Survey (CPS), though, has a somewhat small sample size and may not accurately represent the population. It does, however, provide an indication – particularly when coupled with anecdotal industry reports – that pilots work hours are climbing. In the regulatory period (1972–1978), pilots' average weekly hours approached 36. In the early deregulatory period (1979 through 1984) these weekly hours increased to around 38 and then to over 40 by the late deregulatory era (1985 through 2002). By comparison, weekly hours for other professions remained steady for the CPS survey in general (Kirkland, 2000).

Overall, the rise to 40 hour workweeks is not likely to evoke much sympathy from many at first blush. However, pilot fatigue is considered to be a serious threat to safety particularly when crossing several time zones, working night duty, and experiencing sleep deprivation and long duty periods without breaks (Carmody, 2001; Gloag, 1995; Samel et al., 1997). One study of major accidents between 1978 and 1990 found that prior to their involvement in accidents half the captains and first officers had been awake for more than twelve and eleven hours, respectively (National Transportation Safety Board, 1994). Further compounding the safety

Table 6. Weekly Hours Worked for Airline Pilots and Flight Attendants.

Year	Pilots	Flight Attendants
1970	29.11	–
1971	31.20	24.05
1972	32.04	20.05
1973	37.77	23.41
1974	43.29	30.17
1975	34.89	28.06
1976	35.38	26.71
1977	37.91	33.75
1978	39.61	31.10
1979	36.11	32.07
1980	36.54	30.56
1981	37.15	30.77
1982	37.97	30.85
1983	38.75	30.67
1984	42.03	30.58
1985	38.91	32.63
1986	39.28	34.57
1987	41.28	33.73
1988	39.00	35.27
1989	38.49	32.82
1990	37.66	34.44
1991	39.42	32.04
1992	40.74	32.89
1993	39.24	33.39
1994	43.75	33.78
1995	43.01	33.08
1996	39.54	33.09
1997	41.60	30.65
1998	41.37	32.79
1999	38.85	32.90
2000	40.37	32.80
2001	42.01	33.32

Source: Current Population Survey.

problem airport congestion and crowding often push pilots to test the system limits. Weick (1990) in his detailed analysis of the Tenerife Air disaster attributed part of the system failure to pilots rushing to take-off because they were bumping the limits of the duty time regulations. He contends that increasing the tight coupling of the system increased the probability of such failure (Weick, 1990). Given that air traffic controls and airport capacity are severely limited, this tendency to further constrict system coupling could exaggerate fatigue effects (Subcommittee on Aviation, 2001). As most large disasters have resulted from a series of small events that become linked and amplified, the combined trend effects of pilot fatigue and system complexity may be problematic (Perrow, 1978; Weick, 1990). Recently pilots have been increasingly concerned about the rising hours as indicated by the fact that this issue holds a prominent position on the Air Line Pilots Association (ALPA) web site – the largest union representing pilots. Yet, the death rate from accidents has been declining in the passenger and air cargo markets for a number of years after excluding the deaths associated with 2001 terrorist attacks (Air Transport Association, 2003).

One other factor potentially heightening pilot error is more variation in crew assignments caused by the extreme number of layoffs the industry has experienced at the onset of this decade. The scope of industry layoffs extending to even more senior crew members increased the probability that flight crews lack familiarity with each other. Unfamiliarity among the cockpit crew may serve to exacerbate communication concerns as documented in several studies. Sexton, Helmreich and Thomas' (2000) research finds that pilot error is usually not due to aircraft control mistakes but rather to failures from crew coordination, miscommunication, and flawed decision-making. Weick's (1990) discussion of the Tenerife Air disaster also raises the issue of communication failure between the captain and his first officer as a contributing factor to this accident. The combined effects of increased hours, crew combinations with little experience with each other, and increasingly tightly coupled systems, combine to suggest that the margin for pilot error is declining.

Flight Attendants

Findings reported in Table 6 reveal changing work conditions for flight attendants arising from increased hours. For instance in the regulatory period from 1970 to 1978, flight attendants averaged roughly 28 hours per week but their hours rose to over 30 hours per week in the early deregulatory period from 1979 to 1984. This trend continued to the present when flight attendants hours further increased to an average of 33 hours per week by 2002. In contrast to the hours work trend reported for pilots, flight attendants have only in the last decade become covered by FAA regulations on duty time. Instead, flight attendants relied exclusively upon the collective bargaining agreement to limit their hours. The adoption of these regulations, though, does not appear to have moderated the trend towards increased flight attendant hours.

Weekly hours worked for flight attendants have increased during a period of significantly higher load factors further enhancing the potential for work related stress. Higher load factors indicate that the work environment for flight attendants has increased the number of passengers that flight attendants are required to serve per flight. Although scholars have long recognized that such workplace density is an important determinant influencing how people perceive their jobs, research is equivocal on the relationship between crowded working conditions and stress (Fried, Slowik, Ben-David & Tiegs, 2001). According to several studies examining job stress among flight attendants their critical stressors include limited and overcrowded space, the inability to walk-away from problems and receive prompt outside assistance to emergencies – problems that often rise with the number of passengers (Boyd, 2002; MacDonald, Deddens, Grajewski, Whelan & Hurrell, 2003). In a survey of airline cabin crews in the U.K., 75% of respondents reported being verbally abused by passengers at least one time per month, and 60% of respondents indicated that they had experienced at least one type of physical abuse. Additional evidence on working conditions for flight attendants reported by these authors indicate that the mean scores for psychological job demands and emotional load were higher for female flight attendants than for other working women on average (MacDonald et al., 2003). Despite these relatively high demands, flight attendants reported relatively low levels of anger, anxiety, depression, perceived stress, and job dissatisfaction. Fatigue, the only variable which was moderately high among flight attendants, most likely resulted from circadian rhythms disruptions due to frequent travel across time zones (MacDonald et al., 2003) and which can contribute to cognitive deficits (Cho, Ennaceur, Cole & Chang, 2000). These studies reveal that although flight attendants experience numerous stressors that have increased with deregulation, on average flight attendants are fairly adept at dealing with the stress despite their fatigue.

Compared to flight attendants, travelers may be less adept at handling the stress of long lines and crowding as indicated by the rising cases of "air rage." According to one study, rising incidents of customer abuse are caused by alcohol, delays, poor environmental conditions in the cabin (reduced fresh air), baggage disputes, and failure to meet customer expectations heightened by advertising (American Association of Flight Attendants, 2001; Boyd, 2002). Table 7 contains data from the FAA on the number of enforcement actions taken against passengers in violation of their ruling that states, "no person may assault, threaten, intimidate, or interfere with a crewmember in the performance of the crewmember's duties aboard an aircraft being operated (Federal Aviation Administration, 2000)." The findings in Table 7 indicate the number of enforcement actions executed by the FAA in violation of this regulation. Although the federal statistics do not report non-violent passenger threats, U.S. airlines maintain confidential reports by flight crews and these reports show rising incidents of air rage from 66 to 534 from 1997 to 1999 at the same time that the FAA reports declining incidents (Fogg, 2001).

Flight attendants are likely to experience the brunt of air rage. Anecdotal evidence has reported increased incidents of verbal and physical abuse of flight

Table 7. FAA Report of Crew Interference Enforcement Actions.

Year	Enforcement Actions
1995	140
1996	189
1997	308
1998	292
1999	178
2000	266
2001	100 (first half)

Source: Federal Aviation Administration.

attendants (Boyd, 2002; Fogg, 2001; Subcommittee on Aviation, 1998). The flight attendant has been the first line of defense against unruly passengers. Although these cases represent extreme incidents of passenger misbehavior, it is likely that lesser offenses likely rise in rough proportion to these extreme offenses. The recent increase in federal air marshals might serve to mitigate this trend as passengers may check their behavior given the possibility of law enforcement on board.

Overall, flight attendant productivity has mainly increased through increased hours and increased numbers of passengers served per flight attendant. Although flight attendants work under objectively stressful working conditions, evidence exists suggesting that flight attendants cope well with the stress on average. Fatigue and problem customers appear to be their most significant problems relating to their working conditions.

Mechanics

Post-deregulation working conditions for airline mechanics are characterized by greater pressure for these workers to become more efficient. This pressure arises from greater competition with outsourced maintenance and repair services (Alexander, Reed & Mellnik, 2003). Job pressures from stepped-up competition could create a less safe work environment if mechanics take greater risks to meet efficiency goals. Information presented in Table 4 does reveal evidence of increased industry injury rates. This industry information is taken from the BLS which defines an injury "to include as a cut, fracture, sprain, amputation, etc., which results from a work-related event or from a single instantaneous exposure in the work environment" (Bureau of Labor Statistics, 2004). Figure 4 lists the industry rates per 100 workers and compares manufacturing to air transportation (excluding flight deck and cabin crew). These airline data are thus, heavily influenced by industry injury rates of airline mechanics.

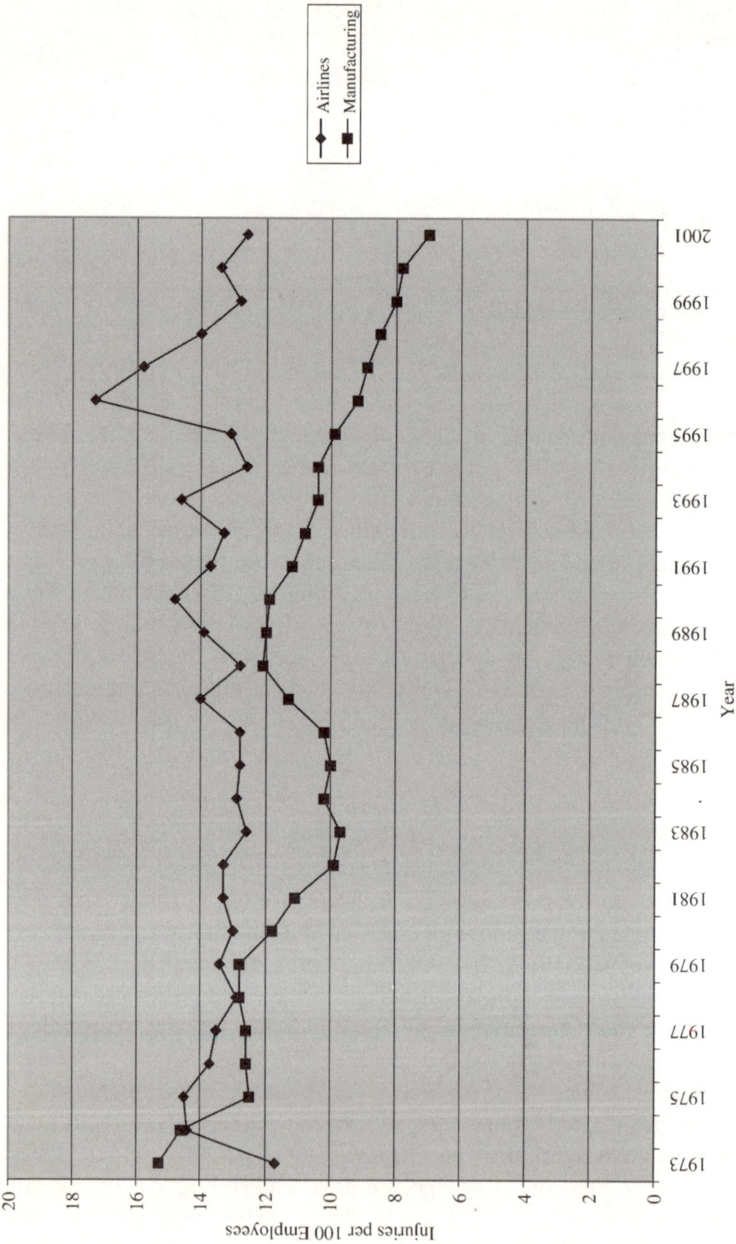

Fig. 4. Industry Injury Rates Including Fatalities. *Source:* Bureau of Labor Statistics (selected years).

Findings reported in Fig. 4 show airlines have always had fairly high injury rates relative to manufacturing but, in recent years, airline rates have risen over time to relatively high levels while manufacturing has been steadily declining.[9] During the regulatory era these trends switched. Airline injury rates declined while manufacturing rates rose. By 1979, airline and manufacturing injury rates were virtually identical. In the early deregulatory era (1979–1984), however, this pattern reversed and the airline injury rates tended to flatten out while manufacturing rates dropped. In the late deregulatory period, these general trends became pronounced with increased volatility in airline injury rates and a noticeably large spike in injuries in the late 1990s. In stark contrast, manufacturing injury rates progressively declined after 1989. In 2002, transportation by air was reported to have the highest rate of total nonfatal cases of injuries and illnesses of any major industry (Bureau of Labor Statistics, 2004) and these injuries and illnesses involved the most lost workday cases.

SUMMARY

At the onset of airline deregulation, most economists focused on deregulatory wage effects. Although wage effects were ultimately realized by flight attendants and pilots, it was more than a decade following the ADA. In the interim, airlines adjusted to the new competitive business environment by increasing employment at a rate lower than the increase in passengers by adopting a hub-and-spoke system that increases efficiency and productivity. Airline carriers also increasingly took steps to lower labor costs by employing more part-time workers, following deregulation. Despite these adjustments, a number of airlines filed for bankruptcy and many of these airlines ultimately failed. As such, airline industry employment has been cyclical with periods of significant adjustments contributing to ongoing job security concerns.

Pressure to become more productive has intensified and evidence exists that productivity has risen but at a rate consistent with other business sectors. Hours have increased for pilots and flight attendants, which raise the specter of increased fatigue and resulting airline safety concerns, that so far have not been realized. Additionally, rising load factors have increased flight attendant and passenger service interactions. Although flight attendants have not shown strong evidence of stress from increasing work pressures, passengers have not always kept calm. There is increasing evidence of passengers interfering with the crew. Such interference includes attacks on flight attendants. Finally, air transportation has the highest injury rates of any industry and highest rates of lost work days – all while injury rates in manufacturing are declining.

In sum, it is difficult to resist the flight metaphor – the turbulence of the industry suggests that its problems have reverberated to their employees. Despite increasing average employment levels, workers have experienced periods of significant employment declines. On average, it appears that workers have become more productive but at a cost to their health and safety. The varying profitability of the airlines and the ongoing bankruptcies suggest that the industry is still facing headwinds and it looks as if significant time will pass before the industry can shift and benefit from a tail wind. In many ways, the seas of deregulation still appear as uncharted today as they did 25 years ago.

NOTES

1. As indicated by Holloway (1997) the distinction between economies of scale and scope in the airline industry can be more or less a question of semantics. Returns to scale are found when average costs decline as firm output expands. Economies-of-scope arise from product line expansion such that the costs of producing both products together are less than the costs of producing them individually. The use of spokes to feed into hubs are often considered to offer the benefits of economies of scope in that the airline is offering separate products (short and long haul flights) but they also offer economies of scale as this combination also increases traffic density.
2. In contrast, UPS only reports 6,000 airline employees for the same time period. Because UPS started as a ground operation, the only employees included in the airline counts are directly involved in air operations.
3. Part-time employment is defined as less than 40 hours per week by the Department of Transportation.
4. According to the Department of Transportation, Federal Express had 47,339 part-time employees in 2002.
5. Estimation results on occupational employment growth are available from the authors upon request.
6. Note that labor costs are the largest variable operating cost and represent slightly over one third of total costs.
7. Note that this also might explain the lack of growth in mechanic's employment.
8. Prior rules were primarily focused on flight time and did not limit time on duty (Lowe, 2001).
9. In 1996, the changes in SIC classification for airlines was anticipated to increase the variability in airline injury rates as noted by the BLS (http://www.bls.gov/iif/oshwc/osh/os/osnr0005.txt).

REFERENCES

Air Transport Association (2003). Safety record of U.S. air carriers operating under 14 CFR 121. http://www.airlines.org/econ/d.aspx?nid=6243.

Air Transport Association (2004). Airline bankruptcies. http://www.airlines.org/econ/d.aspx?nid=6207.

Alexander, A., Reed, T., & Mellnik, T. (2003). Outsourcing up, inspections down: Inexperience, inconsistent oversight raise concerns about contract shops. *Charlotte Observer*, December 8, 1A.

Association of Flight Attendants (2001). Flight attendants issue air rage report card: Government and airlines fail. http://www.afanet.org/afa/default.asp?id=294.

Boyd, C. (2002). Customer violence and employee health and safety. *Work, Employment, and Society, 16*, 151–167.

Bureau of Labor Statistics (2002). Occupational employment and wages, 2002. http://www.bls.gov/oes/2002/oes532011.htm.

Bureau of Labor Statistics (2004). Occupational health and safety definitions. http://www.bls.gov/iif/oshdef.htm#occupinjury.

Card, D. (1998). Deregulation and labor earnings in the airline industry. In: J. Peoples (Ed.), *Regulatory Reform and Labor Markets* (pp. 183–229). Boston MA: Kluwer.

Carmody, C. J. (2001). Enhancing aviation safety. Presented at the alertness management in flight operations symposium. Arlington, VA.

Cho, K., Ennaceur, A., Cole, J. C., & Chang, K. S. (2000). Chronic jet lag produces cognitive deficits. *Journal of Neuroscience, 20*, 66–71.

Crémieux, P. (1996). The effect of deregulation on employee earnings: Pilots, flight attendants, and mechanics, 1959–1992. *Industrial and Labor Relations Review, 49*, 223–242.

Department of Transportation (1995). Flight crewmember duty period limitations, flight time limitations, and rest requirements. http://cf.alpa.org/internet/projects/ftdt/backgr/nprm.htm.

Doganis, R. (2001). *The airline business in the twenty-first century*. London: Routledge.

Federal Aviation Administration (2000). Part 121: Operating requirements – domestic, flag, and supplemental operations: Special federal aviation regulations. http://www1.faa.gov/avr/afs/fars/far–121.txt.

Fogg, M. P. (2001). Air rage: Is it a global problem? *Journal of International and Comparative Law, 7*, 1–25.

Fried, Y., Slowik, L. H., Ben David, H. A., & Tiegs, R. B. (2001). Exploring the relationship between workplace density and employee attitudinal reactions: An integrative model. *Journal of Occupational and Organizational Psychology, 74*, 347–359.

Gittell, J. H. (2003). *The Southwest Airlines way: Using the power of relationships to achieve high performance*. New York: McGraw-Hill.

Gittell, J. H., von Nordenflycht, A., & Kochan, T. A. (2004). Mutual gains or zero sum? Labor relations and firm performance in the airline industry. *Industrial and Labor Relations Review, 57*, 163–180.

Gloag, D. (1995). Rethink urged on pilots' hours. *British Medical Journal, 310*, 895.

Goetz, A. R. (2002). Deregulation, competition and antitrust implications for the U.S. airline industry. *Journal of Transport Geography, 10*, 1–19.

Hirsch, B. T., & Macpherson, D. A. (2000). Earnings, rents, and competition in the airline labor market. *Journal of Labor Economics, 18*, 125–155.

Holloway, S. (1997). *Straight and level: Practical airline economics*. Aldershot: Ashgate.

Johnson, N. B. (2002). Airlines: Can collective bargaining weather the storm? In: P. F. Clark, J. T. Delaney & A. C. Frost (Eds), *Collective Bargaining in the Private Sector* (pp. 15–55). Champaign, IL: Industrial Relations Research Association.

Kim, H. E., & Singal, V. (1993). Mergers and market power: Evidence from the airline industry. *American Economic Review, 83*, 549–569.

Kirkland, K. (2000). On the decline in average weekly hours worked. *Monthly Labor Review, 123*, 26–31.

Lowe, P. (2001). Duty, rest limits top agenda at airline-sponsored seminar. *Aviation International News Online.* http://www.ainonline.com/issues/07_01/july_01_dutyrestlimitspg80.html.

MacDonald, L. A., Deddens, J. A., Grajewski, B. A., Whelan, E. A., & Hurrell, J. L. (2003). Job stress among female flight attendants. *Journal of Occupational and Environmental Medicine, 45*, 703–714.

Meyer, J. R., Oster, C.V., Jr., & Strong, J. S. (1987). Airline financial performance since deregulation. In: J. R. Meyer & C. V. Oster, Jr. (Eds), *Deregulation and the Future of Intercity Passenger Travel* (pp. 17–38). Cambridge, MA.

Morrison, S., & Winston, C. (1995). *The evolution of the airline industry*. Washington, DC: Brookings Institution.

National Transportation Safety Board (1994). A review of flightcrew-involved, major accidents of U.S. air carriers, 1978 through 1990. Safety Study: NTSB/SS-94-01.

Petzinger, T., Jr. (1995). *Hard landing*. New York: Random House.

Robson, J. E. (1998). Airline deregulation: Twenty years of success and counting. *Regulation, 21*, 17–22.

Samel, A., Wegmann, H-M., Vejvoda, M., Drescher, J., Gundel, A., Manzey, D., & Wenzel, J. (1997). Two-crew operations: Stress and fatigue during long-haul night flights. *Aviation, Space, and Environmental Medicine, 68*, 679–687.

Sexton, J. B., Helmreich, R. L., & Thomas, E. J. (2000). Error, stress, and teamwork in medicine and aviation: Cross sectional surveys. *British Medical Journal, 320*, 745–749.

Subcommittee on Aviation (1998). Problems of passenger interference with flight crews and a review of H. R. 3064, the carry-on baggage reduction Act of 1997. Washington DC: U.S. GPO.

Subcommittee on Aviation (2001). Hearing on FAA's capacity benchmarks. http://www.house.gov/transportation/aviation/04–25–01/04–25–01memo.html.

Weick, K. E. (1990). The vulnerable system: An analysis of the Tenerife air disaster. *Journal of Management, 16*, 571–593.

Wilkey, J. R., & MacCartney, S. (2001). American Airlines wins a victory as Judge dismisses antitrust case. *Wall Street Journal*, April 30, A3.

6. PRODUCTIVITY, TECHNICAL CHANGE AND LABOR RELATIONS IN TRANSPORTATION INDUSTRIES

Daniel P. Rich

ABSTRACT

This chapter considers the evidence on productivity growth in transportation industries and provides a critical review of efforts to distinguish the nature and sources of technical progress. Regulatory reform and technological advance have contributed to productivity growth that is nonneutral across occupations and rational labor union responses will be sensitive to these asymmetric labor demand effects. Technical change alters the efficient organization of economic activity as well and a number of labor relation issues in contemporary transportation involve changes that span across the boundaries of firms, across traditional modes and even beyond the transportation sector.

1. INTRODUCTION

One of the basic tenets of economics is that productivity improvement is a prerequisite for sustainable improvements in real earnings and living standards. At the industry level the relationship between productivity growth and labor earnings is much less clear. Under sufficiently competitive labor markets the direct impact might be confined to employment adjustments. Addison and Hirsch (1989) suggest a possible mechanism for earnings gains in a union setting. The

Transportation Labor Issues and Regulatory Reform
Research in Transportation Economics, Volume 10, 109–1

ISSN: 0739-8859/doi:10.1016/S0739-8859(04)10006-1

sources of productivity gains may essentially be taxed by unions that "appropriate the quasi rents from long-lived tangible and intangible capital."

The history of transportation provides a number of heralded innovations that enhanced productivity in the movement of passengers and/or freight. Regulatory reform in a series of transportation industries held out the promise of enhanced productivity growth and there are a number of innovations currently affecting change in the organization of production in transportation. To what extent have these events contributed to productivity growth in transportation and what can be learned regarding employment outcomes and labor relations responses?

The literature supports the view that a number of sources, including regulatory reform, have contributed to productivity growth in transportation industries. While transportation represents only 3–5% of U.S. gross domestic product and employment, the observed productivity gains are a source of cost savings in business operations across various sectors of the national economy. A disproportionate share of transportation employment is unionized and the employment and/or earnings implications for labor appear to be determined less by the overall rate of productivity growth than by the specific nature of technical change.

This chapter explores recent patterns of productivity growth in transportation including the nature and sources of technical change. Section 2 considers the evidence on transportation industry productivity growth, including cost function estimates, and provides a critical review of efforts to distinguish among the sources of technical progress. Section 3 presents evidence of nonneutral technical change across occupational groups and argues that rational union responses will be sensitive to these asymmetric employment effects. Influences on the changing boundaries of firms are considered in Section 4 with application to current developments in sea-rail intermodal coordination, regional jet adoption and supply chain information networks. Concluding observations are provided in Section 5.

2. PRODUCTIVITY GROWTH IN TRANSPORTATION

The production process in transportation is well described by the standard economic theory of production, with a few unique features (Robert J. Gordon, 1992, p. 382).

2.1. Productivity Measurement

The most accessible measures of productivity growth across industries are based on labor productivity. Post-war (1948 to present) patterns of labor productivity growth across different sectors of the U.S. economy have motivated substantial research interest among economists. Concerns over limited prospects for productivity growth in service industries have been amplified with the continuing increase in the service sector share of employment (Triplett & Bosworth, 2002). A broad-based slowdown in productivity growth, outside of selected manufacturing industries, began in the early 1970s. The slowdown persisted through the mid-1990s despite an extended period of information technology investments. Most transportation industries appear to have experienced a corresponding slowdown in labor productivity growth despite the myriad regulatory reforms associated with this period.

Table 1 provides an overview of labor productivity, earnings and employment growth for all private industries and selected industry combinations. The output per hour productivity measure is based on the Bureau of Economic Analysis (BEA) Gross Product Originating series. Corresponding data on compensation and employment are derived from the National Income and Product Accounts (BEA-NIPA). Average annual growth in output per hour declines from 2.27% over 1948–1972 to 1.04% over the 1972–1995 period with a corresponding decline in real earnings growth. The pattern is similar, albeit at lower levels of productivity growth, for retail trade, financial and other service industries. The productivity slowdown is not evident for manufacturing industries taken together; however, the decline of real earnings growth in manufacturing conforms to the pattern for other industries.

The growth of labor productivity and earnings growth in transportation generally outpaced other U.S. industries over the immediate post-WWII period. The 1970s marked the onset of diminished productivity and earnings growth for air transportation and trucking while 1972–1995 appears to be a period of robust productivity growth for rail. Other U.S. industries experienced a broad-based resurgence in productivity growth over the most recent period; however, BEA-NIPA data indicate that the transportation industries shown generally did not participate.

Outcomes for rail industry labor have been reasonably consistent over time (1948–2001) with continued earnings growth and substantial employment decline. On the other hand, workers in air (1972–2001), trucking warehouse (1972–2001) and water transportation (1995–2001) experienced positive employment growth with relatively stagnant earnings. A critical question regarding these asymmetric outcomes across transportation industries is whether they arise from product demand conditions, industry-specific changes in production technology, changes in union representation, or differential union responses relating to preferences for job security.

Labor productivity is a deceptively simple concept subject to a wide range of measurement choices and economic considerations. Among the most influential choices are the definition of output and treatment of intermediate purchases.

Table 1. Labor Productivity, Compensation and Employment: Average Annual Growth.

	1948–1972	1972–1995	1995–2001
Total private industry			
Output per hour	2.27	1.04	1.93
Compensation per employee	2.54	0.86	1.71
Employment	1.02	2.06	1.96
Manufacturing			
Output per hour	2.75	2.79	3.55
Compensation per employee	2.71	1.29	1.15
Employment	0.78	0.02	−0.58
Retail, financial, services			
Output per hour	1.53	0.40	1.95
Compensation per employee	2.46	1.15	2.38
Employment	2.21	3.29	2.61
Rail transportation			
Output per hour	3.86	6.85	4.80
Compensation per employee	2.91	2.35	1.35
Employment	−3.90	−3.93	−1.90
Air transportation			
Output per hour	5.78	1.77	1.47
Compensation per employee	3.62	−0.03	0.81
Employment	5.72	5.16	3.34
Truck and warehouse			
Output per hour	3.93	1.54	0.85
Compensation per employee	2.99	0.09	0.18
Employment	2.73	1.66	2.57
Water transportation			
Output per hour	2.09	2.11	1.98
Compensation per employee	2.77	0.87	0.78
Employment	−1.01	−0.28	1.73

Source: U.S. Department of Commerce, Bureau of Economic Analysis, National Income and Product Accounts, industry tables. Average annual growth of output per hour over selected time periods is provided by Robert Gordon.

Gordon (1992) explains how these are a source of substantial variation between the alternative measures of labor productivity employed by different government agencies. Value added measures of output are used in national income accounting (BEA-NIPA) while physical output measures are the basis for Bureau of Labor Statistics (BLS) and Department of Transportation (BTS) evaluation of transportation productivity. BLS measures, given in Table 2, offer a substantially more

Table 2. Labor Productivity, Multifactor Productivity and Output: Average Annual Growth.

	1972–1977	1977–1987	1987–1995	1995–2000
Total private industry				
Labor productivity	2.01	1.45	1.40	2.63
Multifactor productivity	1.03	0.46	0.55	1.30
Output	3.23	3.24	2.78	4.53
Manufacturing				
Labor productivity	2.92	2.37	2.60	4.24
Multifactor productivity	−0.34	1.19	0.77	2.08
Output	3.09	2.14	2.66	4.01
Retail, financial, services				
Labor productivity	n.a.	n.a.	n.a.	n.a.
Multifactor productivity	n.a.	n.a.	n.a.	n.a.
Output	n.a.	n.a.	n.a.	n.a.
Rail transportation				
Labor productivity	0.33	5.05	5.90	3.76
Multifactor productivity	2.20	4.20	4.12	1.17
Output	1.15	0.37	2.95	1.99
Air transportation				
Labor productivity	3.46	3.89	2.01	0.60
Multifactor productivity	3.06	2.69	1.20	1.71
Output	4.44	6.76	3.30	4.78
Truck and warehouse				
Labor productivity	2.99	3.66	2.82	0.90
Multifactor productivity	n.a.	n.a.	n.a.	n.a.
Output	3.07	−0.58	3.26	2.91
Water transportation				
Labor productivity	n.a.	n.a.	n.a.	n.a.
Multifactor productivity	n.a.	n.a.	n.a.	n.a.
Output	n.a.	n.a.	n.a.	n.a.

Note: Corresponding output and productivity data are not available for selected industries as indicated (n.a.).

Source: U.S. Department of Labor, Bureau of Labor Statistics, Office of Productivity, industry tables.

positive assessment of transportation industry productivity performance over the 1972–1995 period. Additional sources of discrepancy among published sources include choice of employment or hours, treatment of output prices, treatment of multiple outputs, and industry coverage (Dean & Harper, 2001).

The economic interpretation of productivity growth can be examined in the context of a standard production model. Consider a multiple-input production function where capital (X_K), labor (X_L), energy (X_E) and materials (X_M) are combined to produce a single output (Y). The production relationship is not assumed to remain constant over time (t)

$$Y = f(X_K, X_L, X_E, X_M, t) \tag{1}$$

Observed growth in labor productivity may be the result of technical change, that is, where the production function relating inputs to output is altered over time. The quantity of other inputs will clearly influence labor productivity as well. This raises a fundamental requirement for economic interpretation, separating technical change from ordinary substitution responses to relative factor prices. Other influences on observed labor productivity growth include inadequately measured changes in the nature of output, labor composition, or the quality of other inputs.

A common approach toward isolating the growth of multifactor productivity (MFP) or total factor productivity (TFP) as distinct from factor substitution is to construct productivity index measures that incorporate multiple inputs. In terms of Eq. (1), the periodic growth of TFP can be expressed as

$$\frac{\mathrm{dln}f}{\mathrm{d}t} = \frac{\mathrm{dln}y}{\mathrm{d}t} - \Sigma_i S_i \left(\frac{\mathrm{dln}X_i}{\mathrm{d}t} \right) \tag{2}$$

where S_i denotes the cost share of the ith factor of production and $i = K, L, E, M$. Griliches (1994) and Hulten (2001) recount the intellectual development and implementation of the Solow residual, output growth not explained by the growth in inputs. The Divisia-Tornqvist and other index number procedures offer non-parametric measures of TFP growth consistent with Eq. (2). However, unbiased measurement and interpretation should be conditioned on the appropriateness of assumptions regarding allocative efficiency in input demand, constant returns to scale, and Hicks-neutral technical change.

BLS measures of average annual growth in multifactor productivity, labor productivity and output over selected periods are provided in Table 2. The productivity slowdown of 1972–1995 and more recent rebound are both evident in MFP-TFP for the U. S. economy, including manufacturing industries. The BLS provides multifactor productivity series for an expanding range of industries, including rail and air transportation. Multifactor productivity growth in these two industries appears relatively healthy during the periods of economy-wide productivity slowdown. However, the index-based evidence suggests that Solow residual productivity growth in the transportation sector was still cooling off while the post-1995 productivity rebound was heating up in other industries.

It might be noted that a systematic relationship between productivity growth and output growth is not apparent in the transportation industry outcomes in Tables 1 and 2. We would expect reduced costs and increased consumption of transportation services in response to total factor productivity growth. Yet, output growth during some of the most vigorous periods of productivity growth range from healthy (air transportation 1972–1987) to anemic (trucking, 1977–1987). Rail transportation exhibits a particularly weak link between productivity growth and employment-enhancing scale responses. An extraordinary record of post-WWII productivity growth in the rail industry has not induced sufficient output growth to avert employment declines of more than 1 million jobs (Rich, 1986).

2.2. Transportation Firms and Cost Function Estimates

Transportation industry applications occupy a prominent role in the production econometrics literature due in part to the relative availability of firm level data. Characteristics considered unique to transportation, such as network production and the multi-dimensional nature of output, are now recognized as more general concepts with application in a variety of industry settings. Given these conditions, a cost function approach conveys a number of advantages over index number or production function alternatives in the evaluation of productivity growth. Oum, Waters and Yu (1999) discuss recent developments in productivity measurement with application to railroad firms while Braeutigam (1999) offers a review of fundamental issues in the study of transportation costs across modes.

The cost function is particularly well-suited to complex representations of output, either as multiple outputs or using the hedonic approach presented by Spady and Freideander (1978) in which an extensive range of separate output combinations can be represented by a limited set of production characteristics. Consider the expression of a firm's total costs in Eq. (3). Here P represents a vector of input prices, Y represents the primary output, H is an observable output characteristic, and t indicates time.

$$\mathrm{TC} = g(P, Y, H, t) \tag{3}$$

The influence of different output combinations on costs has been evaluated in the empirical literature using commodity type ratios in rail (Berndt et al., 1993) and insurance coverage of shipments in trucking (Daughety & Nelson, 1988). Stage length, or length of haul, is the most common network attribute included in cost function estimation for all modes of transportation (Caves et al., 1984).

Panel data at the firm level commonly employed in transportation cost studies offer an appropriate setting for exploring economies of scale, scope and density. The combination of extensive information on detailed operating characteristics and costs with the development of flexible functional forms has yielded an uncommon wealth of empirical insights into production relationships, the sources of productivity growth and the nature of technical change. A representative specification of the translog total cost function, based on (3), serves as a useful reference.

$$\begin{aligned} \ln TC = {} & \alpha_0 + \Sigma_i \alpha_i \ln P_i + \alpha_y \ln Y + \alpha_h \ln H + \alpha_t t + \frac{1}{2} \Sigma_i \Sigma_j \gamma_{ij} \ln P_i \ln P_j \\ & + \frac{1}{2} \gamma_{yy} (\ln Y)^2 + \Sigma_i \gamma_{iy} \ln P_i \ln Y + \frac{1}{2} \gamma_{hh} (\ln H)^2 + \gamma_{hy} \ln H \ln Y \\ & + \Sigma_i \gamma_{ih} \ln P_i \ln H + \frac{1}{2} \gamma_{tt} t^2 + \gamma_{yt} t \ln Y + \gamma_{ht} t \ln H + \Sigma_i \gamma_{it} t \ln P_i + \varepsilon \end{aligned} \tag{4}$$

Equation (4) contains the full set of second order terms in the single-output, single-attribute case. The straightforward expansion of all Y and H terms provides for the case of multiple outputs and multiple attributes.

Estimates for total factor productivity growth are based on all of the terms involving t, as seen in Eq. (5). In this form we see that TFP growth may be nonlinear (γ_{tt}), scale-augmenting (γ_{yt}), attribute-biased (γ_{ht}) or nonneutral with respect to inputs (γ_{it}).

$$\frac{d\ln TC}{dt} = \alpha_t + \gamma_{tt} t + \gamma_{yt} \ln Y + \gamma_{ht} \ln H + \Sigma_i \gamma_{it} \ln P_i \tag{5}$$

A number of transportation cost studies derive productivity growth estimates using comparable empirical specifications and firm-level panel data. Selected results across transportation modes and different time periods are presented in Table 3.

Caves, Christensen and Swanson (1981) find TFP growth for Class I railroad firms of 3.5% from 1955 to 1963 and 0.6% over the 1963–1974 period. They demonstrate that estimates of productivity growth or technical progress can be sensitive to restrictive assumptions regarding firm behavior and the structure of production. A variable cost specification, with X_K terms included in the cost function, provides for disequilibrium capital stock. The authors find increasing returns to scale and argue that mergers and consolidation introduce a significant upward bias to index measures of productivity growth over the later period. Berndt et al. (1993) and Wilson (1997), with sample periods spanning the Staggers Act of 1980, find cost-reducing effects from deregulation that exceed merger effects and accelerate the rate of technical progress through 1989.

These and several related transportation studies employ a conventional time trend to represent technical progress and a (0,1) dummy variable to indicate years before and after policy reform. This is a popular approach in the empirical literature but ill-suited to distinguishing among the effects of diverse sources of productivity growth. Schwarz-Miller and Talley (2002) chronicle advances in

Table 3. Cost Function Estimates of Productivity Growth.

	Time Period	Average Annual Productivity Growth	Sources of Technical Progress
Rail			
Caves, Christensen and Swanson (1981)	1955–1963	3.5	Increasing returns to scale and railroad mergers.
	1963–1974	0.6	
Berndt et al. (1993)	1974–1986	5.9	Cost-savings from deregulation exceed merger effects.
Wilson (1997)	1978–1980	2.0	Cost-savings from deregulation initially large, decline over time.
	1981–1986	4.7	
	1987–1989	1.3	
Air			
Caves, Christensen and Tretheway (1984)	1970–1977	2.7	Unattributed time effects.
	1977–1981	2.1	
Baltagi, Griffin and Rich (1995)	1971–1978	4.6	Aircraft advances, hubbing, competition.
	1978–1986	3.4	
Truck			
Daughety and Nelson (1988)	1953–1982	Not applicable	Cost-reducing network adjustments attributed to deregulation.
Ying (1990)	1975–1984	Insignificant	
Wong (2001)	1976–1987	4.5	Third order effects for deregulation and trend technical change.
Allen and Liu (1995)	1985–1989	8.6	Cost reductions greatest for high service quality firms.
Water			
Kim and Sachish (1986)	1966–1983	9.4	Productivity growth from containerization exceeds effects from scale.

Note: Estimates based on variable cost specification and sample means unless otherwise noted.

locomotive technology, mechanized track installation, enhanced railcar capacity, computer-assisted traffic control, electronic data interchange and work rule revisions. Unless the combined effect of these production-altering changes follows a linear or quadratic time path, technical progress in the standard empirical model will be misspecified. Whether the appropriate counterfactual to deregulation can be adequately represented with a time-specific structural shift should be considered carefully as well (Winston, 1993, pp. 1270–1271).

The literature on air transportation emphasizes the role of network attributes in productivity patterns observed across carriers and over time. Caves, Christensen and Tretheway (1984) treat stage length, load factor (the ratio of revenue passenger miles to available seat miles) and points served as output characteristics. Residual productivity growth estimates associated with time, including initial years of transition to a deregulated environment, are presented in Table 3.

Baltagi, Griffin and Rich (1995a, b) formalize cost function treatment of technical change as a time-oriented residual not constrained with respect to time path. Given sufficient panel data, separate productivity growth estimates, A(t), are obtained for each period.[1] Proposed determinants of technical change are evaluated in a subsequent round of analysis. An increase in hub-and-spoke operations and increased competition at the city-pair level, measurable outcomes of regulatory change, contribute to productivity growth over the 1978–1986 period. However, the most significant source of technical change is a steady pace of aircraft advances in seating capacity and fuel efficiency adopted into airline fleets before and after deregulation.

An alternative approach is to incorporate specific indicators for proposed sources of technical change directly into the cost function. In the case of an international cargo port, Kim and Sachish (1986) replace the familiar time trend in Eq. (5) with a measure of containerization. Technical progress, in the form of increased containerization, delivered annual TFP growth of 9.4% over the sample period. As in rail, productivity growth observed through index measures would be somewhat higher due to increasing returns to scale and output expansion. While this particular study is limited to the Port of Ashdod (Israel), the argument that containerization represents a singular and substantial source of technical progress at U.S. ports would meet with little objection.[2] Schwarz-Miller and Talley (2002) explore the development and economic impact of containerization in more detail while others discuss implications for geographic concentration (Kuby & Reid, 1992), ship size (Cullinane & Khanna, 1999) and labor relations (Talley, 2002).

All of the above studies rely on second order approximations, as in Eq. (4), where the estimates of substitution relationships are flexible but the effects of technical change on relationships among inputs are limited. To evaluate technical change at a third order degree of flexibility requires a time-varying parameters approach or cost function estimation for discrete time periods. Daughety and Nelson (1988), using firm-level data from the trucking industry, develop cost function estimates at four separate points in time. "The cost functions appear to be relatively similar between 1982 and the 1950s and different during the intervening years," suggesting regulatory-induced distortion "in the isoquants themselves." This approach does not yield estimates of the rate of technical progress.

The impact of the Motor Carrier Act of 1980 on productivity growth is a subject of continuing discussion. Using the approach described above for rail studies, Ying (1990) finds a rate of technical progress for Class I and Class II trucking firms not significantly different from zero but accelerated by deregulation. Wong (2001) employs a "truncated third-order" specification to introduce additional time-varying parameters. The average annual rate of technical progress is 4.5% over 1976–1987 but is slowed by deregulation. McMullen and Okuyama (2000) present results that are qualitatively consistent with Wong using decomposition analysis of MFP index calculations. Unmeasured improvements in service quality appear to be responsible for the seemingly adverse impact of deregulation on trucking costs. Allen and Liu (1995) introduce survey-based indicators of service quality and convenience. They find that the most notable impact of changes in production relationships over 1985–1989 was to reduce costs of service quality provision.

A closely related issue that has received attention in numerous transportation applications is the econometric treatment of heterogeneity across firms. Firm-specific error components are implemented through fixed effects in rail (Berndt et al., 1993) and air transport (Baltagi et al., 1995b). Firm behavior that deviates from allocative or technical efficiency conditions is an especially relevant issue in industries subject to regulatory change. Kumbhakar (1992) demonstrates that estimates of technical progress in air transportation are sensitive to treatment of allocative distortions in carrier input choices. Atkinson and Cornwell (1998) show that rail industry productivity growth is a combination of technical progress (an industry-wide shift of the efficient frontier) and gains in relative firm efficiency (with railroad firms moving toward the efficient frontier). McMullen and Lee (1999) argue that deregulation enhanced the relative cost-efficiency of nonunion trucking firms.

In general, the empirical literature finds contributions from regulatory reform to productivity growth at the margin. However, all else is clearly not constant when we compare productivity growth in the era following deregulation to the preceding periods. The effects of regulatory change are overshadowed in many cases by other sources of technical progress.

3. TECHNICAL CHANGE AND LABOR DEMAND

Also necessary, and probably eventually more useful, are studies that consider the effects of the introduction of specific new technologies on the paths of employment of different types of workers at the level of very small industries (Daniel S. Hamermesh, 1993, p. 352).

3.1. Nonneutral Technical Change

Technical change refers to a residual, observed productivity growth over time not attributable to the growth in measured inputs. Adoption of technological advances, innovations in management of the production process, and production efficiency gains associated with organizational, regulatory or other institutional innovations are all potential sources of residual productivity growth. Technical change is described as biased or nonneutral, as opposed to Hicks-neutral, when the marginal rate of technical substitution between inputs is altered. The impact of technical change on the demand for labor is ambiguous and there can be no uniform theoretical prediction with respect to employment, earnings or rational union responses.

With Hicks-neutral technical change there are conflicting effects on the demand for labor. A reduction in input requirements per unit of output clearly decreases demand for labor and other factors of production if output remains constant. However, reduced marginal costs yield a positive output response that increases demand for all inputs. The relative magnitude of input-saving vs. output-enhancing responses depends on a number of conditions including the price elasticity of consumer demand. *Nonneutral technical change* alters the combination of inputs, reinforcing the input-saving response for some inputs while adding an input-using response for others.

A challenge for empirical evaluation is to distinguish the effects of nonneutral technical change from price-induced input substitution and nonhomothetic responses to output variation. All will tend to alter the cost-minimizing combination of inputs. The cost function framework provides an appropriate setting for estimating the relevant labor demand parameters and Table 4 presents nonneutral technical change results from selected transportation cost function studies. Where estimates are available, technical change is most often identified as labor-saving. In rail transportation, Caves, Christensen and Swanson (1981) find labor-saving technical change over both the 1955–1963 and 1963–1974 periods. Berndt et al. (1993) attribute labor-saving and fuel-using effects over 1978–1986 to deregulation. In trucking, Wong (2001) identifies trend technical change as labor-saving and purchased transportation-using.

The nature of organized labor's accommodation or resistance to anticipated sources of technical change is likely to exhibit recognition of the input-saving versus output-enhancing effects. Schwarz-Miller and Talley (2002) discuss the long history of conflict in U.S. ports over the labor-saving effects of containerization but also document minimal resistance in rail with anticipated gains in intermodal traffic. Dorwick and Spencer (1994) argue that unionized labor may perceive gains from labor-saving technical change with firm-level bargaining in relatively competitive industries while the conditions under which resistance is most likely include inelastic labor demand and union preferences weighted toward employment. Addison and Hirsch (1989) suggest that "unions appropriate quasi rents" from long-lived assets implying that technical progress be viewed

Table 4. Labor Demand Estimates from Cost Function Studies.

	Time Period	Nonneutral Technical Change	Own-Price Elasticity of Labor Demand
Rail			
Caves, Christensen and Swanson (1981)	1955	Labor-saving	−0.13
	1963		−0.16
	1974		−0.18
Berndt et al. (1993)	1974–1986	Labor-saving	−0.19
Air			
Caves, Christensen and Tretheway (1984)	1970–1981		−0.17
Baltagi, Griffin and Rich (1995)	1971		−0.18
	1978		−0.20
	1986		−0.22
Truck			
Daughety and Nelson (1988)	1953–1958		−0.47
	1978		−0.38
	1982		−0.33
Wong (2001)	1976–1987	Labor-saving	−0.35
Allen and Liu (1995)	1985–1989		−0.20
Water			
Kim and Sachish (1986)	1966–1983	Labor-saving	−0.05

Notes: Technical change bias and own-price elasticity of labor demand are derived from reported parameter estimates and means in studies that do not explicitly discuss these findings. Nonneutral technical change is not reported where the empirical specification does not yield a measure of factor bias or where the results are statistically insignificant.

as "taxed" not resisted. Stewart (1990) finds that effective rent appropriation by unions rises with firm-level market share and industry-level union density.

The own-price elasticity of labor demand represents a fundamental tradeoff in alternative models of wage-employment determination in union settings. Labor demand for firms in most transportation industries tends to be relatively inelastic (see the right hand column of Table 4). The results for trucking are within the range of firm-level estimates for other industries (see Hamermesh, 1993). We might expect a change in the marginal rate of technical substitution to alter labor demand elasticities over time; however, nonneutral technical change is typically evaluated as an input-saving or input-using shift in factor shares over time.

In rail and air transportation the own-price elasticity appears to increase over time reflecting, it could be argued, new substitution possibilities from technological, regulatory and other institutional changes. In trucking, separate estimates for distinct time periods incorporate more directly the impact of underlying parameter changes over time (Allen & Liu, 1995; Daughety & Nelson, 1988; Wong, 2001). Allen and Liu (1995) attribute the diminished elasticity of labor demand in trucking (from −0.47 in the 1950s to −0.20 in the 1980s) to lean staffing and conditions in the labor market for qualified truck drivers. The transportation cost studies referenced to this point provide a reasonably extensive and robust collection of labor demand estimates through the late 1980s but one finds little effort in the literature to distinguish among the potential sources of nonneutral technical change.

3.2. Occupational Labor Demand

The broader labor economics literature has focused particular attention to the prevalence and sources of skill-biased technical change, a variant of nonneutral technical change among different classifications of labor. Relative earnings and employment patterns between workers of different educational attainment, skill level or occupation suggest skilled labor-using (or unskilled labor-saving) technical change. While investments in information technology have received substantial attention, Fortin and Lemieux (1997) argue that it is difficult to distinguish empirically among a number of potential sources including industry deregulation, outsourcing and structural changes in labor market institutions.

From an applied perspective, it would be valuable to identify the determinants of labor demand for more detailed occupations. These occupational categories reflect employer-based choices and relate directly to workplace skills, both general and transportation-specific, that form the basis for education and training choices. Occupations serve as a useful vantage point for understanding union behavior in transportation industries. The collective bargaining environment for this sector includes a number of influential craft or occupation-based union organizations.

Stuart Rich (1986) presents employment patterns for the U.S. rail industry over 1952–1984 showing tremendous overall decline and substantial differences across job classifications. The employment shares for each occupational group and average annual employment growth are presented in Table 5. In terms of employment levels, maintenance shop labor (maintenance of equipment and stores) endures the largest decline of more than 300,000 jobs (Rich, 1986, p. 57). The proportion of total employment in this occupational group falls from 28% in 1952 to 19% in 1984. Rich (1986, pp. 59–60) describes two fundamental sources: (1) the transition from steam locomotives, requiring large maintenance facilities in numerous locations, to diesel with less extensive and much less frequent maintenance requirements; and (2) consolidation of maintenance facilities associated with mergers.

Table 5. Occupational Employment in (U.S. Class I) Rail Transportation.

	Shares of Total Employment			Average Annual Employment Growth (%)	
	1952	1968	1984	1952–1968	1968–1984
Executive, officials and staff assistants	0.013	0.027	0.044	+0.14	−0.62
Professional and administrative	0.171	0.216	0.187	−3.04	−4.45
Maintenance of way and structures	0.197	0.151	0.205	−5.79	−1.82
Maintenance of equipment and stores	0.282	0.224	0.190	−5.59	−4.58
Train and engine (conductors, engineers, fireman and brakemen)	0.208	0.280	0.297	−2.66	−3.33
Yardmasters, hostlers and switchtenders	0.013	0.016	0.018	−3.10	−2.99
Other transportation (telegraphers, flagmen and station agents)	0.117	0.087	0.058	−5.90	−5.79

Note: Occupational shares and data for employment growth calculations are taken from Rich (1986, p. 57). Primary source is the Association of American Railroads, *Annual Yearbook of Railroad Facts*.

The diffusion of diesel locomotive technology and the eventual dismantling of restrictive work rule provisions contributed to employment declines for brakemen, firemen and other train and engine occupations (Schwarz-Miller & Talley, 2002). Relative labor-saving effects are more clearly in evidence, with a declining employment share, for the occupational group including telegraphers, flagmen and station agents. Rich (1986, pp. 60–61) observes that labor-saving automation of traffic control, dispatching, waybill transmission and signaling was facilitated by advances in information systems and electronic-based communications.

With application to airline industry firms, a two-step econometric approach to evaluate labor demand and the sources of nonneutral technical is introduced by Chan and Rich (2002). They obtain labor demand parameter estimates for airline occupations and test for nonneutral technical change using a flexible cost system. Unique to this study are input-specific estimates of technical change, $A_j(t)$, that are not constrained with respect to time path. In other words, the effects of technical change for each occupation are identified on a year-by-year basis. This opens the door to a second stage of empirical analysis to distinguish among the potential sources of nonneutral technical change.

Occupational labor demand studies, though uncommon, tend to find price-induced substitution elasticities that exceed estimates based on aggregate labor (Hamermesh, 1993). Chan and Rich (2002) find own-price elasticities for airline occupations ranging from −0.224 to −0.898 that exceed estimates derived from

Table 6. Occupational Employment of Airline Firms: Decomposition of Average Annual Growth (1971–1985).

	Pilots & Copilots	Flight Attendants	Aircraft Mechanics	Pca Handling	Other Personnel
Employment growth	+0.612	+3.647	−1.400	+1.586	−0.013
Output	+4.863	+5.213	+5.484	+4.851	+4.375
Own price	−1.945	−1.880	−6.165	−1.755	−2.610
Cross price	+0.296	+0.518	+4.185	+2.550	+1.554
Technical change	+1.375	+3.254	−2.839	+1.882	+3.488
Elements of tech change	+0.422	+2.129	−2.282	+0.963	+3.537
Hub	−0.094	−0.068	−0.785	−0.731	+0.852
Points	−0.020	−0.003	−0.006	+0.002	−0.077
Stage	−0.020	−0.003	−0.103	−0.248	+0.356
Adoption	+1.350	+2.080	−1.295	+1.686	−0.374
Aircraft hours	−0.096	+0.032	−0.432	−0.011	−0.237
Load factor	−0.463	+0.143	−0.005	+0.076	+1.998
Outsource	+0.008	+0.035	−0.060	−0.002	+0.071
Competition	−0.243	−0.087	+0.405	+0.191	+0.950
Merger	0.000	0.000	0.000	0.000	0.000
Unexplained	−0.087	+0.605	+0.316	−2.087	−3.932

Note: Percent change evaluated at annual means. Unexplained reflects occupational employment growth minus combined effects of output, own price, cross price and attributed technical change elements. Firm effects included in estimation but not reported, see Chan and Rich (2002).

the airline cost studies of Caves, Christensen and Tretheway (1984) and Baltagi, Griffin and Rich (1995). Relaxing the constraints on the nature of technical change implied by aggregate labor yields valuable insights as well. Hicks-neutral technical change across occupations and across all inputs is rejected. While labor productivity increases for all occupational groups, our findings reveal technical change to be labor-saving for aircraft mechanics alone. Flight attendants and central office employees experience substantial labor-using effects.

How do these findings relate to observed patterns of employment and earnings? Employment growth over 1971–1985 is presented in the first row of Table 6 for each occupational group (pilots and co-pilots, flight attendants, aircraft mechanics, pca handling (ground-based employees handling passengers, cargo and aircraft), and other personnel (primarily central office personnel from clerical to executive management). Observed employment outcomes are decomposed into the effects of output growth, price-induced substitution, and technical change. All of these core elements of labor demand are at work. The results indicate substantial employment gains from output growth for all occupations and, for aircraft mechanics, employment-reducing effects of nominal wage growth (*own price*) that exceed output-based gains. Nonneutral technical change clearly contributes to the asymmetric employment patterns across occupations providing over 3% annual growth for flight attendants and other personnel but nearly 3% annual decline for mechanics. Earnings patterns, on the other hand, appear unrelated to our technical change estimates. Hirsch and Macpherson (2000) document a substantial reduction in the industry wage premium for flight attendants but minimal earnings losses for airline mechanics compared to similar workers in other industries.

In a second stage of analysis, Chan and Rich (2002) evaluate several proposed influences on the input-specific, time-oriented residuals from the first round of input demand estimation. Route system concentration into more clearly defined hub-and-spoke networks (*hub*), an adjustment facilitated by deregulation, elicits significant labor-saving responses for airport-based occupations (*pca handling* and *aircraft mechanics*) while increasing labor demand for central office employees (*other personnel*). Aircraft fleet quality changes due to adoption of new wide-bodied and stretch-bodied aircraft are reflected in available seat miles per gallon (*adoption*). New aircraft adoption has the most substantial labor-saving effects for mechanics while increasing labor demand for flight crews (*pilots and copilots* and *flight attendants*). The proportion of aircraft maintenance expenses paid to outside contractors (*outsource*) represents time-related changes in organizational boundaries. The labor-saving impact of aircraft maintenance outsourcing on mechanics at airline firms is statistically significant but relatively unimportant.

In the case of airline occupations, and one might suspect in most applications, there are a variety of sources of nonneutral technical change and the impact on different types of workers is anything but uniform. The concern expressed by Hamermesh (1993) that more studies along these lines are necessary remains largely unanswered. Within the literature on skill-biased technical change, for example, occupational detail is rarely explored beyond the familiar production-nonproduction definitions. Available data on detailed occupations and the adoption of specific technologies need to be incorporated in cost function based studies of labor demand at the industry or firm level.

More recent employment patterns in transportation suggest that ongoing processes of technical change have nonneutral effects across occupations. The Occupational Employment Statistics (OES) program, a joint effort of the Bureau of Labor Statistics and State Employment Security Agencies, develops detailed occupational estimates based on a survey of 400,000 establishments each year. The information in Table 7 is derived from OES data, published or provided by BLS staff. Employment shares in 1988 and 2000 and annual average employment growth over 1988–2000 are presented for selected occupations in three transportation industries.[3]

Table 7. Occupational Employment in Selected Industries: Employment Shares and Employment Growth.

	1988–1990	2000	1989–2000
Private nonagricultural			
Managerial	0.070	0.060	+0.49%
Engineering, science, technical	0.041	0.049	+3.37%
Sales, clerical, service, professional	0.575	0.619	+2.50%
Production & associated	0.281	0.270	+1.48%
	1989	2000	1989–2000
Manufacturing			
Managerial	0.064	0.062	−0.94%
Engineering, science, technical	0.089	0.085	−0.94%
Sales, clerical, service, professional	0.201	0.199	−1.22%
Production & associated	0.651	0.660	−0.44%
	1988	2000	1988–2000
Rail transportation			
Managerial	0.059	0.038	−5.97%
Engineering, science, technical	0.014	0.050	+7.53%
Sales, clerical, service, professional	0.191	0.222	−1.28%
Production & associated	0.736	0.690	−3.04%
Maintenance & track laying	0.182	0.104	−6.46%
Locomotive engineers	0.058	0.130	+4.13%
Conductors & yardmasters	0.098	0.179	+2.41%
Yard engineers, fire starters, brake, signal & switch operators	0.152	0.083	−7.07%
Material moving	0.063	0.047	−4.87%
Truck and warehouse			
Managerial	0.063	0.043	−1.59%
Engineering, science, technical	0.003	0.004	+2.09%
Sales, clerical, service, professional	0.206	0.204	+1.51%
Production & associated	0.726	0.749	+1.86%
Maintenance, installation, repair	0.055	0.047	+0.33%
Drivers, heavy	0.380	0.423	+2.49%
Drivers, light & delivery	0.094	0.072	−0.68%
Drivers, industrial truck & tractor	0.030	0.043	+4.63%
Other material moving	0.114	0.116	+1.17%
Water transportation			
Managerial	0.056	0.051	−0.03%
Engineering, science, technical	0.014	0.022	+4.28%
Sales, clerical, service, professional	0.235	0.238	+0.93%
Production & associated	0.693	0.689	+0.78%
Maintenance, installation, repair	0.092	0.072	−1.24%

Table 7. *(Continued)*

	1988	2000	1988–2000
Captains, mate & pilots	0.102	0.087	−0.53%
Sailors, oilers, ship engineers	0.145	0.157	+1.90%
Crane & tower, industrial truck & tractor	0.021	0.061	+7.34%
Other material moving	0.267	0.121	−5.40%

Note: Calculations based on data from Occupational Employment Statistics survey 1988, 1989, 1990 and 2000.

Looking first at the broad occupational groups, production workers represent a relatively large share of employment in manufacturing industries and an even larger share in transportation. The occupational distribution provides part of the explanation for the high proportion of employees covered by collective bargaining agreements in transportation relative to other industries (Hirsch & Macpherson, 2003). Union density across transportation industries declined over the 1988 to 2000 period; however, only in rail are observed occupational changes a potentially significant factor. In trucking-warehouse, for example, union density declined despite a substantial increase in production relative to managerial jobs.

The engineering, science and technical occupations are a large share of employment in manufacturing relative to other sectors but underrepresented in transportation. Throughout the 1990s this group of occupations represented a growing proportion of employment in transportation. The most dramatic shift occurred in railroads with increased engineering, science and technical accompanied by a much more substantial decline in the employment share of production occupations. Managerial occupations are a declining proportion of total employment in all industries shown.[4]

There are over 400 separate occupations within the "production and associated" group. These occupations represent a wide variety with respect to general training, union representation, firm or industry-specificity of skill requirements, and potential relationships to recent technical change. All of this theoretically important information is lost when empirical research aggregates labor into a single input or relies on the production-nonproduction convention. Over the recent 1988–2000 period alone, substantial variation in employment outcomes is observed in Table 7 across production occupations in transportation industries.

In rail transportation there is a continuing decline for maintenance and other production occupations identified by Rich (1986) while locomotive engineers, in particular, have experienced relative and absolute employment gains. Increased demand for drivers of over-the-road trucks and industrial truck and tractors may reflect increased specialization by trucking and warehouse firms or may simply exhibit the expected nonhomothetic response to output growth. Light and delivery truck driving, a declining occupation in trucking firms, has experienced substantial growth in other industries (air freight, wholesale trade, retail and business services). Occupational employment patterns in water transportation are consistent with the continuing transformation of ports associated with containerization. Stevedores and other material moving occupations continue to experience declining employment while occupations that are most complementary to new port capital, crane and tower operators and industrial truck and tractor drivers, have expanded.

The combination of productive inputs employed by transportation firms, including occupational employment, continues to change over time. These changes are the combined result of price-induced substitution, nonhomothetic responses to different levels of output, or nonneutral technical change. The sources of nonneutral technical change in transportation include investments in technologically advanced capital and other methods of new technology adoption, managerial innovations in production or service delivery, and redefinition of institutional constraints through regulatory reform. Empirical evaluation that seeks to develop unbiased estimates of the impact of any one source must acknowledge, and effectively control for, the wide range of possibilities.

4. ORGANIZATIONAL BOUNDARIES

> We do not believe that a theory of the firm that ignores contracts and other substitutes for ownership will prove useful for empirical studies. The world is replete with alternative instruments and, as always, the economically interesting action is at the margin of these substitutes.
>
> (Bengte Holmstrom & John Roberts, 1998, p. 92)

The productive contribution of any factor of production is not based on the nature of the factor alone but is also determined by numerous characteristics of the context in which the factor is employed. Much of the *economically interesting action* in contemporary transportation involves changes that span across the boundaries of firms, across historically distinct modes of transportation and even beyond the transportation sector. Technical change plays a leading role in all of these developments and regulatory reform, arguably, plays a supporting role in most cases. To understand how deregulation and technical change influence labor relations it is essential to consider their impact on the organization of production.

Separate firms exist for separate production activities to take advantage of economies of scale, scope and learning. The basis for most transportation industry activities derives from these basic elements of the gains to specialization and exchange. A manufacturing firm may enjoy a cost advantage from outsourcing to a trucking specialist serving several clients. There are, however, *transactions costs* associated with market exchange. Most forms of transaction costs can be viewed as a by-product of imperfect information: incomplete contracts due to inadequate observability, agency concerns based on information asymmetries, and information requirements associated with coordinating time-sensitive activities. These transaction costs may give rise to *vertical integration*, for example, the manufacturer may operate its own fleet of trucks despite increased transportation costs to assure the benefits of coordination with production schedules.

Another important determinant of firm boundaries is the degree to which the value of dedicated assets is relationship-specific and the corresponding *holdup problem*. If the trucking firm is required to make investments to serve the manufacturing firm, such as unique trailers or employee training that convey no value in serving other clients, then the trucking firm may be subject to opportunistic behavior by the manufacturing firm. Vertical integration is one approach to protect the return on such investments (Holmstrom & Roberts, 1998, p. 74). Repeated interaction, long term contracts and relational exchange may serve as effective solutions as well.

Relationship-specific capital investments are a prerequisite for intermodal transport of containerized ocean-going freight and double-stack container railroad service. Long term service contracts, of up to ten years, between shipping and rail transportation firms provide the necessary assurance of quasi-rents in this case. Gallamore (1999) and Schwarz-Miller and Talley (2002) recount how the Staggers Act of 1980 and subsequent regulatory reform permitted intermodal arrangements with long-term service contracts, facilitating an important source of technical change and traffic growth for railroads from the mid-1980s to present. Stapleton and Hanna (2002) find that transactions costs are reduced through sea-rail intermodal coordination with the efficiency of door-to-door shipping and sales force integration.

Airline firms organize production by supplementing internal "make" operations with a broad spectrum of external "buy" alternatives. Aircraft leasing, spot market fuel purchases and outsourcing of airport security (until recent federal initiatives) represent market exchange with elements of repeated interaction. Aircraft production, airport facilities, food services, and fuel purchases are in most cases governed by explicit multiperiod contracts. External arrangements with regional affiliate air carriers and international alliance partners, where coordinated performance across organizations may be governed by substantial implicit expectations, are best understood as examples of relational exchange.

Recent developments relating to the boundaries of airline firms have fueled a central conflict in collective bargaining with pilots. The *scope clauses* found in pilot labor agreements are intended to address pilot concerns that outsourcing of flights to regional affiliates or alliance partners serves as a substitute for employment with the mainline carrier. Firms typically describe the benefits in terms of positive effects on traffic growth and new organizational efficiencies while labor representatives tend to emphasize substitution effects and old-fashioned union avoidance. Once again, a combination of regulatory reform and technical change is at work. Deregulation of entry and exit makes it possible for airline firms to reorganize route networks to capitalize on new aircraft technologies.[5] With the introduction of regional jets, often through regional affiliate carriers, more explicit scope clause restrictions have become a pilot bargaining priority. Current agreements include restrictions on the number of regional jets, limits on seating capacity, and conditional clauses based on mainline carrier fleet expansion (U.S. General Accounting Office, 2001). In general, the approach taken to date by pilot unions can be viewed as accommodating the adoption of regional jets where there is assurance that internal output effects will exceed substitution across firm boundaries.

Advances in information technology are particularly disruptive to the organization of production given the preeminence of imperfect information in transactions costs. Baker and Hubbard (2003) consider the impact of two types of on-board computer equipment in trucking on outsourcing decisions of shippers over 1987–1997. Trip recorders provide detailed measures of truck operating performance after a haul is completed. This reduces the monitoring costs of complex job design and encourages a shipping firm, a manufacturing firm for example, to manage transportation as an internal activity. Electronic vehicle management systems provide real time communication capabilities and location information through satellite tracking. This reduces coordination difficulties across firm boundaries, improves capacity utilization for multiple-client trucking firms and encourages the shipping firm to outsource.

With the reassignment of activities across firm or industry boundaries, there may be movement of jobs and workers into different labor relations environments. Calculations from OES survey data, summarized in Table 8, confirm a marginal reduction in the proportion of all truck drivers employed directly by manufacturing and retail firms (from 58.4 to 53.8%). This decline is consistent with the prediction that advances in communication and geographic information systems promote outsourcing to transportation specialists. However, it should be noted that the increase in truck driver employment does not appear in the trucking and warehousing subsector. Air transportation (air freight) and business services (third party logistics) are the beneficiaries.

From a broader perspective, it may be more appropriate to consider productivity in transportation not in industry-specific terms but in the context of supply chain

Table 8. Employment of Truck Drivers Proportion by Industry.

	1988–1990	2000
Manufacturing	0.206	0.165
Retail trade	0.378	0.373
Truck and warehouse	0.317	0.314
Air transportation	0.011	0.065
Business services	0.006	0.014
Other private industries	0.082	0.069

Note: Calculations based on data from Occupational Employment Statistics survey 1988, 1989, 1990 and 2000.

performance. The value of transportation activities has more to do with coordination and less to do with ton-miles when upstream suppliers are expected to respond in real time to point-of-sale data from the retail floor and production schedule adjustments from the manufacturing plant. Leading retailers and manufacturers substitute information for inventory and, as a result, demand unprecedented levels of timeliness in transportation service order fulfillment (Abernathy et al., 1995). Service quality along these dimensions raises transportation costs (Allen & Liu, 1995) but enhances productive outcomes for the supply chain as a whole. Among the challenges for applied research in this area is to develop approaches to productivity measurement that are not industry-specific or constrained by the boundaries of firms.

5. CONCLUSION

In this chapter we have explored recent patterns of productivity growth and the sources of technical change in transportation. A combination of regulatory reform and advanced technologies appear to contribute to residual productivity growth that is nonneutral across occupations and alters the efficient boundaries of firms. Productivity measurement efforts across a wide range of industry settings should benefit from innovations applied in the study of transportation costs, including controls for network and other production characteristics and alternative representations of both the nature and determinants of technical change.

The relationship between the sources of productivity growth and union responses remains unsettled in the literature. Schwarz-Miller and Talley (2002) document the historical propensity of transportation labor unions to anticipate labor-saving technologies and implement restrictive work rules through collective bargaining agreements. Dorwick and Spencer (1994) argue that conditions associated with deregulated transportation industries (competitive product markets, firm-level bargaining and more elastic labor demand) reduce incentives for union resistance. Recent observations include eventual relaxation of long-standing restrictions as well as selective accommodation of potentially beneficial aspects of technical change. Airline pilot contracts with several major carriers, for example, do not preclude adoption of regional jets but do address potentially adverse substitution through negotiated scope clauses.

Accommodation of labor-saving technical progress in exchange for a share of quasi rents represents an alternative response that is consistent with findings in the broader literature on unions and firm performance. Addison and Hirsch (1989) observe that appropriation of quasi rents serves as a tax on investment in the sources of future productivity growth. The conditions most conducive to appropriation of rents, according to Stewart (1990), are greater market share at the firm level and union density at the industry level. The apparent contrast between the rail industry and trucking-warehouse, discussed further in Peoples (1998), is somewhat conspicuous on these conditions for appropriation of quasi rents and the corresponding earnings and employment outcomes.

Promising directions for future research include identification of union preferences given changes in labor demand conditions, additional attention to service quality in cost function studies, and further consideration of productivity growth measurement and union responses as productive activities migrate across traditional firm and industry boundaries.

NOTES

1. Baltagi et al. (1995) include new entrants in their sample and include the effects of network responses to deregulation in their estimates of technical progress.

2. Additional reasons to not consider this estimate representative of U.S. water transportation include redistribution of output among ports and the need to include other water transport subsectors, ocean-going vessels and inland waterways.

3. Prior to 1996 the OES survey involved a rotating set of industries over three years; therefore, 1988–1990 serves as the initial frame of reference for all private industries and 1989 is the initial year for manufacturing. Air transportation is excluded from Table 7. Occupational employment changes observed for air transportation over this period in the OES data are dominated by the relative growth of air courier services.

4. Management analysts/consultants are a growing occupation over this period; however, most of these jobs appear as professional occupations in service industries and not in the industries of the consulting firms' clients.

5. Federal Express was able to establish a concentrated hub-and-spoke network prior to deregulation by initially employing small enough jet aircraft. It is somewhat ironic that one of the anticipated consequences of regional jet diffusion is to increase opportunities to bypass major hubs of passenger carriers.

REFERENCES

Abernathy, F. H., Dunlop, J. T., Hammond, J. H., & Weil, D. (1995). The information-integrated channel: A study of the U.S. apparel industry in transition. *Brookings Papers on Economic Activity, Microeconomics*, 175–246.

Addison, J. T., & Hirsch, B. T. (1989). Union effects on productivity, profits and growth: Has the long run arrived? *Journal of Labor Economics*, *7*, 72–105.

Allen, W. B., & Liu, D. (1995). Service quality and motor carrier costs: An empirical analysis. *Review of Economics and Statistics*, *77*, 499–510.

Atkinson, S., & Cornwell, C. (1998). Estimating radial measures of productivity growth: Frontier vs. non-frontier approaches. *Journal of Productivity Analysis*, *10*, 35–46.

Baker, G. P., & Hubbard, T. N. (2003). Make vs. buy in trucking: Asset ownership, job design and information. *American Economic Review*, *93*, 551–572.

Baltagi, B. H., Griffin, J. M., & Rich, D. P. (1995a). Airline deregulation: The cost pieces of the puzzle. *International Economic Review*, *36*, 245–258.

Baltagi, B. H., Griffin, J. M., & Rich, D. P. (1995b). The measurement of firm-specific indexes of technical change. *Review of Economics and Statistics*, *77*, 654–663.

Berndt, E. R., Friedlaender, A. F., Wang Chiang, J. S., & Vellturo, C. A. (1993). Cost effects of mergers and deregulation in the U. S. rail industry. *Journal of Productivity Analysis*, *4*, 127–144.

Braeutigam, R. R. (1999). Learning about transport costs. In: J. A. Gomez-Ibanez, W. B. Tye & C. Winston (Eds), *Essays in Transportation Economics and Policy: A Handbook in Honor of John R. Meyer* (pp. 57–98). Washington, DC: Brookings Institution Press.

Caves, D. W., Christensen, L. R., & Swanson, J. A. (1981). Productivity growth, scale economies and capacity utilization in U.S. railroads, 1955–1974. *American Economic Review*, *75*, 994–1002.

Caves, D. W., Christensen, L. R., & Tretheway, M. W. (1984). Economies of density vs. economies of scale: Why trunk and local service airline costs differ. *Rand Journal of Economics*, *15*, 471–489.

Chan, W. H., & Rich, D. P. (2002). *Occupational labor demand and the sources of nonneutral technical change*. Presented at Canadian Economics Association Conference, Calgary.

Cullinane, K., & Khanna (1999). Economies of scale in large container ships. *Journal of Transport Economics and Policy*, *33*, 9–42.

Daughety, A. F., & Nelson, F. D. (1988). An economic analysis of changes in the cost and production structure of the trucking industry, 1953–1982. *Review of Economics and Statistics*, *70*, 67–75.

Dean, E. R., & Harper, M. J. (2001). The BLS productivity measurement program. In: C. R. Hulten, E. R. Dean & M. J. Harper (Eds), *New Developments in Productivity Analysis (NBER Studies in Income and Wealth)* (Vol. 63, pp. 55–84). Chicago: University of Chicago Press.

Dorwick, S., & Spencer, B. (1994). Union attitudes to labor-saving innovation: When are unions Luddites? *Journal of Labor Economics*, *12*, 316–344.

Fortin, N. M., & Lemieux, T. (1997). Institutional changes and rising wage inequality: Is there a linkage? *Journal of Economic Perspectives*, *11*, 75–96.

Gallamore, R. E. (1999). Regulation and innovation: Lessons from the American railroad industry. In: J. A. Gomez-Ibanez, W. B. Tye & C. Winston (Eds), *Essays in Transportation Economics and Policy: A Handbook in Honor of John R. Meyer* (pp. 493–529). Washington, DC: Brookings Institution Press.

Gordon, R. J. (1992). Productivity in the transportation sector. In: Z. Griliches (Ed.), *Output Measurement in the Service Sector (NBER Studies in Income and Wealth)* (Vol. 56, pp. 371–422). Chicago: University of Chicago Press.

Griliches, Z. (1994). Productivity, R&D, and the data constraint. *American Economic Review*, *84*, 1–23.

Hamermesh, D. (1993). *Labor demand*. Princeton University Press.

Hirsch, B. T., & Macpherson, D. A. (2000). Earnings, rents and competition in the airline labor market. *Journal of Labor Economics*, *18*, 125–155.

Hirsch, B. T., & Macpherson, D. A. (2003). Union membership and coverage database from the current population survey: Note. *Industrial and Labor Relations Review*, *56*, 349–354.

Holmstrom, B., & Roberts, J. (1998). The boundaries of the firm revisited. *Journal of Economic Perspectives*, *12*, 73–94.

Hulten, C. R. (2001). Total factor productivity: A short biography. In: C. R. Hulten, E. R. Dean & M. J. Harper (Eds), *New Developments in Productivity Analysis (NBER Studies in Income and Wealth)* (Vol. 63, pp. 1–54). Chicago: University of Chicago Press.

Kim, M., & Sachish, A. (1986). The structure of production, technical change and productivity in a port. *Journal of Industrial Economics*, *35*, 209–223.

Kuby, M., & Reid, N. (1992). Technological change and the concentration of the U.S. general cargo port system: 1970–1988. *Economic Geography*, *68*, 272–289.

Kumbhakar, S. C. (1992). Allocative distortions, technical progress, and input demand in U.S. airlines: 1970–1984. *International Economic Review*, *33*, 723–737.

McMullen, B. S., & Lee, M.-K. (1999). Cost efficiency in the U.S. motor carrier industry before and after deregulation: A stochastic frontier approach. *Journal of Transport Economics and Policy*, *33*, 185–208.

McMullen, B. S., & Okuyama, K. (2000). Productivity changes in the U.S. motor carrier industry following deregulation: A malmquist index approach. *International Journal of Transport Economics*, *27*.

Oum, T. H., Waters, W. G., II, & Yu, C. (1999). A survey of productivity and efficiency measurement in rail transport. *Journal of Transport Economics and Policy*, *33*, 9–42.

Peoples, J. (1998). Deregulation and the labor market. *Journal of Economic Perspectives*, *12*, 111–130.

Rich, S. M. (1986). Changing railway technology in the U.S. and its impact upon railroad employment since 1945. *Transportation Journal*, *25*, 55–65.

Schwarz-Miller, & Talley (2002). Technology and labor relations: Railroads and ports. *Journal of Labor Research*, *23*, 513–533.

Spady, R. H., & Friedlander, A. F. (1978). Hedonic cost functions for the regulated trucking industry. *Bell Journal of Economics*, *9*, 154–179.

Stapleton, A., & Hanna, J. B. (2002). Technological innovation adoption: An empirical investigation of steamship line sales force integration. *Transportation Journal*, *36*, 5–21.

Stewart, M. B. (1990). Union wage differentials, product market influences and the division of rents. *Economic Journal*, *100*, 1122–1137.

Talley, W. K. (2002). Dockworker earnings, containerization and shipping deregulation. *Journal of Transport Economics and Policy*, *36*, 447–467.

Triplett, J. E., & Bosworth, B. P. (2002). *"Baumol's disease" has been cured: IT and multifactor productivity in U.S. service industries*. Presented at New York Federal Reserve Bank Conference, Economic Data: New Needs for the 21st Century.

U.S. General Accounting Office (2001). *Aviation competition: Regional jet service yet to reach many small communities*. Report to the Honorable Olympia J. Snowe, U.S. Senate, GAO–01–344.

Wilson, W. W. (1997). Cost savings and productivity in the railroad industry. *Journal of Regulatory Economics*, *11*, 21–40.

Winston, C. (1993). Economic deregulation: Days of reckoning for microeconomists. *Journal of Economic Literature*, *31*, 1263–1289.

Wong, L. (2001). Measuring technological change in the U.S. motor carrier industry. In: B. S. McMullen (Ed.), *Transportation After Deregulation (Research in Transportation Economics* (Vol. 6, pp. 25–54). Oxford, UK: Elsevier.

Ying, J. S. (1990). The inefficiency of regulating a competitive industry: Productivity gains in trucking following reform. *Review of Economics and Statistics*, *72*, 191–201.

7. SHIFTING GEARS IN THE CORNER OFFICE: DEREGULATION AND THE EARNINGS OF TRUCKING EXECUTIVES

Stephen V. Burks, Frederick Guy
and Benjamin Maxwell

ABSTRACT

We study the earnings of executives of for-hire trucking companies from 1977 to 1986. Following deregulation of the U.S. trucking industry in 1979–1980, the real earnings of trucking firm executives (corporate officers) fell for a year or two, but then stabilized and, in the mid-1980s, recovered. Profit rates also fell immediately after deregulation, and then leveled off. The earnings of employee drivers, on the other hand, went into steady decline from 1979 to past the end of the period studied here. To analyze these trends we use a version of the Motor Carrier Financial and Operating Statistics, collected by the Interstate Commerce Commission on all medium-sized and large trucking firms for the years 1977–1986. Our version is unique in breaking out annual employee earnings by employee category for this time period. We document the change in the relative earnings of drivers and executives within the same trucking firms over time. We test the predictions of principal-agent theory and the political constraint model concerning the effect of deregulation on the level and performance sensitivity of executive

Transportation Labor Issues and Regulatory Reform
Research in Transportation Economics, Volume 10, 137–164

ISSN: 0739-8859/doi:10.1016/S0739-8859(04)10007-3

pay, and find evidence favoring political constraint over principal-agent. We also explore the effects of union presence and union busting on the pay of executives, and find that officers in unionized firms get paid more on average, but that officers' pay increases when a unionized firm goes non-union.

1. INTRODUCTION

During the last quarter of the 20th century, the pay of corporate executives soared, both in the U.S. and in other liberal market economies (Mishel & Bernstein, 1994). By contrast, as executive pay soared, the real earnings of semiskilled and unskilled workers fell (Mishel & Bernstein, 1994). Deregulation figures prominently among the factors believed to have contributed to this change, for both groups of employees.[1] Two mechanisms have been offered to explain how deregulation affected the pay of executives. Standard principal-agent models predict that with the increase in competition following deregulation, both the mean level and the performance sensitivity of executive pay would rise. The political constraint theory argues that regulation held down the level of executive pay, but only in industries in which firms were regulated directly, and hence only in such industries did deregulation release this constraint, allowing executive pay to rise.

In this paper we test the principal-agent and political constraint hypotheses using data on executive earnings in for-hire trucking firms serving the intercity (or long haul) market for the transportation of general commodities, between 1977 and 1986.[2] We also compare changes in executive earnings with changes in the earnings of employee drivers in the same firms. The period of our study includes 1979 and 1980, the years of administrative and statutory economic deregulation of the for-hire trucking industry.

Our data comes from the Motor Carrier Financial and Operating Statistics (MCFOS), collected by the Interstate Commerce Commission (ICC), and our version of these data is unique in breaking out the earnings of employees by employee category for this time period.[3] The MCFOS also includes information on a large number of operational and financial variables, such as the firm's size (revenues, number of employees), profitability (operating margins), nature of the firm's business (shares of "truckload" (TL) or "less-than-truckload" (LTL); average length of haul) and union status (proportion of medical and retirement fringe benefit payments going to union-affiliated health, welfare, and pension funds). This information allows us to control for a number of potentially important firm characteristics while studying the relationship between executive pay, regulation, and profit. Moreover, with certain limitations described below (see Section 3.1), we have data not on a sample, but on the entire relevant population of firms.

The central question we address with these data is this: *did the removal of entry and price regulation, such as prevailed in the trucking industry, affect either the level or the performance sensitivity of executive pay?* One view, from the principal-agent literature, is that it should, since the increased competition resulting from deregulation will increase the marginal product of managerial effort, as compared to that in the quiet life under regulation. Under standard models of incomplete contracts, this will in turn lead principals (firm owners) to increase both the expected level and the performance sensitivity of managerial pay. This view receives support from Hubbard and Palia's study (1995) of deregulation in the banking industry.

Another view is that regulation affects the pay of company executives not by changing the optimal contract principals offer executives, but because regulators may impose a political constraint on executive pay. This constraint is not, however, a product of regulation *per se*, but of particular forms of regulation; notably, it should hold where the firm is regulated directly (e.g. rate of return regulation of electric utilities), and not where regulations are a set of rules applied to all firms in an industry, as was the case in the U.S. trucking industry (Joskow et al., 1993). In keeping with this theory, Joskow et al. find only small and statistically insignificant industry effects on the pay of trucking executives in the period covered by our study, whether before or after deregulation.

The Joskow et al. study is valuable because it examines the pay of trucking executives in comparison with those in several other industries. But its conclusions about trucking suffer from the fact that it covers a very small number (approximately five) of very large, publicly traded, trucking companies, which happen to be included in the larger executive compensation database. In addition to being few in number, these firms are likely to be unrepresentative of an industry that has many privately held firms that are medium-sized and smaller.

Analyzing our data, we find that the Joskow et al. (1993) view is supported, and the increasing competition/principal-agent view is not. In particular, when examining the entire population of intercity carriers of general commodities, we find that the advent of deregulation affected neither the level, nor the sensitivity to firm performance, of executive salaries.

In addition to executive pay, we are interested in changes in the pay of executives in relation to what happened to the pay of drivers. The nature of our data allows us to make this comparison not on the basis of aggregates, but on the basis of differences within each of the firms in the population. In this regard we find that unionized firms pay their executives more on average, but that executive salaries increase slightly at union firms that go non-union.

The balance of the paper is structured as follows. Part 2 reviews the nature of regulation in trucking, the process of deregulation, and the changes in industry structure and in drivers' and executives' pay which followed. Part 3 explains the data source, the strengths and limitations of the data, the selection and construction of variables, and some issues in the specification and estimation of econometric models with these data. Part 4 presents estimation results for executives' pay. Part 5 presents concluding remarks.

2. REGULATION AND DEREGULATION IN THE U.S. TRUCKING INDUSTRY

The Motor Carrier Act of 1935 established the economic regulation of the interstate for-hire trucking industry in the U.S. by the Interstate Commerce Commission. This system of regulation prevailed until deregulation began, which is conventionally identified with particular administrative steps taken by the ICC in 1979, which were in turn followed by a more complete statutory deregulation in 1980. The Motor Carrier Act of 1980 broadened and systematized the changes of 1979, and also made the removal of regulation much less likely to be undone later.

Under the regulatory regime that prevailed from 1935 to 1978, competition was severely restricted: routes traveled and commodities hauled by incumbent firms were frozen in their 1935 configuration by a grandfathering process. Entry by new firms into for-hire trucking, and expansion by incumbent firms into new routes, or into different commodities, was sharply limited (although existing authorities to operate became assets that could be, and were, bought and sold; this did permit some firms to greatly increase their geographic scope under regulation) (Rothenberg, 1994).

In addition, prices to shippers that were binding on carriers were set collectively, through the institution of rate bureaus. The price setting actions of the rate bureaus were nominally subject to ICC review, but in practice such reviews were *pro forma*, and the ICC provided a rate enforcement mechanism through an administrative procedure that allowed rates differing from those set by the bureaus to be effectively blocked. This created a government-sponsored cartel, in the form a large set of route-and-commodity-specific oligopolies, which controlled the provision of motor freight services and their prices (Judiciary Committee, 1980; Moore, 1978; Rothenberg, 1994).

In the cartel environment, the industrial organization of the industry was distorted by the inability of new firms to enter, along with the inability of incumbents to feely adjust their output mix. It would have been natural to offer many new routes, and the transport of many new commodities on existing routes, as the industrial geography of the United States underwent significant evolution between 1935 and 1980, but these adjustments were significantly inhibited. This had the result that the technology mix chosen by firms was constrained.

In the long distance transport of general commodities, outside of the parcel segment, there are two basic technologies, in the sense of "overall ways of organizing production." One of these is truckload (TL), or point-to-point service, hauling complete or nearly complete trailer loads of freight. The other is less-than-truckload (LTL), or service in which smaller sized shipments from particular geographic regions are aggregated together, to be moved on a fixed network of routes between carrier-operated terminals. As it turned out, the ways in which the ICC regulated mergers and buyouts in motor freight made growth far more difficult for carriers which used TL methods than for those which used LTL methods. There were two key factors. First, most regulation-era TL firms were limited to specific and narrowly defined commodities, but tended to have significant route flexibility, while most LTL firms had very general commodity rights, but strictly defined routes. It turned out to be easier in practice to put general commodity authorities together in an "end-to-end" fashion to make new long distance connections, since only the routes, and not the commodities, had to match. Second, the ICC had to approve all regulation-era buyouts and mergers, and it arguably gave TL-type firms less favorable treatment over time than it did to LTL-type firms (Rothenberg, 1994).

As a result, during the regulatory era a large amount of full truckload freight was hauled by carriers that used the LTL-type organization of production, with local

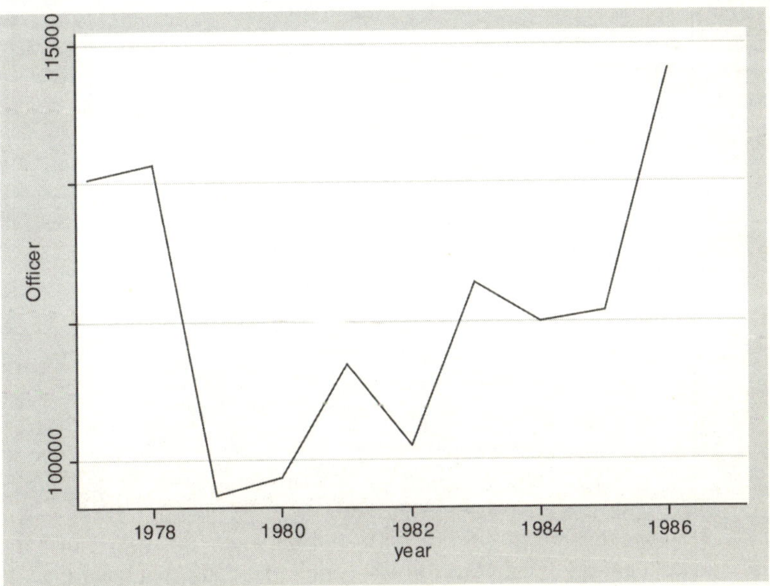

Fig. 1. Adjusted Annual Earnings of Trucking Company Executives 1982–1984 Dollars.

freight-handling terminals and fixed routes. As David Stubblefield, the retiring CEO of national LTL carrier ABF recently put it when discussing the changes deregulation had brought, "When I reflect back on what our life was like in the trucking business prior to deregulation, it was such a different world. In the first place, there were very few truckload carriers. Essentially, the LTL carriers handled all the truckload freight because they had the operating rights" (Cook, 2003).

Deregulation was actively discussed in both industry and government circles beginning in 1975. Administrative measures began to slightly relax restrictions on market entry in 1978, and more significant changes were introduced in 1979. Statutory deregulation of both entry and price was passed in 1980, although some features (notably, changes in the rules governing price setting and rate bureaus) did not take full effect immediately, but were phased in. Following Moore (1986) we take the first year in which there is likely to be much impact on the strategy and performance of firms in the Form M data set to be 1979. The change in regimes from 1978 to 1979 is evident in our data, executives' earnings (Fig. 1) drivers' earnings (Fig. 2) and profits (Fig. 3) all falling sharply from their 1977 to 1978 levels.

When deregulation removed barriers to entry and route adjustments, and made individual pricing possible, the industry underwent a sharp restructuring (Burks,

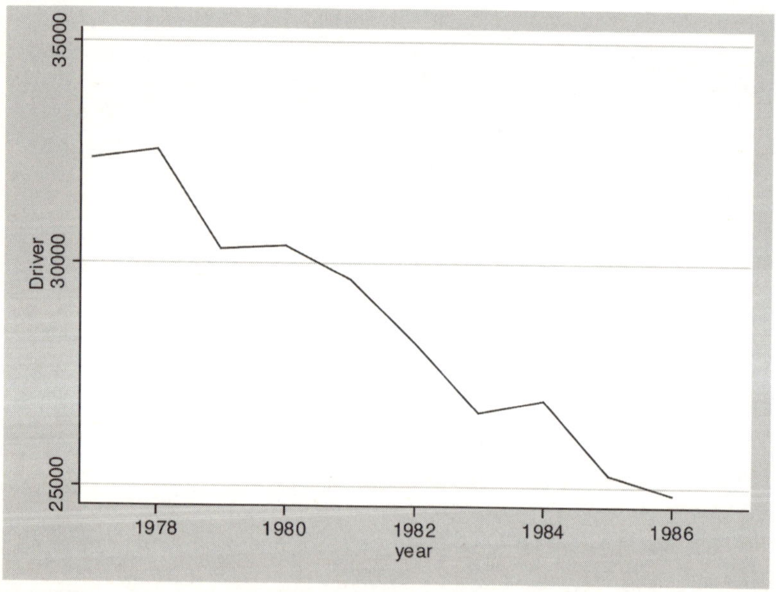

Fig. 2. Annual Earnings of Employee Drivers, For-hire Trucking Companies 1982–1984 Dollars.

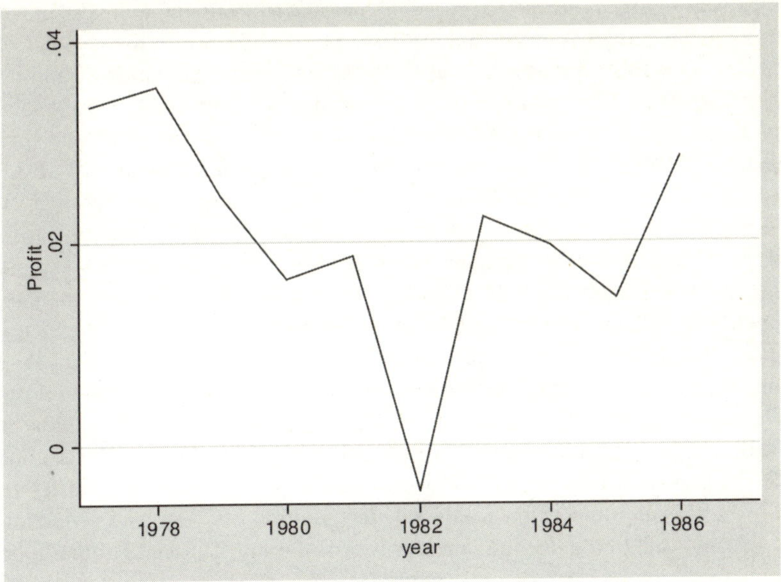

Fig. 3. Mean Operating Profit Margins for For-hire Trucking Companies.

1999; Campbell, 1987; Corsi & Stowers, 1991; Glaskowski, 1990; Perry, 1986). Incumbent TL type firms expanded, and thousands of new small TL firms entered. Without the overhead costs of a terminal system, and paying much less than Teamster wages, these firms sharply cut the cost of TL transportation. Increased competition and lower costs were reflected in freight rates: Moore (1983) finds that TL rates fell 25%, LTL rates 11%, in real terms, during only the first three years of deregulation.

The new and vibrant TL segment took most of the truckload freight that firms using LTL type production had been hauling, and then began taking market share from both railroads and private carriage (Campbell, 1987). LTL firms scrambled to rationalize and expand route structures, while coping with the loss of the majority of their TL freight. The result was a transformation of the technology mix, with the emergence of the focused specialization of individual carriers into TL and LTL types which is reflected in the way the North American Industrial Classification System (NAICS) categorizes trucking firms today (U.S. Census Bureau, 2001).

These changes transformed the competitive context for decision makers within trucking firms, and affected their earnings from salaries. Our data show that the annual (adjusted) average earnings of trucking company executives peaked in 1978, at $110,222 (all values in 1982–1984 dollars; for details of the adjustment that leads us to this figure, see Section 3.2, below). In 1979, the first year in which administrative deregulation had much effect, and also the year of the second OPEC oil price shock, this average fell sharply. It recovered somewhat in 1980 and 1981, then fell again in 1982, and remained low until 1985. After 1985 it rose sharply (Fig. 1). In comparison, the average real annual earnings of employee drivers peaked in 1978, at $32,518, and then fell at a compound annual rate of 3.3%, to $24,858 in 1986 (Fig. 2). The temporary drop in executives' earnings from 1980 to 1985 contrasts with steady upwards earnings trends reported by Joskow et al. for CEOs of large companies, whether in trucking or in a broad sample of industries. We speculate that the 1979 fall is attributable to the sudden increase in competition, perhaps compounded by the spike in fuel prices from the concurrent oil price shock, and the accompanying drop in operating profits (Fig. 3). The second drop in 1981 coincides with a major recession and another dip in profits.

The steady fall in the earnings of employee drivers is in sharp contrast with the fall, stabilization, and recovery of the earnings of executives. The decline in drivers' earnings has been variously attributed to the collapse of industry rents due to increased competition following deregulation, as well as a reduction in rent sharing, due to the decline in the power of the International Brotherhood of

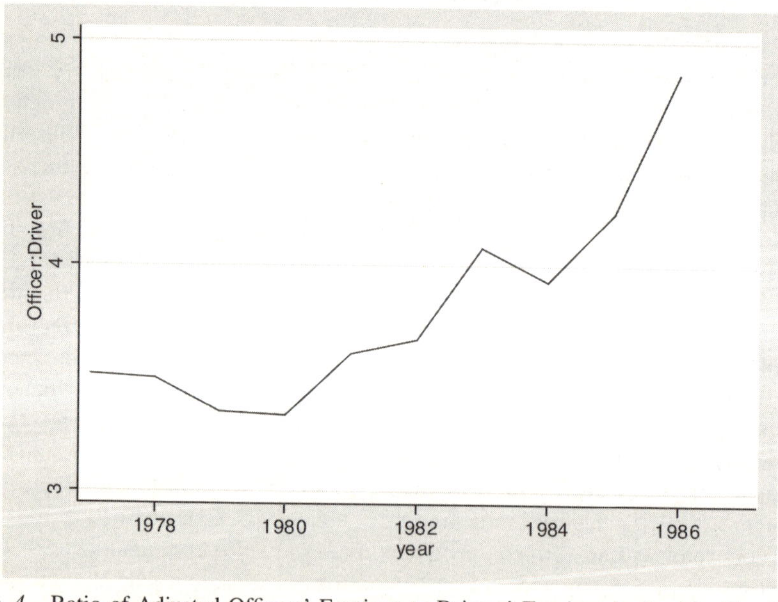

Fig. 4. Ratio of Adjusted Officers' Earnings to Drivers' Earnings in For-hire Trucking Companies.

Teamsters (Rose, 1987), and the nationwide decline in the pay of semiskilled and unskilled workers (Monaco & Brooks, 2001). Whatever the reason for the decline in driver's pay, the relative position of executives shows an upwards trend from 1979 on, with a marked acceleration from 1984 (Fig. 4).

3. DATA

3.1. The Source: The ICC's "Form M"

We use data from the Interstate Commerce Commission's "Form M" to examine the earnings of executives and drivers in the trucking industry. Our version of this data set is unique in providing a breakdown of employee earnings by category for this time period, thus allowing us to compare changes in officers' and drivers' earnings on a firm-by-firm basis, and also to examine the influence of carrier financial performance, carrier size, specialization, and unionization on the pay of executives.

As described in Section 2, during the years 1935–1980 the Interstate Commerce Commission officially had the duty of overseeing the rates collectively charged by regulated firms through the institutions of the rate bureaus, as well as judging the acceptability of all mergers and acquisitions. For these purposes it required all trucking firms subject to economic regulation to file an annual report, called the Form M (for "motor carrier" to distinguish it from the Form R, filed by "rail carriers"), and the contents of these reports were a matter of public record. Interestingly, these reporting regulations were not rescinded by Congress when the ICC itself was "sunsetted" at the end of 1995, and the data collection duties were transferred to the Bureau of Transportation Statistics (BTS). The Motor Carrier Financial and Operating Statistics (MCFOS), the label used by the American Trucking Associations (ATA), which has historically been one of the primary publishers of data from these reports, are thus a unique panel data source on the operations and finances of a key set of firms in the trucking industry, especially since the reporting regulations apply to all firms engaged in interstate freight transport, whether privately or publicly held.

The annual information filed by firms on the paper Form M's was keypunched both by the ATA and by the ICC. Most scholars use the version from the ATA, which is available for more years and had better quality control over the keypunching process, but which contains only part of the information in the paper form. The ICC's version of the Form M electronic data set, which was more complete, albeit with lower quality control, vanished when the agency disappeared. But before that happened, one of us (Burks) obtained an extract from it which includes the breakouts of employee earnings and hours by employee category for 1977–1987, items which are missing from the ATA's version until 1988. We have merged this extract with the more standard version of the Form M information from the ATA, which includes a large subset of the other data items of interest, but which had only the total number of employees and their total annual earnings.

There are two main limitations to data originating in the Form M. First, there was a size threshold below which reporting was not required (annual revenues for three successive years of $.5 million per year until this level was raised to $1 million in 1980), so there is no information on small incumbents, and also none on most of the new entrants in TL, who generally were too small to meet the reporting requirement initially. Second, the ICC relied significantly on voluntary compliance, and once the economic regulations that made it in the immediate interest of firms to report were lifted, this slowly became less effective. Many of the small TL entrants either did not know of the reporting threshold, or else did not choose to obey it, when they became large enough to cross it. In addition, a few (mostly TL) incumbents that had been reporting began to withdraw from doing so, towards the end of the 1980s.

As a result, up to the dawn of deregulation, the data set gives an excellent and complete picture of the entire population of medium and large-sized incumbents. And it provides a very good picture of the attrition and transformation of those incumbents under the impact of deregulation, especially in the earlier years of the process. However, it tells us very little about the new firms that entered the industry at small scale (although it does capture some that entered at larger scale). And its reliability as a picture of the overall population of medium and large firms slowly decreases with time, although it is still an excellent and unique information source for firms that continue to report, to the present day.[4]

We utilize the years 1977 through 1986 in the present paper for two reasons. First, the ICC sharply cut the size and complexity of the Form M in 1988. The size was reduced from 60 pages to (merely!) 30 pages, and the definitions of some variables were rationalized, which improved understandability, but at the cost of some limitations in historical comparability. In particular, the categories into which employee and owner-operator drivers were broken out were changed to better match the empirical reality. This makes 1987 the last year during which all the employee categories are directly comparable with previous years. In addition, during two years, 1981 and 1987, there is a sharp reduction in the number of firms for which the ICC entered the employee earnings and hours breakout information. In 1981 we are able to correct for this problem by interpolating between 1980 and 1982 for those firms that appear in both years. But this cannot be done for 1987, so we have dropped 1987 from our analysis, due to insufficient earnings information.

The quality control limitations on all the electronic data from the Form M, but especially keypunch and processing omissions and errors in the ICC's version, make extensive data cleaning efforts (such as the interpolation just mentioned) necessary before the data can be considered reliable. Fortunately, some systematic redundancies in the variable definitions, plus the panel nature of the data set, make it possible to correct many, perhaps even most, of the errors. Our efforts in this regard are detailed in Appendix 1, available from the authors.

3.2. Observations and Variables Used

The entire data set contains observations on firms of many types, including local and special commodity haulers. We restrict our attention to those meeting the definition of the ICC's "Instruction 27," which applies to firms obtaining at least 75% of their revenues from the intercity common carriage of general commodities (CFR, 1992).[5] We use this subset because we are interested in long distance freight transport, and in firms that use general purpose equipment and therefore compete directly with each other. A further word of explanation is required for the focus on "common carriage," however.

Under economic regulation *common* carriers had to publish their rates through rate bureaus, and offer their services at those rates to all customers, while firms in the contrasting category, *contract* carriers, were permitted to have individualized and confidential contracts with shippers, but were limited to eight customers in total, and no firm could offer both types of pricing and service. Common carriers were what the public thought of as for-hire trucking companies, while contract carriers were a close substitute for private carriage, which might otherwise be engaged in by shippers large enough to consider such an option.[6] After deregulation the limitation on the total number of contract customers was abolished for contract carriers. Also, all firms could easily obtain both types of authority, and nearly all did so.[7] Thus, under deregulation the common/contract carriage distinction quickly came only to apply to different ways the same firm could set its prices. For our purposes, the point is that the Instruction 27 subset captures the relevant set of firms – those that competed with each other to serve the general shipping public – across the regulation/deregulation divide.

Considering Instruction 27 carriers, then, our data set contains 3389 observations on 672 firms, an average of five per firm, from 1977 to 1986. The number of observations in a single cross section peaks at 458 in 1978, and declines to 236 by 1986.[8]

The 1977–1986 Form M uses two categories for employee drivers, linehaul (over-the-road) drivers who are paid on a mileage basis, and drivers who are paid on some other basis. "Drivers who are paid on some other basis" essentially lumps together two disparate categories. One group, the larger one, is local or "city pickup-and-delivery" drivers, who are generally paid by the hour. The second, and smaller one, is road drivers who are paid a percentage of the revenue generated by each load they transport.

We cannot impute a reliable hourly wage on the basis of these data. First of all, we are generally less confident of the hours of work data than we are of the earnings data. Second, for employee drivers paid by the mile, only the number of miles are reported, not the hours of work, which may vary with the amount of on-duty delay time that is experienced by drivers at different firms. Finally, although hours of work are reported for "drivers paid on some other basis," the hours of service regulations for operators of commercial vehicles make it very unlikely that firms recorded the actual work hours for the sub-group that worked over-the-road on a percentage-of-revenue basis.

In order to put observations on all three kinds of drivers on a comparable basis, therefore, we compute, for each firm and year, the average annual earnings for drivers in that firm in that year. The variable *DRIVER* is the natural log of the real (1982–1984 dollars) average annual earnings for drivers in the firm.

We would like to have a measure of the pay of the top executives of the companies in our data set. What we have, instead, are three figures: the combined total pay of all company *officers*, the number of company officers, and the total number of hours worked by all officers. We do not believe the officer hours figures are reliable (where they are not missing they tend to be values reflecting a nominal 40-hour work week), and this leaves us with total pay and number of officers. The number of officers reported varies widely, with a median of four, mean just over five, and a long upper tail leading to a maximum of fifty one. If we use total officers' pay as a proxy for top executive pay, we are accepting a very large error in our measurement. On the other hand, if we use average officers' pay, we simply trade one bias for another.

Our problem is this: we do want to adjust the total paid to officers to account for the number of officers, but a simple average is inadequate, because as the number of officers reported grows larger it tends to include more very "minor" officers. Because every officer is paid a positive salary (even if it is a small one in the case of a minor officer), in firms with a large number of officers the total of all officers' pay overstates the sum of executives' pay. Yet, because many of the minor officers aren't really among the firm's executives, including them in computing a simple average of all officers' pay understates the pay of executives. In addition, total officers' pay and the number of officers are both correlated with total revenue.

Our solution is to divide total pay by the number of officers, but only *after* discounting larger officer numbers. Specifically, we transform total officers' pay in the following manner:

Adjusted Officers' Pay ≡ Total Real Officers' Pay/(Number of Officers^x) where the exponent x is chosen so that in the regression ln(Adjusted Officers' Pay) $= a + b$ (ln Real Revenue) + year dummy $+ e$ the residual, e, is uncorrelated with the number of officers.[9] Our measure of firm size is the natural log of real total *operating revenue* (*REVENUE*). Virtually all studies find firm size to be by far the strongest predictor of executive pay, and we find that e is uncorrelated with the total number of officers when $x = 0.7$. Thus, the variable $OFFICER_{i,t} \equiv$ LN((Total Real Officers' Pay$_{i,t}$)/(Number of Officers$_{i,t}$)$^{0.7}$).

The Form M data includes balance sheet information from which it would in principle be possible to construct a measure of current return on either equity or on total capital employed. However, a large percentage of our firms are privately and closely held, and case study work on the industry suggests that tax considerations, unchecked by the public reporting requirements for stock exchange listing, affect the asset values reported to the ICC by firms of this type (Burks, 1998). The ratio of *operating profit* (before interest payments and profit taxes) to total operating revenues, which we designate as *PROFIT* in the models below, is therefore the best measure of financial performance we have for firms which are, in many cases, not publicly traded.

Our initial measure of *unionization*, UNIONSTATUS is the proportion of total firm expenses on employee health care and retirement that goes to union-affiliated health and welfare funds (Fig. 5). Since most firms in the industry are essentially either union or non-union, this measure is bimodally distributed. In light of this, together with its approximate nature, an appropriate way to use it in regression models is to convert it to a binary variable. For estimation purposes, we transform this into a binary variable, *UNION*, where UNION = 1 when UNIONSTATUS > 0.35.

The ICC marks the dividing line between *LTL and TL* shipments at 10,000 lbs. The exact location of the division is to some degree arbitrary, especially as the maximum cargo weight for a full truckload shipment has essentially doubled since the 1930s, when this number was selected. However, as long as the division is made consistently, and at a level above the average weight of an LTL shipment at firms that are highly LTL-specialized (which is about 1,000 lbs. in our data), it is a useful measure. The variable PERCLTL is the proportion of the firm's total operating revenue which is generated by LTL shipments; the balance is due to truckload shipments.

Nearly all general commodity firms, whatever their primary type, haul some shipments in both size ranges. It is handling shipments smaller than full truckloads above some threshold level that forces a firm to begin to switch from TL to LTL technology, by adding terminals for freight re-handling, and adopting fixed routes between them. In fact, a clear bi-modality of the revenue proportions above and below the 10,000 lb. shipment size emerged by 1986.[10] So, for estimation

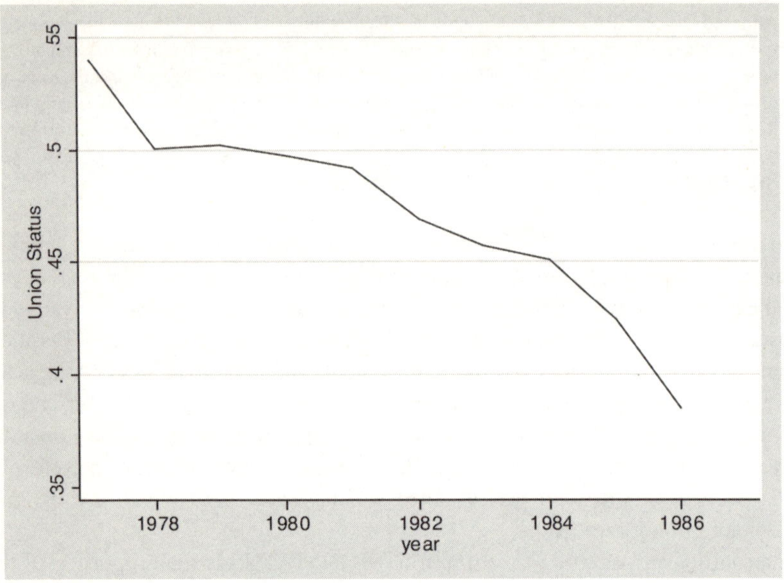

Fig. 5. Proportion of Pension and Welfare Payments Going to Union-affiliated Funds.

purposes, we transform this into a binary variable, *LTL*, where LTL = 1 when PERCLTL > 0.5.

This leaves the question of how intensely a firm that is of *either* type is pursuing a strategy of *specialization* (Fig. 6), *within* its type, which we capture with a specialization index, defined as the absolute value of the difference between PERCLTL and 0.5, divided by 0.5. This forms the variable *SPEC*.

As an indicator of the geographic scope of each firm we use an industry-standard indicator, usually called the *average length of haul*. It is constructed as the ratio of the total ton-miles produced to the total number of tons hauled by the firm. (Ton-miles are the sum over shipments of the weight of the shipment times the distance it is transported.) In its raw form, the distribution of this variable is highly skewed, with a long upper tail. We use the natural log of average length of haul for the variable *HAUL*.

Table 1 shows summary statistics for the variables used in our study. As we will be using both fixed effects (least-squares-dummy-variable, or within-groups) and group means (or between-groups) estimators, we report summary statistics both for the raw data, and for the data after both within- and between-transformations. The "within-group" data is a transformation of the data set in which, for each observation on a variable, the mean value of that variable for the firm in question

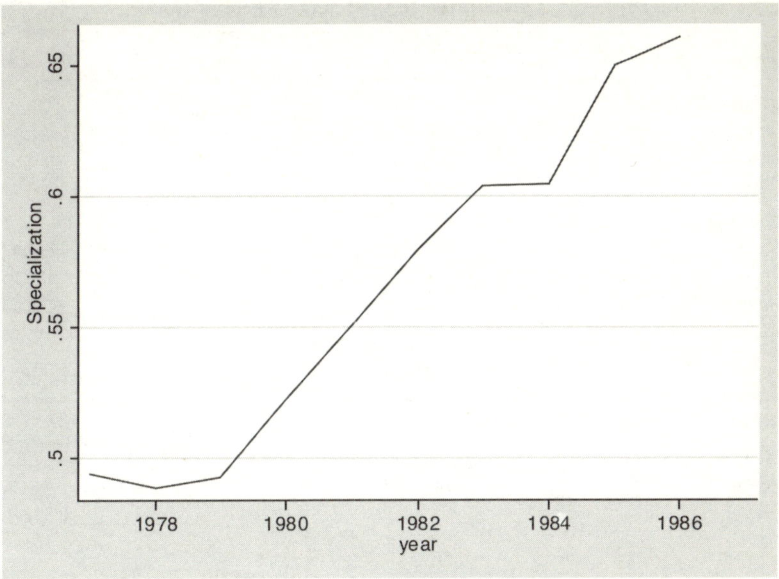

Fig. 6. Index of Specialization by For-hire Trucking Firms in *Either* Truckload or Less-than-truckload.

has been subtracted, so that the data consists of deviations from firm means. The "between-group" values take each firm as a single observation, averaged over the years it is in the data. Figure 6 shows changes over time in mean values for selected variables in our data set.

We have already discussed the trends in executives' pay, and drivers' pay, and profitability, in Section 2, above. Let us review the trends for the other variables used in estimation. Annual averages of the log of real total operating revenues (REVENUE) are roughly constant in our data set, though they also dip in 1982: in other words, mean firm size doesn't change much. Unionization (UNIONSTAT) declines steadily, from 0.55 to 0.4 (see Fig. 5). The average proportion of a firm's business that is LTL as opposed to TL (PERCLTL), varies between 0.64 and 0.71, but shows no trend (graph available from authors). The log of average length of haul (HAUL), however, shows a clear upward trend, so the average firm increased its geographic scope, as it rationalized its routes and added new ones (graph available from authors). Similarly, the specialization index (SPEC) shows a clear upward trend, exhibiting the sharpening segmentation of the product market following the removal of regulatory constraints (see Fig. 6).

Table 1. Descriptive Statistics on Variable Used.

Variable	Mean	Std. Dev.
OFFICER (real levels)		
Overall	104655.3	85557.49
Between		68233.1
Within		38155.25
DRIVE (real levels)		
Overall	29304.29	7733.47
Between		7412.16
Within		4159.58
PROFIT		
Overall	0.022	0.061
Between		0.051
Within		0.038
REVENUE (real levels)		
Overall	4.38e + 0.7	1.29e + 0.8
Between		9.90e + 0.7
Within		2.16e + 0.7
HAUL (real levels)		
Overall	257.8454	246.0658
Between		254.886
Within		62.11517
LTL		
Overall	0.82	0.384
Between		0.403
Within		0.175
SPEC		
Overall	0.55	0.249
Between		0.249
Within		0.110
LTLSPEC		
Overall	0.46	0.288
Between		0.289
Within		0.114
UNION		
Overall	0.59	0.492
Between		0.464
Within		0.192
UNLTL		
Overall	0.51	0.410
Between		0.463

Table 1. *(Continued)*

Variable	Mean	Std. Dev.
Within		0.213
UNSPEC		
Overall	0.31	0.314
Between		0.291
Within		0.149

Note: Variables in the table are as used in estimation, except that those logged in estimation are reported here in levels. "Between" and "within" are between-firm and within-firm standard deviations, corresponding with the transformed data used by the between and fixed effects estimators.

3.3. Estimation Strategy Considerations

Our data is panel data and the conventional way to proceed is with fixed effects estimates. There are at least two relationships that we want to examine, however, for which fixed effects estimation is likely to prove problematic. The fixed effects estimator makes use entirely of within-group (in this case, within-firm) variation in the data, discarding variation that occurs between firms. As a consequence, the estimator is known to be sensitive to errors in variables (Griliches & Hausman, 1986), which biases coefficients towards zero. This is a problem not only when right hand side variables are measured in error, but also when there are un-modeled dynamic effects at work. In the latter case, accurate contemporaneous measurements are serving in part as (error-prone) proxies for missing lagged measurements. The standard remedies for this problem involve the use of lagged observations, as instruments for the current observations (Griliches & Hausman, 1986). However, we have only two years of observations prior to administrative deregulation, and we need to explore structural changes within the ten years of good observations, and these requirements render the use of lagged values infeasible.

The specific variables which concern us here are UNION, LTL and PROFIT. Only 20% of our observations are from firms which changed from union to non-union, or vice versa, during their time in the data set. Thus, 80% of our data will contribute nothing to a "within-firm" estimate of the effect of union status on executives' pay. Furthermore, we know that some unionized TL carriers broke the union after the 1979 Teamsters contract by reopening under new carrier numbers (Burks, 1999), and these firms will be observed as new entrants, if at all, rendering the "within firm" measurement questionable. The problem with the binary variable LTL is not as extreme, but is similar in nature: very few firms switch their primary type, so in a within-firm estimate we would expect the coefficient on the LTL variable to pick up little, with most of the action happening in the coefficient of the SPEC variable.

The problem with PROFIT is different. Here, we need to allow for the possibility that the relationship between financial performance and executives pay could be a dynamic one, with sustained changes in profitability being rewarded differently than one-time gains or losses (Guy, 2000). But dynamic modeling brings us back to the problem of having a short panel with structural change and a number of variables of interest.

A rough and ready solution in such circumstances is to use between-group estimates (regressions in which each observation is an average over the years of observation for firm in question). The between estimator discards all within-group variation, but it picks up the difference between union and non-union, TL and LTL, which vary significantly across firms. It also captures long-run dynamic relationships (Pesaran & Smith, 1995), which should be important in (at least) the relationship between profit and executives' pay. It does this at the cost of failing to control for unobserved firm-specific characteristics which may be sources of bias.

A random effects (or error components) estimator might seem to offer a reasonable compromise, as it would compute a weighted average of the within and between estimates, but there are two problems with straightforward use of such an estimator. One is that the assumptions required for it to be an unbiased estimator are essentially that the expected value of its estimate is no different from that of the fixed effects estimate: in other words, if we tried use it to make up for what we suspect to be bias (as opposed to lack of precision) in our fixed effects estimates, we have no guide to the statistical properties of the estimator. The second problem is that, even if we managed to avoid the first problem, the random effects estimator imposes the same weighting of the within- and between estimates for all coefficients (the weighting may vary by *observation*, but that is separate question). Since our problem is precisely that the relative importance of within- and between-group variation differs quite a bit from one variable to another, this could be a problem.

In light of these considerations, we report both the within- and between estimates, separately. Given the differences in their biases, we are able in some cases to use the two sets of estimates as extreme bounds for the relationship in question. We also report random effects estimates, for comparison.

4. DETERMINANTS OF OFFICERS' PAY

We begin with a very general specification of the pay equation for officers, $\text{OFFICER}_{i,t} = \alpha_i + \beta_1\text{REVENUE}_{i,t} + \beta_2\text{PROFIT}_{i,t} + \beta_3\text{HAUL}_{i,t} +$

$\beta_4 LTL_{i,t} + \beta_5 UNION_{i,t} + \beta_6 SPEC_{i,t} + \beta_7 LTL_{i,t} \times UNION_{i,t} + \beta_8 LTL_{i,t} \times SPEC_{i,t} + \beta_8 UNION_{i,t} \times SPEC_{i,t} +$ interaction terms for all variables with transition (1979–1983) and full deregulation (1984–1986) + year dummies $+ u_{i,t}$.

For reasons discussed in the previous section, we will be estimating this model using both fixed effects and between estimators. We also present random effects estimates for comparison. Starting with the general specification above we tested, variable by variable, for structural change between the transition period and the fully deregulated period, and between the regulated period and the two periods afterwards. We selected interactions and variables for inclusion on the basis of the Schwartz Bayesian Information Criterion. We developed our specification using the fixed effects estimator, but the testing-down of structural changes followed the same path with all three estimators.

Standard F- and χ^2 tests fail to reject a hypothesis of no structural change in the overall model between the transitional and fully-deregulated periods, but reject this hypothesis between the regulated period (1977–1978) and after. At the level of individual coefficients, moreover, the regulated and deregulated periods are different only in the cases of PROFIT and HAUL, and for reasons discussed below we believe the apparent structural change in the PROFIT coefficient to be spurious. The Schwartz criterion favors the elimination of the variables LTL, SPEC and their interactions; in regressions using standardized data, none of the coefficients on these variables is large enough to attract interest. Table 2a reports estimates from the model that resulted from these tests.

Using REVNEUE as our measure of firm size, we find a firm-size elasticity of executive pay of between 0.29 (between) and 0.34 (fixed effects). Both are within the 0.20–0.35 range of estimates for firm size elasticity of CEO pay indicated by Baker, Jensen and Murphy (1988). The difference between the between and fixed effects estimates is statistically significant, but not large enough to be of substantive interest. We found no change in this effect following deregulation. Firm size explains far more of the variation in officers pay than any other variable, in both the fixed effects and between estimates (Table 2b).[11]

For reasons we discussed in Section 3.3, we expect the between estimates to give us an upper bound for the long-run relationship (i.e. over several years) between officers' pay and profitability, and for the fixed effects estimates to capture a shorter period effect (i.e. year-to-year) but to be biased downward, if interpreted as estimates of the long-run effect. In the between estimates, there is a large and statistically strong relationship between profitability and officers' pay, but no significant change following deregulation; in the within estimates, the situation is reversed, with a small and insignificant effect under regulation, and a much larger, statistically significant one, after deregulation (Tables 2a and 2b). The random effects estimates fall somewhere in between, as we would expect. Taken together, the

Table 2a. Officers' Pay Between, Random Effects, and Fixed Effects $n = 3389$.

Variable	Fixed Effects	Random Effects	Between
REVENUE	**0.34*****	**0.32*****	**0.29*****
	0.023	0.012	0.015
PROFIT	**0.02**	**0.63*****	**2.92*****
	0.208	0.191	0.782
PROFIT × p2&3	**0.67****	**0.41***	**0.31**
	0.213	0.202	1.064
HAUL	**−0.09*****	**−0.08*****	**−0.06**
	0.022	0.018	0.033
HAUL × p2&3	**0.07*****	**0.08*****	**0.07***
	0.014	0.014	0.033
UNION	**−0.05***	**−0.06****	**0.09***
	0.025	0.021	0.040
Period 2			**−0.26**
			0.172
Period 3			**−0.26**
			0.220
1978	**−0.04***	**−0.03**	
	0.020	0.020	
1979	**−0.15*****	**−0.13*****	
	0.021	0.021	
1980	**−0.57*****	**−0.55*****	
	0.077	0.075	
1981	**−0.59*****	**−0.57*****	
	0.078	0.075	
1982	**−0.59*****	**−0.56*****	
	0.078	0.075	
1983	**−0.62*****	**−0.60*****	
	0.078	0.076	
1984	**−0.65*****	**−0.62*****	
	0.078	0.076	
1985	**−0.68*****	**−0.64*****	
	0.079	0.076	
1986	**−0.65*****	**−0.61*****	
	0.079	0.077	

Note: Estimated coefficients in bold, with standard errors. Period 2 = transition period, 1979–1983, Period 3 = full deregulation, 1984–1986, Periods 2&3 = both of the above.

*$p < 0.05$.

**$p < 0.01$.

***$p < 0.001$.

Table 2b. Officers' Pay Fixed Effects and Between Estimates Levels and Standardized Data $n = 3389$.

Variable	Levels		Standardized	
	Fixed Effects	Between	Fixed Effects	Between
REVENUE	**0.34*****	**0.29*****	**0.28*****	**0.68*****
	0.023	0.015	0.017	0.038
PROFIT	**0.02**	**2.92*****	**0.00**	**0.19*****
	0.208	0.782	0.025	0.046
PROFIT × p2&3	**0.67****	**0.31**	**0.08*****	**0.00**
	0.213	1.064	0.023	0.047
HAUL	**−0.09*****	**−0.06**	**−0.08*****	**−0.09***
	0.022	0.033	0.017	0.039
HAUL × p2&3	**0.07*****	**0.07***	**0.58*****	**0.20****
	0.014	0.033	0.101	0.075
UNION	**−0.05***	**0.09***	**−0.03***	**0.01**
	0.025	0.040	0.015	0.032
Period 2		**−0.26**		**−0.42***
		0.172		0.177
Period 3		**−0.26**		**−0.41**
		0.220		0.249
1978	**−0.04***		**−0.14***	
	0.020		0.063	
1979	**−0.15*****		**−0.52*****	
	0.021		0.066	
1980	**−0.57*****		**−2.00*****	
	0.077		0.242	
1981	**−0.59*****		**−2.07*****	
	0.078		0.244	
1982	**−0.59*****		**−2.09*****	
	0.078		0.246	
1983	**−0.62*****		**−2.19*****	
	0.078		0.247	
1984	**−0.65*****		**−2.28*****	
	0.078		0.246	

Note: Estimated coefficients in bold, with standard errors. Period 2 = transition period, 1979–1983, Period 3 = full deregulation, 1984–1986, P 2&3 = both of the above.

$^{*}p < 0.05$.

$^{**}p < 0.01$.

$^{***}p < 0.001$.

estimates for the de-regulated period are quite similar, but the short-run (within) and long-run (between) estimates for the regulated period are substantially different.

We might be tempted to treat the change in the fixed effects estimates from the regulated to the de-regulated periods as indicating a structural change: if deregulation led to a stronger short-term relationship between profitability and officers' pay, but left untouched the long-term relationship, we would expect to see results such as those reported in Tables 2a and 2b. We did not trust this result, however, because the results for the regulated period are estimated on just two years' data. As Griliches and Hausman (1986) show, the downward bias of the absolute value of coefficients, due to errors in variables in fixed effects models, gets worse as the panel gets shorter; the lower limit is of course a panel of two, which is equivalent to a first-difference estimate. The between estimator is not subject to this sensitivity. It is possible, then, that the apparently small and insignificant effect of profitability on officers pay, in the fixed effects estimates for the regulated period, is an artifact of the shortness of that period in our data.

To check this, we estimated the model on first-differenced data for a series of two year periods (1977–1978, 1979–1980, etc.). The results are reported in Table 2c. The profit coefficients here are statistically insignificant in every period. On the basis of this, we would discount the suggestion that the results in Tables 2a and 2b indicate any structural change in the pay-profit relationship for officers. Similar regressions on longer periods (three years, then five years) yield larger coefficients by no particular pattern. We therefore re-estimated the models in Table 2a, after eliminating the de-regulation interaction term for PROFIT. These results are reported in Table 2d.

We find, then, that the relationship between profitability and officers' pay in trucking companies did not change with deregulation. What are we to make of this fact? It is contrary to the competition hypothesis (Hubbard & Palia, 1995), but consistent with the political constraint hypothesis (Geddes, 1997; Joskow et al., 1993). This is a corroboration of Joskow et al.'s finding in a much larger and more varied set of firms. We confirm that the political constraint was never binding in this industry: it is the constraint that wasn't there.

Under regulation, companies with a longer average length of haul paid officers less; this effect disappeared following deregulation. We interpret this as reflecting the difficulties of operating a long-haul firm under regulation, when long-haul routes often had to be cobbled together from disparate grandfathered operating authorities. After deregulation the typical firm expanded its geographic scope, and hence increased its average length of haul. It appears that a wide consensus on the advisability of this strategy meant that choosing it carried neither a pay penalty nor a pay premium for executives.

Unionization has a small but statistically significant effect on the pay of officers. This effect takes opposite signs in the fixed effects and between estimates. The between estimate tell us that unionized firms pay their executives more on

Table 2c. Officers' Pay First Difference Estimates Two Year Periods.

Variable	77–78	79–80	80–81	81–82	82–83	83–84	84–85	85–86
REVENUE	**0.63*****	**0.50*****	**0.40*****	**0.22****	**0.42*****	**0.14**	**0.30***	**0.51*****
	0.126	0.098	0.102	0.081	0.101	0.162	0.139	0.143
PROFIT	**0.08**	**0.23**	**−0.33**	**−0.56**	**0.14**	**−0.87**	**0.04**	**−0.15**
	0.556	0.462	0.421	0.405	0.351	0.508	0.259	0.467
HAUL	**−0.08**	**−0.10***	**−0.08**	**0.11**	**−0.03**	**0.07**	**−0.00**	**−0.04**
	0.098	0.052	0.060	0.059	0.080	0.069	0.065	0.075
LTL	**0.09**	**−0.08**	**0.13**	**0.06**	**0.01**	**−0.02**	**−0.04**	**0.02**
	0.171	0.144	0.145	0.095	0.190	0.155	0.158	0.225
SPEC	**0.18**	**−0.51***	**0.01**	**0.44**	**0.46**	**0.30**	**0.28**	**0.58**
	0.356	0.250	0.284	0.230	0.323	0.407	0.344	0.332
UNION	**0.03**	**0.18**	**−0.03**	**−0.29***	**0.29**	**−0.20**	**0.66***	**0.07**
	0.194	0.160	0.172	0.140	0.219	0.235	0.295	0.256
LTL × SPEC	**−0.59**	**0.53***	**−0.19**	**−0.29**	**0.03**	**−0.17**	**0.50**	**−0.26**
	0.350	0.233	0.251	0.182	0.339	0.458	0.356	0.348
UNION × LTL	**0.00**	**0.11**	**0.24***	**0.17**	**−0.18**	**0.09**	**−0.33**	**0.03**
	0.157	0.131	0.119	0.108	0.171	0.166	0.176	0.232
UNION × SPEC	**−0.06**	**−0.36**	**−0.07**	**0.07**	**−0.28**	**0.12**	**−0.69**	**−0.28**
	0.305	0.195	0.208	0.197	0.252	0.324	0.357	0.337
Constant	**−0.07*****	**−0.00**	**−0.02**	**−0.07*****	**−0.02**	**−0.02**	**−0.05***	**0.01**
	0.021	0.019	0.015	0.020	0.022	0.024	0.024	0.022
N	353	343	300	296	268	247	217	210

Note : Estimated coefficients in bold, with standard errors.

$^{*}p < 0.05$.

$^{**}p < 0.01$.

$^{***}p < 0.001$.

Table 2d. Officers Pay Assuming no Structural Change in Coefficient on Profit Fixed Effects, Random Effects and Between Estimates $n = 3389$.

Variable	Fixed Effects	Random Effects	Between
REVENUE	**0.35*****	**0.33*****	**0.29*****
	0.022	0.012	0.015
PROFIT	**0.49*****	**0.92*****	**3.12*****
	0.147	0.132	0.356
HAUL	**−0.10*****	**−0.09*****	**−0.06**
	0.022	0.018	0.033
HAUL × p2&3	**0.07*****	**0.08*****	**0.07***
	0.014	0.014	0.033
UNION	**−0.05***	**−0.06****	**0.09**
	0.025	0.021	0.040
Period 2			**−0.26**
			0.172
Period 3			**−0.25**
			0.219
1978	**−0.04**	**−0.03**	
	0.020	0.020	
1979	**−0.14*****	**−0.12*****	
	0.021	0.021	
1980	**−0.55*****	**−0.54*****	
	0.077	0.075	
1981	**−0.57*****	**−0.56*****	
	0.078	0.075	
1982	**−0.58*****	**−0.56*****	
	0.078	0.075	
1983	**−0.60*****	**−0.59*****	
	0.078	0.076	
1984	**−0.63*****	**−0.61*****	
	0.078	0.076	

Note: Estimated coefficients in bold, with standard errors. Period 2 = transition period, 1979–1983; Period 3 = full deregulation, 1984–1986; p2&3 = both of the above.

$^{*}p < 0.05$.

$^{**}p < 0.01$.

$^{***}p < 0.001$.

average. Since unionized firms pay drivers more, and since the existence of firm-level pay equity effects is well established (Frank, 1985; Akerlof & Yellen, 1990), a positive overall relationship between unionization and officers' pay is not surprising. However, the negative coefficient on union status in the within estimate indicates that following the de-unionization of a firm (when the value of this binary variable declines from 1 to 0), officers are rewarded with an increase in pay.

5. CONCLUSION

The deregulation of trucking took place at a time when the real earnings of unskilled workers were beginning a sustained decline, and those of company executives were beginning to skyrocket; both trends contributed to the large rise in earnings inequality in the U.S. during this period (Gottschalk & Smeeding, 1997). By examining changes in the pay of drivers and company executives both within and between trucking carriers, we have hoped to shed some light on the causes of this increase. We have examined the role of competition and that of political constraints in two competing models of executive behavior and remuneration. We have also examined the effect of union presence and various business strategy variables on the pay of executives. And, finally, we have documented changes in the relative pay of drivers and executives in these companies.

Administrative deregulation in 1979, followed by statutory changes in 1980, sharply increased the competition faced by for-hire trucking firms. The executives of for-hire trucking firms took a big hit, as did firm profits, and the earnings of other employees, in the immediate aftermath of administrative deregulation, and the impact of two macroeconomic recessions. Unlike their employees, trucking executives did not continue to lose ground as the industry restructured, and firm profits returned to previous levels. From 1985 onward they received pay increases in line with the wider boom in executive pay.

Yet deregulation does not appear to have brought these executives increased risk as the price of their increased rewards, or at any rate not risk in the form of variations in annual salary income: the responsiveness of pay to profitability and to firm size remained as it was before deregulation. This is consistent with the view that trucking, having been regulated on an industry basis in terms of entry and rates, not rate of return, would not have been politically constrained in setting executives' pay under regulation. It is contrary to the expectation that the greater competition brought by deregulation should have shifted the optimal executive contract towards higher powered incentives.

We find two further industry-specific effects. One is that executives' earnings have a small negative elasticity with respect to average length of haul under regulation, which is sharply reduced after deregulation. We interpret this change as a change, when regulatory restrictions were lifted, in the rewards to executives of firms that were aggressive at extending their geographic scope. Finally, we find that unionized firms paid their executives more by a small amount, but that breaking the union also resulted in a small but statistically significant increase in executives' earnings. This speaks to the active role of executives in bringing about the increase in earnings inequality.

The increase in executives' earnings, alongside the steady slide in drivers' earnings, raises the same disturbing questions about a secular increase in inequality in the trucking industry as it does for the economy as a whole. The likelihood of drivers recovering something of their former position seems slight in the post-regulation organization of the trucking industry.

NOTES

1. For the case of workers, see the discussion in DiNardo et al. (1996).

2. "For-hire carriage" contrasts with "private carriage." Private carriers are firms primarily in some other line of business, which haul goods which they also own. For-hire carriers haul goods that others own, for compensation, and make up what is normally called the "trucking industry." In 1982 for-hire carriers utilized 35% of the heavy freight vehicles in the total (non-governmental) U.S. fleet, and operated 54% of the miles traveled by such vehicles. They dominated longer hauls (over 200 miles), however, utilizing 69% of the heavy freight vehicles, and running 71% of the miles (Burks et al., 2004).

3. The contemporary successor to the ICC's MCFOS is collected by the Bureau of Transportation Statistics (BTS) of the U.S. Department of Transportation (USDOT).

4. The Bureau of Transportation Statistics (BTS), U.S. Department of Transportation (USDOT), current statutory recipient of the Form M reports, has been making significant efforts in recent years to improve the coverage and overall quality of the data, at the same time as it has undertaken to reduce the size of the Form, and hence the reporting burden on individual firms. As of the 1999 data year, the Motor Carrier Financial and Operating Statistics, are available on the web directly from the BTS.

5. The definition "Instruction 27" and of the variables reported in the Form M, up to 1994, is based on the Uniform System of Accounts for Motor Carriers of Property, which made up most of section "49CFR1207" of the Code of Federal Regulations, during this era.

6. The "rule of eight" had the effect of preventing contract carriers from easily filling empty backhauls by matching customers in different locations, and thus competing more effectively with common carriers (Rothenberg, 1994).

7. Thus, some of the "new" entrants at large enough scale to be in the Instruction 27 data set are actually contract carriers that acquired common carrier authority and began to compete more widely for customers.

8. The number of observations, by year, is as follows: 1977, 440; 1978, 458; 1979, 419; 1980, 386; 1981, 321; 1982, 316; 1983, 279; 1984, 273; 1985, 261; 1986, 236.

9. Appendix 2, available from the authors, provides further details on this calculation.

10. Graph available from the authors; see also (Belzer, 1994; Burks, 1999).

11. To get approximate effect sizes, we ran the within- and between regressions on standardized data. The results are reported in Table 2b. Such standardization is not a routine

procedure with these panel estimators. We standardized the data prior to the within- and between-groups transformations. The results should be treated with caution.

ACKNOWLEDGMENTS

Stephen Burks gratefully acknowledges the assistance of Tom Corsi and Ed Welkener in acquiring different parts of the data utilized. Ben Maxwell acknowledges the Undergraduate Research Opportunities Program (UROP) of the University of Minnesota for financial support. We are also indebted to Kristen Monaco, James Peoples, Bart Finzel, Pareena Lawrence, and especially to three referees, for their comments on earlier versions of the paper. Errors remain the responsibility of the authors.

REFERENCES

Akerlof, G. A., & Yellen, J. L. (1990). The fair wage-effort hypothesis and unemployment. *Quarterly Journal of Economics*, *105*, 1003–1016.

Baker, G. P., Jensen, M. C., & Murphy, K. J. (1988). Compensation and incentives: Practice vs. theory. *Journal of Finance*, *43*, 593–616.

Belzer, M. H. (1994). The motor carrier industry: Truckers and teamsters under siege. In: P. B. Voos (Ed.), *Contemporary Collective Bargaining in the Private Sector* (pp. 259–302). Madison, WI: Industrial Relations Research Association.

Burks, S. V. (1998). *Field notes on LTL firm site visits*. Amherst, MA: University of Michigan Trucking Industry Program. Unpublished.

Burks, S. V. (1999). *The origins of parallel segmented labor and product markets: A reciprocity-based agency model with an application to motor freight*. Amherst, MA: Graduate School of the University of Massachusetts, 81.

Burks, S. V., Monaco, K., & Myers-Kuykindall, J. (2004). How many trucks, how many miles: Trends in the use of heavy freight vehicles in the U.S., 1977–1997. Atlanta, GA: Trucking Industry Program, Georgia Institute of Technology, Working Paper.

Campbell, B. G. (1987). Deregulation and the motor carrier industry. *Data Resources U.S. Review*, 24–29.

CFR (1992). Code of federal regulations. 49CFR1207: 249.

Cook, J. (2003). A leader for changing times. *Logistics Management* (electronic edition, 11/01/03).

Corsi, T., & Stowers, J. R. (1991). Effects of a deregulated environment on motor carriers: A systematic multi-segment analysis. *Transportation Journal*, *30*, 4–28.

DiNardo, J., Fortin, N. M., & Lemieux, T. (1996). Labor market institutions and the distribution of wages, 1973–1992: A Semiparametric approach. *Econometrica*, *64*, 1001–1044.

Frank, R. (1985). *Choosing the right pond*. New York: Oxford University Press.

Geddes, R. R. (1997). Ownership, regulation, and managerial monitoring in the electric utility industry. *Journal of Law and Economics*, *40*, 261–288.

Glaskowski, N. A. (1990). *Effects of deregulation on motor carriers*. Westport, CT: Eno Transportation Foundation.

Gottschalk, P., & Smeeding, T. M. (1997). Cross-national comparisons of earnings and income inequality. *Journal of Economic Literature*, *35*, 633–687.

Griliches, Z., & Hausman, J. A. (1986). Errors in variables in panel data. *Journal of Econometrics*, *31*, 9318.

Guy, F. (2000). CEO pay, shareholder returns and accounting profits. *International Journal of the Economics of Business*, *7*, 263–274.

Hubbard, R. G., & Palia, D. (1995). Executive pay and performance: Evidence from the U.S. banking industry. *Journal of Financial Economics*, *39*, 105–130.

Joskow, P., Rose, N., & Shepard, A. (1993). Regulatory constraints on CEO compensation. *Brookings Papers on Economic Activity (Microeconomics)*, 1–72.

Judiciary Committee, U.S. S. (1980). Federal restraints on competition in the trucking industry: Antitrust immunity and economic regulation. Washington, DC: Judiciary Committee, U.S. Senate: 351.

Mishel, L., & Bernstein, J. (1994). *The state of working America 1994–1995*. Ithaca, NY: Cornell University Press.

Monaco, K., & Brooks, T. (2001). Deregulation and wages in trucking: A time series approach. *Research in Transportation Economics*, *6*, 55–69.

Moore, T. G. (1978). The beneficiaries of trucking regulation. *Journal of Law and Economics*, *21*, 327–343.

Moore, T. G. (1983). Rail and truck reform – The record so far. *Regulation*, 33–41.

Moore, T. G. (1986). Rail and trucking deregulation. In: *Regulatory Reform: What Actually Happened* (pp. 14–39). Boston: Little, Brown.

Perry, C. R. (1986). *Deregulation and the decline of the unionized trucking industry*. Philadelphia, PA: Industrial Research Unit, The Wharton School, University of Pennsylvania.

Pesaran, M. H., & Smith, R. (1995). Estimating long-run relationships from dynamic heterogeneous panels. *Journal of Econometrics*, *68*, 791–803.

Rose, N. (1987). Labor rent sharing and regulation: Evidence from the trucking industry. *Journal of Political Economy*, *95*, 1146–1178.

Rothenberg, L. S. (1994). *Regulation, organizations, and politics: Motor freight policy at the interstate commerce commission*. Ann Arbor, MI: University of Michigan Press.

U.S. Census Bureau (2001). *1997 Economic census, establishment and firm size statistics*. Washington, DC: U.S. Department of Commerce.

8. EARNINGS OF LOW TO MID-LEVEL MANAGERS IN THE AIRLINE, TRUCKING, AND RAILROAD INDUSTRIES

John D. Bitzan

ABSTRACT

This study examines the earnings and characteristics of low to mid-level managers in the airline, trucking, and railroad industries and changes since deregulation. Moreover, the study examines the hypotheses that managerial quality has improved and that there is a stronger pay for performance relationship as a result of deregulation.

The study finds general support for the idea that managerial quality and the returns to managerial quality increased as a result of deregulation. Furthermore, a direct estimation of managerial earnings of railroad workers provides support for a strengthening of the pay for performance relationship as a result of deregulation.

INTRODUCTION

Although regulatory reform of the transport industries occurred more than two-decades ago, the impacts of such reform on workers in these industries is still not completely understood. Several recent studies have examined the impacts of regulatory reform on the earnings of union and nonunion workers in the

Transportation Labor Issues and Regulatory Reform
Research in Transportation Economics, Volume 10, 165–189

ISSN: 0739-8859/doi:10.1016/S0739-8859(04)10008-5

transportation industries. These studies have found varying impacts from regulation, probably owing to the differences in regulation among the different industries and differences in deregulation's impacts on pricing, service, and productivity.

However, while a great number of studies have examined the impacts of deregulation on workers in these industries, most have focused on unionized and non-unionized workers in operating occupations. This study performs a preliminary examination of the impacts of deregulation on low to mid-level managers employed in the transport industries. An examination of low to mid-level managerial earnings and deregulation is especially interesting, since these managers are integral to the success of transport firms in a deregulated environment. The decisions made by purchasing agents, sales managers, office managers, and others in low to mid-level managerial positions directly influence the profitability of transport firms – particularly in the more competitive environment associated with deregulation.

Specifically, this study examines the impact of regulatory reform on mid to low-level managers in the airline, trucking, and rail industries. In addition to examining the impact of regulatory reform on the earnings of managers, this study explores the hypotheses that managerial quality has increased as a result of deregulation in these industries and that there is a closer relationship between firm performance and managerial compensation resulting from deregulation.

The next section of the paper examines the reasons why deregulation may impact managerial earnings and reviews studies that have examined the earnings changes of workers in transportation industries resulting from deregulation. This is followed by estimations of earnings level changes in the transport industries resulting from deregulation. The third section presents a discussion of the pay for performance hypothesis, along with its implications for managerial quality. This is followed by an examination of managerial quality changes since deregulation. The fifth section presents a decomposition of managerial earnings changes resulting from changes in managerial quality and in the rewards for managerial quality. Finally, a direct test for the pay for performance relationship and how it has changed as a result of deregulation is presented for the rail industry.

REVIEW OF PREVIOUS STUDIES EXAMINING DEREGULATION AND LABOR EARNINGS

Labor economists have long been interested in the impacts of regulation and market structure on the earnings levels in a given industry. Theory does not provide a unique prediction of the effects of regulation on the wages of workers. On the one hand, regulation may create economic rents for firms by restricting entry into the industry and by price setting. These economic rents provide an opportunity for increased wages, particularly when the industry is characterized by a significant union presence. Moreover, these rents may be shared with non-unionized labor, as well. On the other hand, regulation may limit the firm's ability to make productivity gains through various restrictions on pricing and service. An inability to make productivity gains will limit the growth of the marginal product of labor, and therefore limit earnings of workers. Other potential effects of regulation result from requiring regulated firms to serve markets that are not profitable. Such a requirement is likely to enhance employment, but to reduce productivity and wages.

Several studies have examined the relationship between regulation and the earnings of workers in operating occupations. These studies have found varying impacts of regulatory reform among the airline, trucking, and railroad industries. In the trucking industry, a variety of studies have found a decrease in the earnings of unionized drivers, a decline in the union non-union wage differential, and little evidence of non-union rent sharing in the regulatory period.[1] In the airline industry, studies have found small impacts on wages from deregulation, though the most recent study finds about a 10% decline in airline worker earnings as a result of deregulation.[2] Finally, in the railroad industry, studies have found varying impacts on earnings across occupations. For example Talley and Schwarz-Miller (1998) found slight declines in earnings relative to the regulated sector for engineers, while Belzer (1998) found increases in earnings relative to the regulated sector for conductors.[3]

In addition to these potential impacts of regulation on operating occupation earnings, the pay for performance hypothesis suggests a different effect of regulation on the earnings of high level managers. The pay for performance hypothesis is based on principal-agent theory. The firm's owners (the principals) cannot observe or monitor all the actions of the high level managers (the agents). Because the managers may have incentives to pursue their own interests (large staff, perks) rather than those of the owners (profits), managerial compensation is often tied to the performance of the firm. Such pay for performance schemes attempt to reduce the principal-agent problem of differing goals between firm managers and owners. However, as discussed in the following section, because the ability of high level managers to affect firm performance is limited by regulation, the pay for performance relationship may not be as strong in a regulated environment. Moreover, if managers cannot affect performance as much in a regulated environment, the need for high quality managers may not be as great in a regulated environment. Thus, according to this theory, the earnings of high level managers may be lower in a regulated environment due to a lower demand for high quality managers. In fact, a number of studies discussed later find such a result for CEOs. The likelihood of this result carrying over to low-level and mid-level managers is discussed in a subsequent section.

While there have been several studies of the effects of deregulation on the earnings of transport operators and CEOs, there has been very little study of the earnings of low to mid-level managers. As part of a broader study of airline earnings and deregulation, Card (1998) finds that the earnings premiums of airline managers relative to managers in other industries declined by about 10% between 1979 and 1989. Using 1973 through 1991 Current Population Survey data, Belzer (1998) finds that railroad managers experience wage declines after deregulation, but that they experience wage increases relative to managers in other industries.

DEREGULATION AND EARNINGS OF LOW TO MID-LEVEL MANAGERS

This study uses March Current Population Survey (CPS) data from 1968 through 1998 to assess the impact of deregulation on the earnings of airline, trucking, and railroad workers in managerial occupations. Because of the limited number of female managers in these industries in the pre-deregulation period, only male manager earnings are considered in this study. The March CPS provides data on the previous year's annual earnings and weeks worked, along with information on personal characteristics of workers. Because earnings and weeks worked data are for the previous year, the data used are really 1967 through 1997 earnings.[4]

A preliminary examination of the impact of deregulation on low to mid-level manager earnings in the three transportation industries is provided through the estimation of a pooled regression of the log of earnings on human capital characteristics, time, deregulation, and a time-deregulation interaction variable. The initial model is specified for all three industries in equation 1. In this specification, the coefficient on time shows the pre-deregulation earnings trend, the coefficient on the deregulation dummy shows the initial impact of deregulation on earnings, and the interaction term between deregulation and time shows any change in the pre-deregulation earnings trend that may have occurred as a result of deregulation.

$$\begin{aligned}\ln \mathrm{Earn}_{it} = {} & \beta_0 + \beta_1 \mathrm{Assoc}_{it} + \beta_2 \mathrm{Coll}_{it} + \beta_3 \mathrm{Age}_{it} + \beta_4 \mathrm{Age}_{it}^2 + \beta_5 \mathrm{White}_{it} \\ & + \beta_6 \mathrm{Married}_{it} + \beta_7 \mathrm{Weeks}_{it} + \beta_8 \mathrm{Time} + \beta_9 \mathrm{Dereg} + \beta_{10} \mathrm{Dereg} \\ & \times \mathrm{Time} + \varepsilon \qquad (1)\end{aligned}$$

where:

Earn = Real Annual wage and salary income (2002 prices)

Assoc = Dummy – at least an associate's degree

Coll = Dummy – at least a college degree
White = Dummy – white
Married = Dummy – married
Weeks = weeks worked
Dereg = Dummy (Air = 1978, Motor Carrier = 1980, Rail = 1980)

Table 1 shows the estimation results for male managers in all three industries. As the table shows, there does not appear to be a significant earnings impact

Table 1. Estimates of the Impacts of Deregulation on the Natural Log of Earnings for Workers in Managerial Occupations.[a]

Independent Variable	Airlines	Trucking	Railroads
Intercept	6.8496*	7.1760*	7.2472*
	(0.3903)	(0.3086)	(0.3766)
Dummy – Associate	−0.0089	0.0830**	0.1020*
	(0.0471)	(0.0375)	(0.0345)
Dummy – College	0.1598*	0.1277*	0.1994*
	(0.0438)	(0.0400)	(0.0404)
Age	0.0872*	0.0582*	0.0562*
	(0.0125)	(0.0087)	(0.0105)
Age^2	−0.0009*	−0.0006*	−0.0005*
	(0.0001)	(0.0001)	(0.0001)
Dummy – White	0.1602*	0.1633	0.2329**
	(0.0608)	(0.1102)	(0.0936)
Dummy – Married	0.0220	0.1638*	0.1012**
	(0.0501)	(0.0483)	(0.0448)
Weeks worked	0.0319*	0.0349*	0.0323*
	(0.0055)	(0.0044)	(0.0056)
Time	0.0100	0.0017	0.0092**
	(0.0093)	(0.0056)	(0.0046)
Dummy – Deregulation	0.0115	−0.0646	0.1183
	(0.1010)	(0.1035)	(0.1035)
Time × Dereg	0.0057	0.0015	−0.0090
	(0.0103)	(0.0074)	(0.0069)
N	490	1023	610
Adj. R^2	0.2318	0.1724	0.2357
F	15.76	22.29	19.78
DW	1.82	1.98	2.08

Note: Standard errors in parentheses.
[a] The deregulation years used for the airline, trucking, and railroad industries are those starting in 1978, 1980, and 1980 for the three industries, respectively.
* Significant at the 1% level.
** Significant at the 5% level.

from deregulation in any of the three industries. Managerial earnings in the airline industry show increases over time with a one shot increase from deregulation and then a reduced earnings trend after deregulation. In the trucking industry, a one time decrease in managerial earnings occurs with deregulation, but an increasing trend occurs thereafter. Finally, in the railroad industry there is a one time increase in earnings from deregulation, but a decreased earnings trend after deregulation. However, none of these trends are significant.

While Table 1 shows no apparent impact on the earnings of low to mid-level managers as a result of deregulation, a full assessment should consider the impacts of deregulation on managerial earnings in these industries relative to those in unregulated industries. Yearly earnings equations were estimated with a sample of managers from each of the above industries plus managers in manufacturing.[5] Earnings premiums were obtained by estimating a model including the same human capital and personal characteristics as in the above specification and dummy variables for the airline, trucking, and railroad industries. The results showed no consistent earnings premium in any of the three industries, nor any major change in earnings premiums.[6]

Although there does not appear to be a significant change in the level of earnings realized by low to mid-level managers resulting from deregulation, the relationship between firm performance and low to mid-level managerial compensation may have been altered by deregulation. The following sections examine the pay for performance hypothesis and the potential impacts of regulation on pay for performance of managers in transportation industries.

PAY FOR PERFORMANCE OF MID-LEVEL MANAGERS AND THE EFFECTS OF DEREGULATION

Why should the sensitivity of managers' compensation to firm performance be affected by regulation? Regulation implies an increase in the number of restrictions placed on the firm, potentially including restrictions on pricing, on which customers are served, and on the firm's ability to stop serving a particular segment of customers. Along with this increase in the number of restrictions, comes a decreased ability of managers to influence the firm's performance. If the manager has a limited role in the overall success of the firm, it is difficult to reward the manager based on firm performance.

A number of studies have examined the relationship between executive compensation and firm performance, and most have found evidence consistent with the hypothesis that the sensitivity of managerial compensation to firm performance diminishes with regulation. Some of these studies are discussed briefly here.

Carroll and Ciscel (1982) find significantly lower base salaries for executives in utilities and transportation than for those in unregulated industries. They argue that this lower base pay reflected more risk averse CEOs finding regulated industries and less incentive by regulated sectors to seek innovative managers. However, one surprising result of their study was a finding that transportation executives receive more rewards for cost efficiency than unregulated firms, while utility executives are punished for cost efficiency. Carroll and Ciscel explain these results based on differences in the nature of regulation among transportation and utilities – transportation firms had a price floor meaning more rewards for cost savings, while utility firms faced cost plus pricing.

Joskow, Rose and Shepard (1993) find that CEOs of regulated firms earned much less than CEOs of unregulated firms. They explain this finding with an alternative explanation for the relationship between regulation and managerial compensation – political constraints. The authors argue that regulators, under political pressure, may act to limit the compensation of executives due to a belief by the general public that such executives are often overcompensated. Interestingly, Joskow, Rose, and Shepard also find that executive compensation in regulated firms is less sensitive to stockholder earnings than that in unregulated firms.

Like the previous studies, Palia (2000) also finds a smaller compensation package for executives in regulated industries vs. those in unregulated manufacturing. In comparing the pay for performance sensitivity of regulated utilities with unregulated manufacturing firms, the author also finds a much stronger pay for performance relationship among the unregulated firms. The author explains this relationship based on a combination of lower corporate returns to ability among regulated firms and the political constraints hypothesized by Joskow et al.

While several studies have examined the relationship between executive compensation and firm-performance, and most have found support for such a relationship, there have not been any studies that have examined this relationship for low to mid-level managers. Purchasing agents, sales managers, office managers, and others in low to mid-level managerial positions certainly have an important impact on the costs and revenues realized by the firm. However, the pay for performance relationship for such workers does not necessarily mirror that of the chief executive. On the one hand, mid-level managers' contributions to the firm's overall success may be less visible than that of high-level executives. This may suggest a limited role of pay for performance among low to mid-level managers. However, on the other hand, to the extent the performance of the firm depends on the performance of the low to mid-level managers, and to the extent that firm performance determines the compensation level of the chief executive, the CEO has some incentive to make sure that low to mid-level managers are rewarded for performance.

One difficulty in examining the pay for performance hypothesis among low to mid-level managers, and how it has changed as a result of deregulation, is that there is a lack of firm-level data. That is, an ideal way to examine pay for performance is to match compensation and individual characteristics of workers with firm level data on performance. For CEOs, these types of data are readily available through executive compensation surveys published in popular business magazines. However, low to mid-level managerial earnings and individual characteristics are not available on a firm-level basis.

Because of this difficulty, it is useful to consider other implications of the pay for performance hypothesis and regulation. Jensen and Murphy (1990) and Palia (2000) show how the pay for performance hypothesis has implications for the quality of managers hired in an industry. In essence, managers with high ability, move into industries where performance is rewarded heavily. Because regulation limits the ability of managers to influence firm performance, managers in regulated industries are less likely to be held accountable for poor performance and less likely to be rewarded for exemplary performance. On the supply side, this suggests that managers that are more risk averse or who have lower ability are more likely to select into positions in regulated industries. On the demand side, this suggests that regulated industries have less incentive to seek high ability managers. This suggests an alternative test of the pay for performance/regulation hypothesis. That is, the quality of managers in regulated industries is likely to be lower than that in unregulated industries.

Palia (2000) examines CEO quality in unregulated and regulated industries to test the hypothesis that unregulated industries selected higher quality managers. The author finds that a sample of regulated utility executives had statistically significantly lower quality of education than a similar sample of unregulated manufacturing executives during the 1988 through 1993 time period. Similarly, the author finds a statistically significant increase in educational quality among airline executives as a result of deregulation. The following paragraphs provide a brief discussion of the transportation industries prior to deregulation, explaining why such a managerial quality-regulation relationship may exist.

In the case of airlines, the Civil Aeronautics Board (CAB) set prices and awarded routes to carriers in an attempt to limit competition. Prices were set based on industry average costs in a way that protected the least efficient carriers. Once the inability to compete in price led to capacity competition, some major carriers petitioned the CAB to restrict such competition. Thus, the only type of competition that existed was service competition – e.g. more comfortable seats, better entertainment, and better meals. In such an environment, it is apparent that the rewards to managerial ability would be limited. Outside of developing creative service promotions to attract new passengers, managers had very little discretion to influence the firm's revenues, costs, or long-term viability.

The trucking industry was also heavily restricted by regulation. Entry into the common carrier segment of the trucking entry was restricted by the Interstate Commerce Commission (ICC). Moreover, common carriers in the industry were restricted in the geographic regions they could serve, the exact routes they could serve (in some cases), and the commodities they could carry. Further, rates were set jointly by rate bureaus comprised of groups of trucking firms. Although the restrictions were not quite as heavy for contract carriers, they still had to obtain operating authority from the ICC, were not allowed to participate in common carriage, and could not serve more than 8 customers. Private carriers were not regulated, but such carriers' primary business was not motor carriage and they could only haul freight for their own firm (e.g. Walmart). As in the airline industry, the ability of managers to influence profits was likely reduced by such an environment.

Finally, the railroad industry was also heavily restricted by regulation. Regulation by the ICC limited the ability of railroads to change rates, to abandon unprofitable lines, to merge with other railroads, and to introduce new services. One spectacular example of regulation limiting innovation was highlighted by MacAvoy and Sloss (1967), who point out that hauling a single commodity in trainloads was shown to result in large cost savings in the 1920s, yet trainload service for coal was not introduced to the eastern seaboard until 1963. The inability of managers to influence profits was perhaps most apparent in the railroad industry. In fact, in highlighting railroad industry problems with regulatory underpinnings, the U.S. Department of Transportation cited inflexible management, outdated operating procedures, and a lack of intermodalism and innovation in the industry (MacAvoy & Snow, 1977).

Grimm, Kling and Smith (1987) examine top management characteristics in the railroad industry before and after deregulation. They hypothesize several changes in railroad management that are consistent with the pay for performance – regulation hypothesis. These include shifts toward younger managers willing to take more risks, managers that have experience in unregulated environments, more female managers, more educated workers, more managers with business backgrounds, a management structure more focused on marketing and less on operations, and more decision-making shifted to lower level managers. In testing for differences in the characteristics of top managers before and after deregulation, they find general support for most of these hypotheses. The following section of the paper examines the hypothesis that low to mid-level managerial quality has increased since deregulation in airlines, trucking firms, and railroad firms.

CHANGES IN MANAGERIAL QUALITY SINCE DEREGULATION

As highlighted in the previous section, there is reason to believe that managerial quality may have improved in the transportation industries as a result of deregulation. Table 2 provides a comparison of average characteristics of male workers in low to mid-level managerial occupations in airlines, trucking, and railroads before and after deregulation from the 1968 through 1998 March Current Population Surveys. The table also shows *t*-values obtained from a *t*-test of equal means between pre-deregulation characteristics and post-deregulation characteristics. The March Current Population Surveys provide information on individual worker characteristics, as well as information on earnings and weeks worked in the previous year. Thus, the earnings data reflect the years 1967 through 1997. As the table shows, there have been large and statistically significant increases in the proportion of low to mid-level managers having at least an associate's degree and at least a college degree in all three industries. Particularly striking is the change in the proportion of low to mid-level managers with college degrees since deregulation. These proportions increased by 60, 58, and 56% in the airline, trucking, and railroad industries, respectively.

Other characteristics shown in Table 2 are an increase in average age of managers in the airline industry and decreases in the trucking and railroad industries (although differences in age are not statistically significant), decreases in the proportion of workers who are white, decreases in the proportion of workers who are married, and increases in the number of weeks worked per year (not statistically significant). There are two ways to look at the change in age. On the one hand, a decrease may represent reduced human capital accumulation through reductions in on the job training. On the other hand, as suggested by Grimm et al., a decrease in age may represent a switch to managers more open to change and innovation. The statistically significant decrease of the proportion of workers who are white may suggest a reduction in racial discrimination after deregulation – a result that has been found in many other studies. It is unclear what the significant reduction in the proportion of workers who are married represents, though it may at least partially reflect a slightly younger group of workers.[7]

While many of these changes are statistically significant, one might also expect similar changes in managerial characteristics in non-regulated industries – i.e. the change in characteristics may not be the result of deregulation. In fact, *t*-tests of mean comparisons also show significant increases in the proportion of workers with associate's degrees or more and college degrees or more for manufacturing managers. *t*-Tests of managerial characteristics in manufacturing show statistically significantly lower ages, lower proportion of workers who are

Table 2. Mean Characteristics of Male Workers in Managerial Occupations Before and After Deregulation.[a]

	Airlines		Trucking		Railroads	
	Pre-Dereg	Post-Dereg	Pre-Dereg	Post-Dereg	Pre-Dereg	Post-Dereg
Proportion with associates degree or higher	0.649	0.726 (1.73)***	0.484	0.606 (3.94)*	0.393	0.516 (3.02)*
Proportion with a college degree or higher	0.318	0.509 (4.00)*	0.250	0.396 (5.07)*	0.194	0.303 (3.06)*
Age	41.51	42.01 (0.50)	42.36	41.33 (1.55)	46.37	45.19 (1.4)
Age^2	1822.36	1873.32 (0.58)	1894.84	1828.34 (1.13)	2251.85	2149.44 (1.35)
Proportion that are white	0.948	0.890 (2.35)**	0.996	0.972 (3.13)*	0.994	0.957* (2.81)
Proportion that are married	0.909	0.801 (3.40)*	0.952	0.841 (6.04)*	0.949	0.803* (5.31)
Weeks worked	51.01	51.26 (0.95)	51.13	51.20 (0.36)	51.24	51.48 (1.13)
N	154	336	457	560	356	234
ln earnings	10.781	10.847 (1.70)***	10.789	10.760 (0.95)	10.784	10.854 (2.30)**

Note: t-ratios for significant difference of means in parentheses.

[a] The deregulation years used for the airline, trucking, and railroad industries are those starting in 1978, 1980, and 1980 for the three industries, respectively.

* Significant at the 1% level.

** Significant at the 5% level.

*** Significant at the 10% level.

white, lower proportion of workers who are married, and higher number of weeks worked during the period coinciding with transportation deregulation.

Although the same types of changes in managerial characteristics occurred in unregulated manufacturing as in the regulated transportation industries, the magnitude of change was not necessarily the same. Table 3 provides a simple comparison of percentage changes in managerial characteristics in the airline, trucking, and railroad industries coinciding with deregulation, along with changes in the characteristics of manufacturing managers over the same time periods. As the table shows, the percentage increase in the proportion of managers with at least a college degree was more than 56% in each of the three transportation industries in a period coinciding with deregulation, while it was only 30% in manufacturing over the same time period. Moreover, the percentage increases in the proportion of managers with at least an associate's degree was over 25% in the trucking and railroad industries, while it was only 16% in manufacturing. In terms of other characteristics, the table shows that the percentage changes in other managerial characteristics were similar between the unregulated manufacturing industry and the previously regulated transportation industries. These numbers provide some support for the idea that at least part of the increase in education levels among managers in the transportation industries was a result of deregulation.

As a further test of the hypothesis that part of the increases in quality measures may have occurred from deregulation, I estimate a model of the log-odds of a worker having at least a college education for managerial workers in the manufacturing, air, trucking, and rail industries. The model includes time as an independent variable to account for the fact that the likelihood of managers having a college education or more is likely to grow over time. It also includes dummy variables for managers in the airline, trucking, and railroad industries. These will account for differences in the likelihood of managers having at least a college education in these industries before deregulation. The interaction terms between the deregulation period (1978 and later) and the manufacturing, airline, trucking, and railroad industries will measure whether a change in the likelihood of managers having at least a college education occurred in each of these industries following deregulation. The logit model is specified as:

$$\ln\left(\frac{P_c}{1-P_c}\right) = \beta_0 + \beta_1\text{Time} + \beta_2\text{Air} + \beta_3\text{Truck} + \beta_4\text{Rail} + \beta_5\text{MFGDEREG} + \beta_6\text{AIRDEREG} + \beta_7\text{TRUCKDEREG} + \beta_8\text{RAILDEREG} + \varepsilon \qquad (2)$$

Table 3. Comparison of Percentage Changes in Manager Worker Characteristics Between Manufacturing, Air, Trucking, and Railroads.

Characteristic	Percentage Change				
	MFG Post-1978 vs. Pre-1978	Air Post-1978 vs. Pre-1978	MFG Post-1980 vs. Pre-1980	Trucking Post-1980 vs. Pre-1980	Rail Post-1980 vs. Pre-1980
Proportion with an Associate's Degree	16.3	11.9	15.6	25.2	31.3
Proportion with a College Degree	30.2	60.1	30.0	58.4	56.2
Age	−2.2	1.2	−2.6	−2.4	−2.5
Proportion that are White	−3.0	−6.1	−3.0	−2.4	−3.7
Proportion that are Married	−11.2	−11.9	−10.7	−11.7	−15.4
Weeks worked	0.5	0.5	0.4	0.1	0.5

where:

Air, Truck, Rail are dummy variables for those industries.
MFGDEREG, AIRDEREG, TRUCKDEREG, and RAILDEREG are industry specific dummy variables coinciding with 1978.

Table 4 shows the estimation results from this model. As the table shows, the probability of managerial workers having at least a college education is much lower in the transportation industries than in manufacturing, especially before deregulation. Moreover, the probability of managerial workers having at least a college education increases over time, as one would expect. Finally, although only statistically significant for trucking, the model shows while the probability of having a college education increases in 1978 for every industry, the magnitude of the increase is much larger in the transportation industries than in manufacturing. In fact, at the mean value of the proportion of managers having at least a college education, deregulation increases the probability of having at least a college education for manufacturing managers by 1.4 percentage points, while it increases the probability of having at least a college education for airline, trucking, and rail managers by 7.9, 7.1, and 6.3 percentage points, respectively.[8] Thus, while not all of the increases in quality are the result of deregulation, it appears likely that some portion of the increases may be attributable to deregulation.

Table 4. Estimate of the Log-Odds of Having At Least a College Education (Managerial Occupations 1968–1998).[a]

Variable	Parameter Estimate	Probability Change
Intercept	−0.3754* (0.0277)	
Time	0.0379* (0.0032)	0.0095
Dummy – Air	−0.5773* (0.1748)	−0.14
Dummy – Truck	−1.038* (0.1257)	−0.26
Dummy – Rail	−1.3698* (0.1532)	−0.34
Mfg × Dereg	0.0550 (0.0501)	0.014
Air × Dereg	0.3160 (0.2096)	0.079
Truck × Dereg	0.2842** (0.1533)	0.071
Rail × Dereg	0.2538 (0.2022)	0.063
Likelihood ratio = 974.45		
$N = 23{,}600$		

Note: Standard errors in parentheses.
[a] 1978 is used as the start of deregulation.
*Significant at the 1% level.
**Significant at the 10% level.

DECOMPOSITION OF MANAGERIAL EARNINGS CHANGES

If the hypothesis that managerial quality has increased in the transportation industries as a result of deregulation is correct, we would also expect to see changes in the returns to managerial characteristics that are proxies for quality. That is, managerial hiring practices in the transportation industries should change by increasing the reward to personal characteristics that are associated with high ability.

Table 5 shows estimated regressions of managerial earnings on human capital characteristics and other control variables for male managers before and after deregulation in each of the three transportation industries. As the table shows, while the returns to having at least an associate's degree do not change in the expected direction for two of the three industries, the returns to having at least a college education increase in all three. This is an important finding, since the percentage increase in characteristics serving as a proxy for managerial quality was largest for the proportion of workers having at least a college degree (see Table 3). Moreover, the returns to age (a proxy for experience) increase in two of the three industries after deregulation. While one view suggests that deregulation should result in a decrease in the returns to age due to the need for more innovative managers, an alternative view is that the industry-specific human capital acquired by managers that are in the transportation industries for long periods of time may become more valuable in a competitive environment. This alternative view may be particularly true among low to mid-level managers – a group that is likely to need a better understanding of the operational details of the firm than higher-level managers. Finally, the table shows that for two out of the three industries, there is an increase in the returns to weeks worked. An increase in returns to weeks worked is also consistent with the pay for performance – regulation hypothesis.

Additional insight into changes in managerial characteristics and compensation since deregulation might be obtained by examining earnings changes since deregulation and decomposing those changes into those attributable to changes in worker characteristics and those attributable to changes in the ways such characteristics are rewarded. The Oaxaca decomposition is a method for separating the total earnings gap between two groups into two portions; one portion is explained by differences in personal characteristics, and the other is due to differences in estimated coefficients between the two groups. Generally, the Oaxaca decomposition is applied to different racial groups or different sexes to measure such wage differences. However, it is equally applicable to changes in low to mid-level managerial earnings between the regulatory period and the deregulation period. Oaxaca (1973) showed that the log wage differential between

Table 5. Estimates of the Natural Log of Earnings for Workers in Managerial Occupations Before and After Deregulation.[a]

Independent Variable	Airlines		Trucking		Railroads	
	Pre-Dereg	Post-Dereg	Pre-Dereg	Post-Dereg	Pre-Dereg	Post-Dereg
Intercept	7.5978* (0.7359)	6.8230* (0.4610)	7.8622* (0.6698)	6.9772* (0.3578)	6.0047* (0.6103)	7.5979* (0.5119)
Dummy – Associate	0.0337 (0.0676)	–0.0451 (0.0637)	0.0739 (0.0520)	0.1011*** (0.0536)	0.1137* (0.0428)	0.0979*** (0.0555)
Dummy – College	0.1235*** (0.0689)	0.1840* (0.0566)	0.1035*** (0.0602)	0.1481* (0.0534)	0.1707* (0.0534)	0.2419* (0.0594)
Age	0.0751* (0.0211)	0.0886* (0.0155)	0.0701* (0.0146)	0.0551* (0.0109)	0.0331** (0.0133)	0.0822* (0.0163)
Age^2	–0.0007* (0.0002)	–0.0009* (0.0002)	–0.0007* (0.0002)	–0.0005* (0.0001)	–0.0003** (0.0002)	–0.0008* (0.0002)
Dummy – White	0.1535 (0.1299)	0.1598** (0.0703)	0.3005 (0.3189)	0.1556 (0.1185)	0.2159 (0.2215)	0.2567** (0.1043)
Dummy – Married	–0.0603 (0.0979)	0.0341 (0.0599)	0.1330 (0.0986)	0.1461* (0.0565)	0.0896 (0.0767)	0.1022*** (0.0556)
Weeks worked	0.0247*** (0.0132)	0.0335* (0.0063)	0.0169*** (0.0099)	0.0387* (0.0051)	0.0696* (0.0092)	0.0149** (0.0070)
N	154	336	457	566	356	254
Adj. R^2	0.1563	0.2434	0.0774	0.2413	0.2252	0.3016
F	5.05	16.40	6.47	26.67	15.74	16.61
DW	1.66	1.85	2.00	1.96	2.03	2.17

Note: Standard errors in parentheses.

[a] The deregulation years used for the airline, trucking, and railroad industries are those starting in 1978, 1980, and 1980 for the three industries, respectively.

* Significant at the 1% level.

** Significant at the 5% level.

*** Significant at the 10% level.

two groups can be separated into an explained portion and an unexplained portion as follows:

$$\ln \bar{W}_D - \ln \bar{W}_R = (\bar{X}_D - \bar{X}_R)\hat{\beta}_R + \bar{X}_D(\hat{\beta}_D - \hat{\beta}_R) \quad (3)$$

where:

$\bar{W}_D$ = mean deregulation wage
$\bar{W}_R$ = mean regulation wage
$\bar{X}_D$ = vector of mean post – deregulation characteristics
$\bar{X}_R$ = vector of mean pre-deregulation characteristics
$\hat{\beta}_D$ = vector of estimated post-deregulation coefficients
$\hat{\beta}_R$ = vector of estimated pre-deregulation coefficients

In the above expression, the first term is the portion of the differential explained by differences in characteristics between pre-deregulation and post-deregulation managers, while the second portion is the portion explained by differences in the rewards to personal characteristics between the regulatory and deregulatory environments. The above estimate of differences in characteristics uses regulation weights. A similar expression can be formulated using deregulation weights:

$$\ln \bar{W}_D - \ln \bar{W}_R = (\bar{X}_D - \bar{X}_R)\hat{\beta}_D + \bar{X}_R(\hat{\beta}_D - \hat{\beta}_R) \quad (4)$$

In this study, both weights are presented.

Table 6 presents the Oaxaca decomposition of earnings differences between the pre-deregulation and post-deregulation environments for airline, trucking, and railroad managers. For each industry, the first two columns of the table show the percentage of the earnings gap explained by changes in managerial characteristics, while the last two columns show the percentage of the earnings gap explained by changes in the rewards to such characteristics. In discussing this table, it will be useful to discuss each of the three transportation industries separately.

As the table shows, airline managers received real annual earnings that were about 6.9% higher after deregulation in comparison to before deregulation. In examining the percentages of this change resulting from changes in worker characteristics, between 39 and 48% of the gap can be explained by an increase in education levels among airline workers over this period. Changes in age had very little effect on earnings, while an increase in the number of weeks worked for the year accounted for approximately 9–13% of the differential. Examining the percentages resulting from changes in the rewards to personal characteristics shows a reduction in earnings resulting from decreased returns to at least an associate's degree and increases due to increased returns to at least a college degree. In total, though, the change in returns to education explains

Table 6. Managerial Earnings Changes Resulting from Changes in Worker Characteristics and in the Rewards for Various Characteristics (Pre-Deregulation to Post-Deregulation).

	ln Airline Earnings Change = 0.0664				ln Motor Carr. Earnings Change = −0.0296				ln Railroad Earnings Change = 0.0709			
	Worker Chars.		Reward for Chars.		Worker Chars.		Reward for Chars.		Worker Chars.		Reward for Chars.	
	Pre-Dereg. Coeff. (%)	Post-Dereg. Coeff. (%)	Pre-Dereg. Chars. (%)	Post-Dereg. Chars. (%)	Pre-Dereg. Coeff. (%)	Post-Dereg. Coeff. (%)	Pre-Dereg. Chars. (%)	Post-Dereg. Chars. (%)	Pre-Dereg. Coeff. (%)	Post-Dereg. Coeff. (%)	Pre-Dereg. Chars. (%)	Post-Dereg. Chars. (%)
Proportion with Assoc.	3.9	−5.2	−77.0	−86.1	−30.5	−41.8	−44.4	−55.6	19.6	16.9	−8.7	−11.4
Proportion with College	35.5	52.8	29.0	46.3	−51.1	−73.2	−37.6	−59.7	26.3	37.3	19.4	30.4
Education total	39.4	47.6	−48.0	−39.8	−81.6	−114.9	−82.0	−115.3	45.9	54.2	10.7	19.0
Age	56.5	66.6	842.1	852.3	241.9	190.1	2147.7	2095.8	−55.0	−136.8	3213.5	3131.7
Age^2	−56.8	−67.4	−378.1	−388.7	−164.7	−106.8	−1650.3	−1592.4	44.7	112.8	−1497.7	−1429.6
Age total	−0.3	−0.7	464.1	463.6	77.2	83.3	497.3	503.4	−10.3	−24.0	1715.8	1702.1
Education and Exper. Total	39.1	46.9	416.0	423.9	−4.4	−31.7	415.3	388.1	35.6	30.2	1726.5	1721.1
Proportion that are White	−13.4	−14.0	8.9	8.4	24.2	12.6	486.8	475.1	−11.5	−13.6	57.1	55.0
Proportion that are Married	9.8	−5.6	129.1	113.7	49.8	54.7	−42.2	−37.2	−18.5	−21.1	16.9	14.3
Weeks worked	9.3	12.6	671.8	675.0	−3.9	−9.0	−3774.8	−3780.0	23.4	5.0	−3946.6	−3964.9
Intercept			−1166.2	−1166.2			2987.6	2987.6			2245.7	2245.7
Total	44.7	39.9	59.7	54.8	65.6	26.5	72.7	33.6	29.1	0.5	99.7	71.1

a negative portion of the gap (i.e. earnings went down as a result of changes in the return to education). However, increases in the returns to experience (age) accounted for a huge portion of the gap (in excess of 400%). This may provide support for the idea that human capital resulting from industry-specific training increased in importance for airlines following deregulation.[9] Finally, there is also a large portion of the gap (670+%) explained by increased returns to the number of weeks worked during the year. This supports the hypothesis of an increasing pay for performance relationship following deregulation. In summary, the decomposition of airline manager earnings provides some support for an increase in managerial quality and an increase in the rewards for quality following deregulation.

For trucking managers, there was a decrease in real annual earnings between the regulatory period and deregulation of about 2.9%. The first two columns of the trucking portion of Table 6 show that between −82 and −115% of this drop was explained by an increase in the education level of managers in trucking. That is, earnings dropped despite large gains in education that would suggest increased earnings. The first two columns of the trucking portion of the table also show that between 77 and 83% of the drop in earnings is explained by a drop in the age of managers in the industry. Finally, these columns show a small negative portion of the gap explained by increased weeks worked. Again, this suggests a drop in pay despite a suggested increase resulting from increased weeks of work for the year. The last two columns of the trucking portion of Table 6 show the percentages of the earnings gap resulting from changes in the rewards for personal characteristics. As the table shows, large negative percentages of the gap are explained by an increase in returns to associate's degrees and college degrees – the drop in earnings occurred despite these increased returns. In excess of 400% of the drop in earnings was the result of decreased returns to age in the trucking industry. Finally, large negative portions of the gap are explained by an increase in the returns to weeks worked. In summary, the motor carrier decomposition supports the idea that there were increases in education and the returns to education, but decreases in age and in the returns to age after deregulation.

As shown in Table 6, railroad industry managers experienced a 7.4% increase in earnings after deregulation. The first two columns of the Oaxaca decomposition for railroads show that 46–54% of this gap is explained by increases in education levels of railroad workers after deregulation, that −10 to −24% of this increase is explained by reductions in the age of railroad managers (earnings increased despite the reduction), and that an increase in weeks worked explains 5–24% of the increase. The last two columns of the table show that 10–19% of the increase is explained by increased returns to education, large amounts of the increase are explained by increased returns to experience, and large negative amounts of the increase are explained by a decrease in returns to the number of weeks worked (the increase in earnings occurred in spite of the decrease in returns to weeks worked). In summary, the railroad decomposition supports the idea that earnings of railroad managers increased after deregulation because of greater levels of education and returns to education, and greater returns to experience, although they increased in spite of a decrease in the level of experience.

For the most part, these decompositions support the idea that managerial quality improved after deregulation and the rewards for managerial quality increased as well. However, it should be kept in mind that these changes in managerial quality and the returns to managerial quality were not solely the result of deregulation. A general increase in human capital characteristics appears to have occurred in other industries, as well.

DIRECT MEASUREMENT OF PAY FOR PERFORMANCE AND DEREGULATION

One final test of the pay for performance hypothesis and the impact of regulation is to relate managerial pay to firm performance before and after deregulation. Ideally, the pay for performance hypothesis could be tested by estimating an earnings equation that accounts for human capital characteristics and some measure of the firm's performance in the previous year. The change in the relationship between firm performance and managerial pay could be tested through an interaction term between the deregulation period and the firm's performance in the previous year.

Unfortunately, the Current Population Survey does not identify the firm in which the manager is employed. Moreover, because transportation firms have large networks, with managers in different parts of the country, it is not possible to identify the firm based on the state where the worker is located.

However, a proxy for firm performance is available for the railroad industry. Railroad return on investment (ROI) is available regionally from the 1920s until today (Railroad Facts, various years). Prior to 1986, ROI is available for three regions – the west, which is roughly everything west of the Mississippi River, the east, which is the east north of Kentucky and Virginia, and the south. Starting in 1986, the east and south regions were combined. While these regions are large, they coincide with the operational areas of several railroads over this period. Based on the state of residence of managers from the March Current Population Survey files, managers are matched to these regions.

The following model is used for the direct test of the pay for performance-regulation hypothesis in the railroad industry:

$$\begin{aligned}\text{lnEarn}_{it} = {} & \beta_0 + \beta_1\text{Assoc}_{it} + \beta_2\text{Coll}_{it} + \beta_3\text{Age}_{it} + \beta_4\text{Age}_{it}^2 + \beta_5\text{White}_{it} \\ & + \beta_6\text{Married}_{it} + \beta_7\text{Weeks}_{it} + \beta_8\text{ROI}_{i(t-1)} + \beta_9\text{Dereg} \\ & \times \text{ROI}_{i(t-1)} + \varepsilon \end{aligned} \tag{5}$$

where:

Earn = Annual wage and salary income
Assoc = Dummy – at least an associate's degree
Coll = Dummy – at least a college degree
White = Dummy – white
Married = Dummy – married
Weeks = weeks worked
ROI = regional ROI coinciding with the worker's state of residence

Table 7. Estimation of Pay for Performance of Railroad Managers (Dep. Var. = Natural Log of Earnings).[a]

Variable	Parameter Estimate
Intercept	7.2919* (0.3766)
Dummy – Associate	0.1057* (0.0345)
Dummy – College	0.2049* (0.0405)
Age	0.0565* (0.0105)
Age^2	−0.0005* (0.0001)
Dummy – White	0.2193** (0.0938)
Dummy – Married	0.0893** (0.0446)
Weeks worked	0.0338* (0.0056)
ROI	−1.2831 (0.9283)
Dereg × ROI	1.5287*** (0.8242)
N	610
Adj R^2	0.2296
F	21.17
DW	2.06

Note: Standard errors in parentheses.
[a] The deregulation years used are 1980 and later.
* Significant at the 1% level.
** Significant at the 5% level.
*** Significant at the 10% level.

In this model, the coefficient on ROI will measure the relationship between return on investment and managerial earnings, while the coefficient on the deregulation-ROI interaction term will measure whether this relationship has changed as a result of deregulation. Table 7 shows the estimated model. As the table shows, all human capital variables have their expected signs and all are significant at conventional levels. The variables of interest ROI and Dereg × ROI show a very interesting result. Prior to deregulation there is no statistically significant relationship between return on investment and earnings, while after deregulation there is a positive and statistically significant relationship. Moreover, the parameter estimate on the deregulation-ROI interaction term suggests a 361% increase in the association between managerial earnings and return on investment since deregulation.[10] This provides support for the hypothesis that pay for performance of low to mid-level managers increased in the rail industry as a result of deregulation.

SUMMARY AND CONCLUSIONS

This study examines the earnings of low to mid-level managers in the airline, trucking, and railroad industries and how they have changed as a result of deregulation. Moreover, the study examines the hypotheses that managerial quality has improved in these industries and that there is a stronger pay for performance relationship of managers in these industries as a result of deregulation.

In estimating pooled earnings equations accounting for human capital and other personal characteristics, the study finds no significant change in the earnings of low to mid-level managers resulting from deregulation. Further, yearly earnings equations show no significant changes in earnings premiums in comparison to manufacturing for managers in the transport industries following deregulation.

In examining managerial quality and changes from deregulation, the study finds significant increases in education levels among managers in the airline, trucking, and railroad industries following deregulation. While significant increases in education levels also occurred in unregulated manufacturing during this same period, percentage increases in education levels were much higher in the transport industries. Moreover, a log-odds model shows that the probability of managers having at least a college education increases much more rapidly in the transportation industries following deregulation than in unregulated manufacturing.

An Oaxaca decomposition of earnings changes in the three transportation industries from pre to post-deregulation environments provides general support for the idea that managerial quality and the returns to managerial quality increased as a result of deregulation.

Finally, a direct estimation of managerial earnings of railroad workers as a function of personal characteristics and regional return on investment provides support for the hypothesis that the pay for performance relationship has strengthened as a result of deregulation.

While the findings of this study provide support for a stronger pay for performance relationship and improvements in managerial quality following deregulation, limitations in the data used suggest that these conclusions should be considered preliminary. Data with larger sample sizes, data relating managerial characteristics and earnings to firm performance, and data with additional proxies for managerial quality (e.g. more details on degrees received) may provide additional insight into pay for performance and its relationship to regulation.

NOTES

1. See Rose (1987), Hirsch (1988), Hendricks (1994), and Hirsch and Macpherson (1998).
2. See Card (1996), Hendricks (1994), and Card (1998).
3. See Hendricks (1994), Talley and Schwarz-Miller (1998) and Belzer (1998).
4. All references to a particular year in this study refer to the year in which wages and salary were earned. Thus, deregulation for railroads (which occurred in 1980) coincides with the 1981 March CPS.
5. Managers from all durable and non-durable manufacturing industries are included in the comparison group.
6. Table A1 of the appendix presents the variance-weighted pre and post-deregulation premiums over manufacturing for the three transportation industries. None of the changes in earnings premiums following deregulation is statistically significant.
7. Table 2 shows that in the trucking industry the average age of low to mid-level managers declines from 42.4 to 41.3 years from the pre-deregulation period to the post-deregulation period, while it decreases from 46.4 to 45.2 years in the railroad industry over the same periods.
8. These are obtained by $Pc \times (1-Pc)\,\beta$. e.g. for manufacturing, $0.522 \times 0.478 \times 0.055$, for airlines, $0.522 \times 0.478 \times 0.316$, for trucking, $0.522 \times 0.478 \times 0.2842$, for railroads $0.522 \times 0.478 \times 0.2538$.
9. However, industry tenure is unmeasurable with these data.
10. This is measured as $e^{1.5287} - 1$.

ACKNOWLEDGMENTS

I am grateful to James Peoples and Wayne Talley for valuable comments and suggestions on earlier drafts of this paper.

REFERENCES

Belzer, M. (1998). Commentary on railroad deregulation and union labor earnings. In: J. Peoples (Ed.), *Regulatory Reform and Labor Markets*. Boston, MA: Kluwer.

Card, D. (1998). Deregulation and labor earnings in the airline industry. In: J. Peoples (Ed.), *Regulatory Reform and Labor Markets*. Boston, MA: Kluwer.

Carroll, T., & Ciscel, D. (1982). The effects of regulation on executive compensation. *The Review of Economics and Statistics*, *64*, 505–509.

Grimm, C., James, K., & Smith, K. (1987). The impact of U.S. rail regulatory reform on railroad management and organizational structure. *Transportation Research A*, *21A*, 87–94.

Hendricks, W. (1994). Deregulation and labor earnings. *Journal of Labor Research*, *15*, 207–234.

Hirsch, B. (1988). Trucking regulation, unionization and labor earnings, 1973–1985. *Journal of Human Resources*, *23*, 296–319.

Hirsch, B., & Macpherson, D. (1998). Earnings and employment in trucking: Deregulating a naturally competitive industry. In: J. Peoples (Ed.), *Regulatory Reform and Labor Markets*. Boston, MA: Kluwer.

Jensen, M., & Murphy, K. (1990). CEO incentives – It's not how much you pay, but how. *Journal of Applied Corporate Finance*, *3*, 36–49.

Joskow, P., Rose, N., & Shepard, A. (1993). Regulatory constraints on CEO compensation. *Brookings Papers on Economic Activity, Microeconomics*, 1–72.

MacAvoy, P., & Sloss, J. (1967). *Regulation of transport innovation*. New York, NY: Random House.

MacAvoy, P., & Snow, J. (Eds) (1977). *Railroad revitalization and regulatory reform*. Washington, DC: The American Enterprise Institute for Public Policy Research.

Oaxaca, R. (1973). Male-female wage differentials in urban labor markets. *International Economic Review*, *14*, 693–709.

Palia, D. (2000). The impact of regulation on CEO labor markets. *Rand Journal of Economics*, *31*, 165–179.

Rose, N. (1987). Labor rent-sharing and regulation: Evidence from the trucking industry. *Journal of Political Economy*, *95*, 1146–1178.

Talley, W., & Schwarz-Miller, A. (1998). Railroad deregulation and union labor earnings. In: J. Peoples (Ed.), *Regulatory Reform and Labor Markets*. Boston, MA: Kluwer.

APPENDIX

Estimated wage premiums for airline, trucking, and railroad managers over managers in manufacturing:

Period	Airline Differential	Trucking Differential	Railroad Differential
Pre-deregulation	−0.00997 (0.1142)	0.007395 (0.0732)	−0.02405 (0.0816)
Post-deregulation	−0.00035 (0.0997)	−0.04896 (0.0730)	0.019129 (0.1075)
Overall	−0.0034 (0.1043)	−0.02564 (0.0731)	−0.00627 (0.0923)

- Estimated differentials are the variance weighted average differentials estimated in yearly wage equations.
- Standard errors in parentheses.
- Yearly wage equations were estimated on a cross section of male manufacturing and transportation mid-level managers. Independent variables include dummy variables for having at least an associate's degree and for having at least a college degree, dummy variables for race and marital status, age and age squared, the number of weeks worked, and dummy variables for the airline, trucking, and railroad industries.
- Deregulation years used for airlines, trucking, and railroads were 1978, 1980, and 1980, respectively.

9. OWNER-OPERATOR TRUCK DRIVER EARNINGS AND EMPLOYMENT: PORT CITIES AND DEREGULATION

James Peoples and Wayne K. Talley

ABSTRACT

This chapter tests the hypothesis that ocean transportation deregulation presents owner-operators with greater job opportunities and the opportunity to increase earnings at port cities. The pre- and post-deregulation earnings estimates of owner-operator drivers in the fifty busiest port-cities are compared to estimates for other owner-operators. Earnings findings indicate a statistically significant increase in the relative earnings for port-city owner-operators following deregulation. Employment findings reveal that compared to the pre-deregulation period, a greater share of owner-operator drivers are employed at port cities in the shipping post-deregulation period.

1. INTRODUCTION

Ocean transportation is the primary transportation mode for world trade.[1] The ocean transportation of bulk commodities advanced during the first half of the twentieth century. For example, ships were specially designed to transport oil, coal and grain; however, general cargo continued to be handled as break-bulk

Transportation Labor Issues and Regulatory Reform
Research in Transportation Economics, Volume 10, 191–213

ISSN: 0739-8859/doi:10.1016/S0739-8859(04)10009-7

(on pallet) cargo. Pallets were moved, generally one at a time, onto a truck or rail car that carried them from the factory or warehouse to the docks. There, each pallet was unloaded and hoisted by cargo net and crane from the dock and onto the ship. Once the pallet was in the ship's hold, it had to be positioned precisely and braced, protecting it from damage during the ocean crossing. This process was then reversed at the other end of the voyage, making the ocean transportation of general cargo a slow, labor-intensive and expensive process.

In 1955 Malcom McLean realized that individual pieces of general cargo needed to be handled only twice – at their origin when stored in a standardized container box and at their destination when unloaded. He purchased a small tanker company, renamed it Sea-Land, and adapted its ships to transport truck trailers. The first voyage of a Sea-Land container ship left Newark, New Jersey for Puerto Rico on April 26, 1956. The first international voyage of a container ship (from the U.S. to Rotterdam) occurred ten years later. The containerization of world trade had begun. In the years that followed, standardized containers were constructed, generally 20 or 40 feet long without wheels, having locking mechanisms at each corner that could be secured to a truck chassis, a rail car, a crane, or to other containers inside a ship's hold or on its deck.

As opposed to the transportation of break-bulk cargo, the transportation of containerized cargo is fast, capital intensive and relatively inexpensive. While a break-bulk ship often took a week to unload and reload, a container ship might be in port for only several hours for the same amount of cargo. Unlike break-bulk ships, most container ships would become non-self-sustaining, i.e. without cargo cranes aboard. Therefore, container ships found it necessary to call at ports equipped with dockside container cranes. Break-bulk ports aspiring to become container ports had to become more capital intensive – not only investing in dockside cranes but also in other types of mobile and infrastructure capital.

Containerization also radically altered cargo handling tasks, as capital was substituted for labor. The demand for dockworkers dramatically declined, with job losses ranging from 40 to 60% in many countries (Zarocostas, 1996).[2] In the Port of New York/New Jersey, 30,000 longshoremen were employed in 1970; by 1986 this number had declined to 7,400 dockworkers (Chadwin et al., 1990).[3]

Whereas containerization reduced the demand for dockworkers, shipping deregulation led to an increase in dockworker demand. The U.S. Shipping Act of 1984, which amended the Shipping Act of 1916,[4] eased government regulation of ocean transportation.[5] The 1984 Act permitted service contracts between shippers and carriers/conferences[6] and authorized door-to-door (intermodal) rather than just port-to-port rates.[7] The real hourly and weekly wages of U.S. union dockworkers increased 14.3% and 15.3%, respectively, in the post-deregulation period (Talley, 2002). These wage increases are attributed to an increase in the bargaining power of dockworkers which, in turn, is attributed to: (1) an increase in demand for dockworkers; (2) a decrease in the likelihood that dockworker employers will chance a strike; and (3) an increase in port capital-labor ratios (Talley, 2002).

The 1984 Act enabled shipping lines to develop more cost efficient networks – cargo could now move by an intermodal (i.e. door-to-door) rate, leaving the choice of port-of-call to the shipping line. Shipping lines could also take advantage of economies of ship size and save cost by using larger containerships to call at load-center ports where containers were accumulated. The lower rates from passing cost savings onto shippers and from improvements in quality of service,[8] stimulated the growth in containerized cargo. Such industry growth also influenced the industry's labor market by increasing the demand for dockworkers.[9]

To handle the growth in container traffic, U.S. ports and shipping lines of all countries invested billions of dollars in container terminals and infrastructures and in larger and larger container ships, thereby increasing the costs from disruptions in the utilization of port infrastructures and containerships. As a consequence, dockworker employers are more reluctant to chance a strike – agreeing to settle labor contract extensions prior to contract expiration, which is much earlier than in the past. In addition, dockworker employers are more likely to agree to higher dockworker wage demands than would have occurred under more lengthy negotiations.[10] The significant increase in port capital investments also resulted in higher port capital-labor ratios, thereby reducing dockworkers' share of port costs and in turn increasing their bargaining power in negotiating higher wages.

Shipping deregulation has also led to an increase in demand for intermodal truck drivers, who move cargo to and from ports, and would therefore benefit from increased business activity at ports. The impact of shipping deregulation on driver earnings, however is unclear *a priori*. While greater demand for the services of intermodal truck drivers should lead to higher earnings for this group of workers, changing labor market conditions such as increased negotiation advantages for shipping employers and increased operating costs for these drivers suggest that shipping deregulation poses significant limitations on the ability of drivers to enhance their earnings. This paper contributes to our understanding of the impact of shipping deregulation on labor earnings by investigating the earnings of owner-operator truck drivers at port cities vs. other locations during shipping pre- and post-deregulation periods. Owner-operator employment patterns for these periods are also investigated. Owner-operator truck drivers (also referred to as independent truck drivers) own the trucks that they drive and are the principal drivers in the provision of intermodal truck service.

The remainder of the paper is structured as follows. Section 2 discusses the deregulation of trucking and its impact on truck labor, followed by a discussion of intermodal trucking and ports in Section 3. Data and the empirical approach are discussed in Section 4, followed by presentations of the earnings and employment results of owner-operators in Sections 5 and 6, respectively. Conclusions are set forth in Section 7.

2. TRUCKING DEREGULATION AND LABOR

The demand for owner-operator as well as other truck drivers increased following trucking deregulation. The Motor Carrier Act of 1935 placed truck carriers, engaged in intercity, interstate for-hire truck services, under the economic regulatory authority of the Interstate Commerce Commission (ICC). By the early 1970s critics of ICC truck regulation noted waste and inefficiency, absence of competition and high rates in the industry.[11] By the late 1970s ICC administrative deregulation of the for-hire truck carrier industry was underway. In July 1980 Congress passed the Motor Carrier Act of 1980 (1980 MCA) which substantially reduced ICC regulation of the industry, accelerating ICC administrative deregulation. Entry restrictions were eased; contract carriers were permitted to hold common carrier certificates; and the discounting of rates was permitted within a zone of rate freedom.

Following passage of the 1980 MCA the number of trucking firms increased dramatically, more than doubling by 1988. New entrants in the truckload (TL) sector, due to ease of entry, account for most of this increase. The demand for TL truck drivers increased markedly. Owner-operator TL drivers benefitted disproportionately from trucking deregulation; their share of the trucking industry work force increased significantly (Hirsch & Macpherson, 1998). The number of truck carriers acting as brokers for TL truck service also increased dramatically. The broker negotiates a price per TL with the shipper and with the independent TL carrier, the difference in price being his/her commission. By using a broker, the owner-operator TL carrier avoids having to maintain an office and a sales force.

Compared to TL carriers, who are mostly nonunion, less-than-truckload (LTL) carriers are heavily unionized. Following trucking deregulation, union jobs and membership in the Teamster union (the primary union representing truck carriers) declined, while the size of the driver work force increased from 1.1 million in 1978 to 1.9 million by 1996 (Peoples, 1998). LTL carriers, though, remained heavily unionized following deregulation. The differing market structures of the LTL and TL sector helps explain the contrasting employment patterns of truck drivers. In contrast to the large number of relatively small competitors in the TL sector, the four-firm concentration ratio of LTL carriers actually increased following deregulation, due primarily to the barriers of entry associated with shipping operations in this sector of the trucking industry.[12] This increase in LTL market concentration enhances the ease of unions maintaining a relatively higher membership rate because of the low per worker cost of organizing an industry sector consisting of a few large carriers.

In addition to changing employment patterns in the trucking industry, trucking deregulation also influenced the ability of trucking carriers to pay high wages. Prior to deregulation, ICC entry and rate restrictions provided the opportunity for union truck drivers to share rents with carriers (Rose, 1987). For example, the Teamsters instituted a strategy of negotiating labor National Master Freight Agreements (NMFA) with carriers. NMFAs are determined by negotiation among the Teamsters and major for-hire carriers and usually sets the pattern for labor negotiations for other union carriers (Hirsch & Macpherson, 1998, p. 121). The strategy of negotiating the NMFA provides a whipsawing advantage to enable union members to share rents with trucking carriers. The decline in the overall percentage of union drivers in the trucking industry combined with the decline in carrier participation in NMFA has led to the erosion of bargaining power of trucking unions.[13] This erosion has in turn contributed to the decline in truck drivers wages following trucking deregulation. For instance, the 1982 NMFA contract froze wages for three years and established new work rules to make NMFA carriers more competitive with nonunion carriers. The 1985 NMFA included a two-tier wage structure, where new hires would start at 70% of scale and reach full scale in three years. The 1988 NMFA institutionalized Employee Stock Ownership Plans (ESOPs); when substituted for wage increases, the profit sharing plans resulted in wage cuts for employees of financially troubled carriers. The 1994 NMFA (expiring in 1998), preceded by a 24 day strike, the longest strike in the history of NMFAs, provided for modest wage increases; new hires would start at 75% of scale and reach full scale in two years (Belzer, 1995).[14] For the post-deregulation period, Talley (2001) found that the real hourly wage and weekly earnings of for-hire union truck drivers declined 15.8 and 16.0%, respectively, while the nonunion hourly wages and weekly earnings declined 11.1 and 12.4% respectively. Owner-operators also experienced declining earnings immediately following trucking deregulation, but not to the extent experienced by company drivers in the for-hire sector (Peoples & Peteraf, 1999).

3. INTERMODAL TRUCKING AND PORTS

Truck drivers who provide truck service to ports include: harbor drayage and over-the-road drivers. The former provides local truck service. For example, moving containers from (to) the port to (from) local distribution warehouses and railyards. Over-the-road drivers provide intercity truck service, such as, moving containers from (to) the port to (from) locations other than in the local area of the port. The form of payment for these two types of drivers differs markedly. For example, drayage truckers are typically paid by the number of trips, while over-the-road drivers are paid by the mileage incurred. Both types of drivers are usually owner-operators. Brokerage firms typically keep 25–30% of the freight revenue of harbor drayage service with the remainder going to owner-operators (Mongelluzzo, 2001).

The 1984 Act stimulated growth in container cargo, leading to an increase in demand for intermodal truck carriage and its work force. The increase in demand for intermodal truck drivers is expected to result in higher driver wages, all else held constant. However, the Act's door-to-door rate provision is expected to have a negative impact on driver wages. Specifically, it requires that the shipping line arrange for all transportation services for a shipment, often contracting for land transportation services. The large volume of containers handled by shipping lines enhances their bargaining position when negotiating truck rates; often resulting in rates lower than those that would be negotiated by individual shippers.

The earnings of intermodal truck drivers are also negatively affected by time-related and other costs imposed on them by ports and shipping lines. The higher costs when subtracted from trucking revenues result in lower driver earnings. For example, truck drivers often incur port congestion from waiting in lines. Consequently, harbor drayage drivers, who are paid by the trip, have their earnings reduced when long waits result in fewer port trips per day. Solutions for reducing the waiting time of truckers while in port include providing additional truck lanes, extending gate hours, establishing port reservation systems, and encouraging local warehouses and distribution centers to remain open longer hours. In 1999 the Port of Vancouver (Canada) agreed to pay harbor drayage truckers by the hour as opposed to the trip as a solution to the problem of lost trucker earnings while waiting in long lines at the port. In 2002 the California legislature passed a truck idling (the Lownthal) bill that stipulates a $250 fine on marine terminals for every truck that must wait in line for more than 30 minutes. However, fines may be avoided by terminals keeping their gates open 60–70 hours per week.

Owner-operators providing port services also face additional cost associated with hauling shipping containers. Containers and their (truck trailer) chassis are owned or leased by shipping lines. While in port, shipping lines are responsible for repair of defective chassis, e.g. brakes, lights and tires, and damaged containers. Once containers and their chassis have been turned over to a driver and have departed the port, the trucker is responsible for any highway fines that might occur. A trucker may not be aware of container and chassis defects – they may not have been reported or if reported, not repaired by the shipping line or his/her agent. Alternatively, a trucker may know of the defects but may accept the defective equipment and risk a fine to avoid losing the cargo or future cargoes to a competitor. If the trucker acknowledges the defects prior to departure, he/she will be delayed in port while repairs are made. In 2002 the California legislature passed a chassis roadability (the Romero) bill that makes marine terminals responsible for providing safe, roadworthy chassis to harbor truckers. Specifically, terminal operators must certify that the chassis they tender to truckers are roadworthy and pay any fines that truckers receive for operating defective chassis.

Similar chassis roadability legislation has been passed by South Carolina, Louisiana and Illinois and proposed in New Jersey, Pennsylvania, Florida, Virginia and Texas. The Intermodal Association of North America is also lobbying for a uniform national policy on equipment roadability. In 2003 the Teamsters plan to sponsor nationwide legislation similar to the California Romero and Lowenthal bills, as well as an overweight container bill, that would require that marine terminals weigh all inbound containers before tendering them to truckers – thereby addressing the issue of truckers paying overweight highway fines. Last, government legislation further limits owner-operators from easily matching the wage gains of unionized company drivers. As independent contractors, owner-operator truck drivers are prohibited under antitrust laws (in contrast to truck carrier employees) from forming collective-bargaining organizations. In 2001 the Teamsters and the dockworker unions, the International Longshoremen's Association (ILA) and the International Longshore and Warehouse Union (ILWU), agreed to form a national alliance to organize harbor truck drivers. The alliance seeks to persuade broker truck carriers to hire the estimated 50,000 nationwide harbor truck drivers as direct employees and lease the trucks from the drivers. If successful, the alliance will then have unionized the major links of intermodal maritime cargo movements – the vessel, the port, and local truck drayage – i.e. dockworkers working for shipping lines and stevedores, dockworkers working for ports, and truck drivers providing harbor drayage transportation.

In sum, a comparison of trucking and shipping post-deregulation labor market environments suggests the following employment and earnings patterns. Trucking deregulation facilitated major employment gains for nonunion drivers, and especially for owner-operators. In comparison, it is hypothesized that shipping deregulation promotes greater demand for owner-operators at major ports. Trucking deregulation affected drivers pay by substantially reducing the rent that carriers could share with company and owner-operator drivers. It is hypothesized that shipping deregulation should affect the earnings of port-city owner-operators. However, how such deregulation affects the earnings of these drivers is not obvious *a priori*. This uncertainty about shipping deregulation's earnings effect emphasizes the need for an empirical assessment of owner-operator earnings. In addition, an empirical test of the hypothesis on port-city owner-operator employment patterns is also important since such a test has yet to be undertaken.

4. DATA AND EMPIRICAL APPROACH

Information on individual truck drivers is taken from the 1973–1998 March Current Population Survey (CPS) files to empirically examine earnings and employment patterns of owner-operator truck drivers. These files report information on drivers' age, years of schooling, U.S. region of residence, industry of employment, occupation, race, gender, marital status, weeks worked per year and weekly hours worked. A limitation of the data is that the union status of truck drivers is not reported. However, owner-operators as independent contractors are prohibited from union membership.

Several benefits are associated with using the March CPS files to examine the earnings and employment of owner-operators. For instance, these files report MSA-FIPS (metropolitan) codes to identify drivers' place of residency which are then matched with port-city rankings (from the U.S. Army Corps of Engineers) to identify whether a driver resides near one of the fifty busiest U.S. ports.[15] The CPS files also identify whether a driver is an owner-operator or company driver and whether employed in the for-hire or private truck carriage sector. Owner-operators are self-employed truck drivers working in either the for-hire or the private truck carrier sector. Drivers reporting trucking as their employing industry are classified as working in the for-hire carriage sector, whereas drivers reporting non-trucking operations as their employing industry's primary business are classified as working in the private carriage sector. In this study, annual profits generated by owner-operators represent their annual salaries.[16] Among the sample population of 14,479 truck drivers listed in the 1973–1998 March CPS files, 967 are owner-operators.

Descriptive statistics of the CPS owner-operator data are presented in Table 1. The data are partitioned into three sample periods, depicting the major regulatory regimes faced by owner-operators. The 1973–1978 observation sample depicts the period of extensive rate and entry regulation of the truck carrier industry.[17] The 1979–1983 observation sample depicts the period of initial (administrative) trucking regulatory reform initiated by the Interstate Commerce Commission in 1979 and relaxation of rate and entry restrictions legislated by the U.S. Congress with passage of the 1980 MCA. Last, the 1984–1998 observation sample depicts the period of regulatory reform in both the trucking and ocean shipping industries, i.e. from passage of the 1980 MCA and the Shipping Act of 1984.[18] The latter impacted owner-operators via its impact on intermodal trucking.

Table 1. Owner-Operator Descriptive Statistics.

Variables	1973–1978		1979–1983		1984–1998	
	Port-City (1)	Others (2)	Port-City (3)	Others (4)	Port-City (5)	Others (6)
Mean salary of owner-operators (1983 dollars)	$18,138	$20,695	$14,000	$16,036	$17,973	$17,775
Percentage of owner-operators who are for-hire drivers	76.25%	89.79%	84.82%	81.35%	79.23%	78.75%
Percentage of owner-operators who are male	98.75%	100%	99.10%	98.30%	95.46%	95.55%
Percentage of owner-operators who work over 48 weeks annually	51.12%	67.34%	64.36%	66.66%	64.36%	73.50%
Mean weekly hours	40.06	47.85	42.25	44.26	44.61	48.78
Percentage of owner-operators who received a high school diploma	32.50%	34.69%	48.27%	40.01%	43.59%	39.37%
Regional residence percentage of owner-operators who reside in the following regions[a]						
North east	21.25%	10.20%	26.43%	4.40%	31.14%	20.76%
North central	22.50%	30.61%	17.24%	15.55%	21.10%	22.67%
South	20.0%	28.57%	16.09%	35.55%	28.37%	36.51%
Percentage of owner-operators who are married	82.50%	85.71%	78.16%	86.67%	71.28%	76.84%
Mean age of owner-operators	41.45	40.16	41.16	46.17	42.64	42.47
Percentage of owner-operators who are white	80.00%	87.75%	83.03%	86.67%	85.60%	88.88%
Percentage of owner-operators who are employed full-time	65.00%	83.67%	74.71%	75.55%	90.53%	92.59%
Number of observations	80	49	87	45	289	419

[a] The western U.S. quadrant depicts the benchmark regional residence location.

Table 1 reveals distinct profile differences between owner-operators of major port cities and owner-operators residing in other locations. A listing of these major ports is presented in the Appendix. The pre-deregulation findings in columns 1 and 2 indicate that in general the profile of port-city owner-operators is one that is not associated with relatively high earnings. For instance, port-city owner-operators worked fewer hours per week and fewer weeks per year compared to other owner-operators. In addition, port-city owner-operators were less likely than other owner-operators to be employed in the higher paying for-hire trucking industry. The only characteristic associated with higher earnings for port-city than for other owner-operators for the pre-deregulation period is residence in the northeast region of the U.S. Nonetheless, port-city owner-operators still earned annual salaries in 1983 dollars that were 14% less than other owner-operators. The higher annual salaries for the latter may reflect a compensating wage differential, i.e. a higher salary is paid to compensate these drivers for undesirable working conditions such as being away from home at night.

Truck post-deregulation statistics for the 1979–1983 sample observation period, found in columns 3 and 4 of Table 1, indicate that the relative profile differences between the two groups of owner-operators resemble the differences reported for the pre-deregulation period. The major profile changes are the much higher relative share of port-city owner-operators residing in the high wage northeast, and the slightly larger share of these drivers operating in the now relatively less lucrative for-hire sector.[19] While the disproportionate share of port-city owner-operators residing in the northeast might possibly contribute to improving their earnings relative to other owners, the significant decline in wage rates of for-hire truck drivers in the post-deregulation period (Hirsch, 1988; Rose, 1987) has reduced the earnings of port-city owner-operators. Indeed, the 1979–1983 mean port-city owner-operator earnings is 22.81% less than the pre-deregulation mean.

In contrast to the earnings results reported for the first two observation periods, the findings in columns 5 and 6 indicate that following shipping deregulation port-city owner-operators earned mean salaries that closely resemble that of owner-operators residing in other locations. This earnings result arises even though port-city owner-operators still work fewer hours per week and fewer weeks per year than other owner-operators. In addition, compared to other owner-operators, port-city owner-operators are no longer as overwhelmingly employed in the high wage northeast as was the case for the two previous regulatory regimes. For example, compared to owner-operators in other locations, port-city owner-operators are 2.1 and 6.007 times as likely to reside in the northeast for the 1973–1978 and 1979–1983 observation periods, respectively.[20] This ratio fell to 1.5 for the 1984–1990 observation period. Apparently, factors other than their worker profiles help contribute to the dramatic change in the relative earnings of port-city owner-operators following shipping deregulation.

Finding mean differences in the characteristics, regional residence, sectoral employment and working time among port-city owner-operators and owner-operators residing in other locations indicates the possibility of wage bias when using mean earnings to examine the influence of shipping deregulation on the annual earnings of owner-operators. We estimate the following earnings equation to address the bias that results from driver profiles differing among the two groups of owner-operators:

$$\begin{aligned}\text{Salary}_k = \beta_0 + \beta_1 X_k + \beta_2 \text{Dereg}_k + \beta_3 \text{PortCity}_k \\ + \beta_4 \text{Dereg}_k \times \text{PortCity}_k + \varepsilon_k \qquad (1)\end{aligned}$$

where k indexes individual owner-operators. The variable Salary denotes the annual earnings of owner-operators in 1983 dollars.[21] The vector X consists of individual driver information including age, age-squared, educational attainment, weeks worked per year, hours worked per week and dummy variables identifying marital status, race, sex, U.S. region of residence, employed full-time and driver employment in the for-hire or private carriage sector of the truck carrier industry. In addition, the annual national unemployment rate and motor fuel price are included as earnings determinants to control for time-variant distortions such as changes in the business cycle and changes in the cost of truck carrier operations.[22] The variable Dereg is a dummy depicting the observation period following shipping deregulation, equaling one if the observation year is 1984 or greater and zero if it is before 1984.[23] The variable PortCity is a dummy equaling one if an owner-operator resides in one of the fifty busiest U.S. port cities. The final variable presented in Eq. (1) is the interaction of the Dereg and PortCity dummies.

Two sample populations are used to estimate Eq. (1). Initially, the five year period immediately preceding shipping deregulation is excluded from the observation sample to focus on the comparison of port-city owner-operator earnings prior to trucking deregulation with those following shipping deregulation. The other sample population excludes the six year period immediately preceding trucking deregulation to focus on the comparison of port-city owner operator earnings immediately following trucking deregulation with their earnings immediately following shipping deregulation. In addition, separate earnings equations are estimated for each of the three regulatory regimes to attempt to distinguish among the effects of trucking and shipping deregulation on the relative earnings of port-city owner-operators.

The primary coefficients of interest are β_2, β_3, β_4, $\beta_2 + \beta_4$, and $\beta_3 + \beta_4$. The coefficient β_2 measures the shipping post-deregulation change in the earnings of owner-operators who do not reside in one of the fifty busiest port-cities.

The coefficient β_3 measures the shipping pre-deregulation earnings differential between port-city owner-operators and owner-operators residing in other locations. β_4 measures the change in the earnings differential of port-city owner-operators and owner-operators residing in other locations following shipping deregulation. $\beta_2 + \beta_4$ measures the shipping post-deregulation change in the earnings of port-city owner-operators. Last, $\beta_3 + \beta_4$ measures the shipping post-deregulation earnings differential between port-city owner-operators and owner-operators residing in other locations.

Trucking employment share equations are also estimated to examine whether shipping deregulation enhances the employment opportunities of port-city owner-operators compared to truck drivers residing in other localities. The specification of the employment share equation is depicted by Eq. (2):

$$\Pr(\text{owner-operator}_k = 1) = \phi\{\gamma_0 + \gamma_1 X_k + \gamma_2 \text{Dereg}_k + \gamma_3 \text{PortCity}_k + \gamma_4 \text{Dereg}_k \times \text{PortCity}_k + \upsilon_k\} \quad (2)$$

where ϕ is a normal probability function and owner-operator is a binary variable with a value of one if the driver is classified as an owner-operator and zero if the driver is classified as a company driver. The explanatory variables are the same as those used in the earnings equation. The coefficients of key interest are γ_2, γ_3, γ_4, $\gamma_2 + \gamma_4$, and $\gamma_3 + \gamma_4$. The coefficient γ_2 measures the marginal effect of shipping deregulation on the probability a non-port-city driver is an owner-operator rather than a company driver. The coefficient γ_3 measures the pre-deregulation probability differential that a port-city driver compared to a driver in other locations is an owner-operator rather than a company driver. The coefficient γ_4 measures the change in the port-city – non-port-city probability differential that a driver is an owner-operator rather than a company driver following shipping deregulation; $\gamma_2 + \gamma_4$ measures the shipping deregulation effect on the probability that a port-city driver is an owner-operator rather than a company driver; and $\gamma_3 + \gamma_4$ measures the post-deregulation probability differential that a port-city driver compared to a driver in other locations is an owner-operator rather than a company driver.

5. EARNINGS RESULTS

Column 1 of Table 2 presents the regression results from estimating Eq. (1). The findings on the control variables reveal two contrasting associations between owner-operator characteristics and earnings. For instance, the descriptive statistics reported in Table 1 show a disproportionate share of port-city owner-operators residing in the high wage northeast region of the U.S., which should enhance

Table 2. Owner-Operator Earnings Results.[a]

Explanatory Variables	Dependent Variable: Annual Earnings of Owner-Operators (1983 Dollars)				
	1973–1978, 1984–1998 (1)	1979–1998 (2)	1973–1978 (3)	1979–1983 (4)	1984–1998 (5)
Intercept	−22521 (−2.143)	−35390 (−2.835)	−92385 (−2.356)	−25199 (−0.843)	−18910 (−1.495)
For-hire driver	998.57 (0.743)	2111.70 (1.515)	−9228.13 (−1.764)	3690.27 (1.200)	1750.51 (1.149)
Male	9074.90 (2.849)	8121.77 (2.819)	2325.46 (1.076)	1702.55 (0.119)	7994.22 (2.672)
Working more than 48 weeks per year	4142.69 (3.054)	3951.58 (3.196)	4180.63 (0.902)	2633.39 (0.980)	4090.08 (2.890)
Weekly hours	140.65 (4.038)	160.83 (4.329)	130.44 (1.308)	−40.78 (−0.533)	191.25 (4.624)
High school diploma	−1468.39 (−1.186)	−308.06 (−0.269)	−8253.47 (−2.003)	−752.34 (−0.297)	−490.05 (−0.380)
Regional residence					
North east	830.82 (0.463)	463.015 (0.279)	4901.68 (0.859)	2042.88 (0.626)	134.69 (0.035)
North central	−963.53 (−0.533)	−720.78 (−0.424)	2561.90 (0.490)	4686.51 (1.415)	−1803.0 (−0.938)
South	−772.83 (−0.453)	−226.67 (−0.145)	71.99 (0.0128)	5019.67 (1.553)	−915.26 (−0.519)
National unemployment rate	−270.19 (−0.460)	26.64 (0.042)	−1590.65 (−0.786)	−314.44 (−0.343)	521.78 (0.613)
White	−2131.29 (−0.419)	2472.67 (1.472)	6217.67 (1.055)	6467.21 (1.944)	−1846.8 (−0.364)
Married	3396.27 (2.589)	2777.38 (2.067)	7703.97 (1.499)	6409.04 (2.191)	2516.53 (1.722)
Age	957.40 (3.188)	754.64 (2.385)	2388.19 (2.434)	981.39 (1.491)	670.62 (1.896)
Age-squared	−10.33 (−3.092)	−7.95 (−2.271)	−26.71 (−2.362)	−10.81 (−0.950)	−7.090 (−1.816)
Employed full-time	4261.91 (2.450)	41.02 (0.498)	4874.15 (0.498)	7582.37 (2.308)	5239.19 (2.301)
Dereg	−4729.41 (−1.753)	900.28 (0.247)	–	–	–
PortCity	−1578.59 (−0.571)	−3099.16 (−1.185)	−387.68 (−0.097)	−412.23 (−0.151)	2278.34 (1.733)
Dereg × PortCity	4870.35 (1.587)	5946.38 (2.651)	–	–	–
Fuel price	−72.73 (−0.669)	29.57 (0.359)	363.68 (0.731)	−35.12 (−0.232)	−84.48 (−0.892)
Number of observations	836	839	128	131	707
R^2 (%)	13.42	11.52	26.33	19.95	10.73
F-score	7.739	5.936	2.502	1.791	4.881

[a] *t*-Statistics are presented in parentheses.

the relative earnings of these drivers. However, the estimated coefficient on this variable presented in column 1 of Table 2 indicates that owner-operators residing in the northeast region of the U.S. do not receive statistically significantly higher earnings than owner-operators residing in other regions of the U.S.

A much different result is found when examining the earnings effect associated with port-city drivers working fewer weeks per year and fewer hours per week. The estimated coefficient on these variables is statistically significant. Information on the mean value of hours worked and the estimated coefficient on hours worked can be used to examine the extent to which relatively fewer hours worked for port-city owner-operators restricts their ability to enhance their relative earnings. Taking the product of the pre-deregulation mean of hours differential of −7.79 and the estimated coefficient on hours worked (140.65) gives a mean port-city owner-operator earnings discount of $1,081 per week. The post-deregulation finding on weekly hours shows how the smaller hours-worked differential for port-city owner-operators improves the chances of these drivers receiving higher relative weekly incomes following deregulation. Taking the product of the post-deregulation mean hours differential of 4.17 and the estimated coefficient on hours worked (140.65) gives a mean port-city owner-operator earnings discount of only $586 per week.

The finding on the estimated coefficients of the other control variables reported in column 1 of Table 2 suggest that these parameter estimates have signs that are consistent with labor theory on worker earnings. Owner-operator earnings are statistically significantly higher for older drivers, men, drivers employed full-time, and drivers who are married. Apparently, controlling for differences in owner-operator characteristics helps explain the pre-deregulation mean earnings differential presented in Table 1. The estimated coefficient on the PortCity variable indicates that port-city owner-operators receive an annual earnings discount that is not statistically significant from owner-operators residing in other locations for the 1973–1978 pre-deregulation period.

The estimated coefficient on the Dereg dummy suggests statistically significantly declining earnings for the shipping deregulation period for owner-operators who do not reside in one of the fifty busiest U.S. port cities. Real earnings for this group of drivers is $4,729 lower than in the 1973–1978 pre-deregulation observation period. Alternatively, the sum of the estimated coefficients on the Dereg × PortCity interaction term and the Dereg dummy suggests an insignificant increase in earnings of $141 for port-city owner-operators following shipping deregulation.[24] The sum of the estimated coefficients on the PortCity and Dereg × PortCity dummies suggest that following deregulation, port-city owner-operators received a $3,292 earnings premium above that of owner-operators residing in other locations.[25] Thus, the results suggest a relative increase in the earnings of port-city owner-operators following shipping deregulation. These results support the notion that shipping deregulation promotes a business environment that increases the relative earnings of port-city owner-operators.

The findings obtained from estimating Eq. (1) for the trucking and shipping post-deregulation observation periods are presented in column 2. The estimated coefficient on the Dereg dummy suggests that owner-operators who did not reside in the fifty busiest U.S. ports did not receive statistically significantly different earnings during the transition from trucking deregulation to additional deregulation in shipping. The real annual earnings for these drivers do not change significantly following shipping deregulation compared to the five year period immediately following trucking deregulation. In contrast, the real annual earnings of port-city owner-operators increased appreciably over the same period. For instance, the sum of the estimated coefficients on the Dereg × PortCity interaction dummy and the Dereg dummy suggests a $6,847 increase in the real annual earnings of port-city owner-operators following shipping deregulation.[26] This is in contrast to an earnings increase of $141 relative to the trucking pre-deregulation period.

Columns 3–5 of Table 2 contain results from estimating separate earnings equations for each regulatory regime. A particularly interesting result that arises from using these less restrictive specifications of the earnings equation is the absence of a significant trucking deregulation earnings effect. For example, the findings in column 4 indicate that the estimated coefficient on the PortCity dummy lacks statistical significance. The shipping post-deregulation findings in column 5 do reveal a non-trivial change in the relative earnings of port-city owner-operators. The estimated coefficient on the PortCity dummy in column 5 is positive and statistically significant. This finding which is consistent with the finding in column 2 suggests that the transition from trucking deregulation to one that includes shipping deregulation is characterized by port-city owner-operators receiving significantly higher earnings. Such a dramatic change in the earnings of port-city owner-operators suggests that the earnings effect of shipping deregulation is unique from that of trucking deregulation.

6. EMPLOYMENT RESULTS

Column 1 of Table 3 presents the probit driver employment results from estimating Eq. (2). The findings on the control variables reveal that trucking employment probabilities are possibly associated with trucking regulation and that anti-trust legislation that prohibits owner-operators from joining a union possibly places these drivers at an earnings disadvantage. For example, the estimated coefficient on the for-hire dummy is positive and statistically significant suggesting that,

Table 3. Owner-Operator Employment Results.

Explanatory Variables	Dependent Variable: Trucking Sector Identifier Equals one if Driver is an Owner-Operator and Zero if Driver is a Company Driver				
	1973–1978, 1984–1998 (1)	1979–1998 (2)	1973–1978 (3)	1979–1983 (4)	1984–1998 (5)
Intercept	–2.49 (–83.03)	–2.996 (–6.83)	–8.08 (–0.0001)	–7.769 (–0.00001)	–3.013 (–92.59)
For-hire driver	0.911 (102.80)	1.002 (118.82)	0.943 (81.44)	1.0385 (128.48)	0.853 (377.6)
For-hire × Dereg	–0.0718 (–0.5097)	–0.1627 (–2.522)	–	–	–
Male	–0.165 (–4.238)	–0.1999 (–3.86)	–0.219 (–0.197)	0.108 (0.101)	–0.190 (–3.419)
Working more than 48 weeks per year	–0.158 (–12.48)	–0.106 (–5.897)	–0.309 (–5.176)	–0.048 (–0.197)	–0.124 (–6.630)
Weekly hours	0.007 (28.59)	0.0075 (28.979)	0.007 (6.040)	0.002 (0.377)	0.0077 (25.30)
High school diploma	–0.072 (–3.341)	–0.025 (–0.4127)	–0.307 (–9.009)	–0.035 (–0.689)	0.025 (0.069)
Regional residence					
North east	0.0591 (1.332)	0.0831 (2.196)	–0.088 (–0.422)	–0.016 (–0.217)	0.091 (2.187)
North central	–0.015 (–0.094)	–0.0464 (–0.6477)	0.084 (0.437)	–0.133 (–1.888)	–0.037 (–0.336)
South	0.087 (3.086)	0.0784 (2.119)	0.179 (1.714)	0.0856 (0.502)	0.080 (1.069)
Married	0.0479 (1.104)	0.0763 (2.875)	–0.109 (–0.669)	0.198 (2.617)	0.065 (1.788)
Age	0.0142 (76.42)	0.0145 (77.612)	0.0113 (8.576)	0.0108 (6.834)	0.0152 (70.73)
National unemployment rate	0.004 (0.050)	0.0135 (0.404)	–0.070 (–1.850)	0.003 (0.009)	0.014 (0.249)
White	0.036 (0.412)	0.0653 (1.342)	–0.149 (–1.265)	0.0687 (1.215)	0.075 (0.303)
Employed full-time	–0.067 (–1.067)	–0.063 (–0.938)	–0.055 (–0.167)	–0.129 (–1.039)	–0.030 (–0.226)
Dereg	–0.0422 (–0.234)	0.211 (2.098)	–	–	–
PortCity	–0.1774 (–4.136)	0.0476 (0.2431)	–0.1909 (–3.488)	0.068 (0.4303)	0.0823 (3.52)
Dereg × PortCity	0.2638 (7.303)	0.0405 (0.1701)	–	–	–
Fuel price	0.001 (0.566)	0.0005 (0.0287)	0.014 (1.477)	0.0007 (0.027)	0.0009 (0.092)
Number of observations	11354	11408	2104	2158	9250
Log likelihood	–2627	–2622.67	–426.05	–416.45	–2234.3

Note: Asymptotic *t*-statistics are presented in parentheses.

ceteris paribus, compared to company drivers owner-operators were more likely to be employed in the for-hire carrier sector prior to trucking deregulation. Such an employment outcome is to be expected given the enforcement of truck regulation that severely restricted owner-operators from servicing the private carriage sector. The estimated coefficient on the For-hire × Dereg interaction dummy indicates that compared to company drivers the probability of owner-operators working in the for-hire carriers sector did not change significantly following shipping deregulation. This outcome is also consistent with past research indicating that the tradition of limited use of owner-operators continued even after legislation was passed to ease restrictions on the employment of these drivers in the private carriage sector (Peoples & Peteraf, 1999). The other statistically significant coefficients on the control variables suggest that compared to company drivers, owner-operators are likely to work more hours per week, to reside in the southern region of the U.S., to be older and to be women. The employment probability findings on owner-operators' hours is a labor market outcome that is less common when workers are represented by a union. The fact that owner-operators are prohibited from joining a union promotes a labor market environment that is conducive to them working longer hours. Typically unions negotiate lower hours and full-time positions for their members. The employment probability results of southern residency indicates greater employment opportunities for owner-operators in a region that has proven difficult for unions to organize, especially given the enactment of right-to-work laws in many southern states.[27] The results for older and female drivers possibly indicate that they prefer the independence and flexibility associated with operating their own truck.

The results in column 1 also indicate contrasting employment probability results for owner-operators across regulatory regimes. The estimated coefficient on PortCity indicates that the probability that an owner-operator resides near a port-city is statistically significantly less than the probability that a company driver resides near these locations in the pre-deregulation period. The estimated coefficient on the Dereg dummy indicates that the probability a non-port-city driver is an owner-operator rather than a company driver does not change significantly following deregulation. In contrast, the estimated coefficient on the Dereg × PortCity dummy indicates that the change in the port-city-non-port-city probability differential that a driver is an owner-operator rather than a company driver increases substantially following shipping deregulation. This shipping post-deregulation result is consistent with the notion that regulatory reform facilitated greater employment opportunities for owner-operators at port cities.

The findings derived from estimating Eq. (2) for the trucking and shipping post-deregulation periods are presented in column 2 of Table 3. The estimated coefficient on the PortCity dummy suggests that for the five year period immediately following trucking deregulation in 1978, the probability differential that a port-city driver compared to a driver in other locations is an owner-operator rather than a company driver is statistically insignificant. The estimated coefficient on the Dereg dummy indicates that compared to the five years immediately following trucking deregulation, the probability a non-port-city driver is an owner-operator rather than a company driver increases significantly following shipping deregulation. The estimated coefficient on the Dereg × PortCity dummy indicates that compared to the five years immediately following trucking deregulation, the change in the port-city-non-port-city probability differential that a driver is an owner-operator rather than a company driver is not statistically significant.

The estimated coefficient on the PortCity dummy in column 3 suggests a statistically significantly lower probability differential that a port-city driver compared to a driver in other locations is an owner-operator rather than a company driver driver. In contrast, the coefficient on the PortCity dummy in column 4 indicates that compared to company drivers the probability of a truck driver being an owner-operator is not significantly different for port-city drivers compared to drivers residing in other locations for the five year observation period immediately following trucking deregulation. The estimated coefficient on the PortCity variable in column 5, which is slightly larger than that reported in column 4 and statistically significant, suggests increased employment opportunities for port-city owner-operators in the shipping post-deregulation period.

7. CONCLUSION

The Shipping Act of 1984 authorized door-to-door rates for ocean transportation in U.S. trades, leaving the port-of-call to the container shipping line. The more cost efficient container shipping networks, lower rates (from cost savings passed onto shippers), and improvements in the quality of service that followed stimulated the growth in U.S. containerized cargo. The demand for port dockworkers and their wages increased in lockstep with these product market changes. Theory suggest that such economic growth at port cities should also facilitate greater demand for owner-operator truck drivers, since they are the primary truck drivers in the provision of intermodal truck service at ports. Economic theory, however, does not provide a definitive hypothesis on the expected impact of shipping deregulation on the wages of port-city owner-operators. For instance, the increase in demand for drivers is expected to result in higher owner-operator wages at port cities. Alternatively, the increase in the bargaining power of shipping lines in negotiating owner-operator truck rates attributed to the door-to-door rate provision of the 1984 Act may result in lower wages. Port congestion costs attributed to the growth in containerized cargo are also expected to have a negative impact on owner-operator wages.

An empirical investigation of the earnings of U.S. owner-operator truck drivers at port cities vs. other locations during shipping pre- and post-deregulation periods revealed that the wages of port-city owner-operators have increased in the shipping post-deregulation period. These wage increases are in sharp contrast to the decline in driver wages in the trucking industry that followed passage of the 1980 MCA. They suggest that the increase in port-city owner-operator wages from an increase in demand for owner-operators more than offsets any negative impacts on these wages from the enhanced bargaining power of shipping lines in negotiating truck rates and from port congestion. The investigation also revealed that the earnings of port-city owner-operators in the shipping post-deregulation period exceed those of other owner-operators.

An investigation of the employment shares of owner-operators at port cities vs. other locations during shipping pre- and post-deregulation periods reveals that a greater share of owner-operator drivers are employed at port cities in the shipping post-deregulation period. Hence, shipping deregulation has not only lead to an increase in the wages of owner-operators at port cities, but also an increase in their employment at these cities.

NOTES

1. Ocean transportation is especially important for U.S. trade, with 95% of its intercontinental commerce moving by ship (Staff, 2000).

2. In the United Kingdom, dock jobs fell from 80,000 in 1967 to 11,400 in 1986 (Chadwin, Pope & Talley, 1990). Even in recent years, significant losses have occurred. In the United Kingdom, port employment declined by 44% between 1989 and 1992. In France, work rule reforms, introduced in 1992, led to employment declines of up to 66% in six major ports. In Australia, waterfront reforms introduced in 1989 led to a 42% two-year reduction in stevedore labor.

3. For further discussion of ocean container shipping, see Talley (2000).

4. The U.S. Shipping Act of 1916 created the U.S. Shipping Board (renamed the Federal Maritime Commission in 1961) to have jurisdiction over common carriers by water operating in interstate or foreign commerce on the high seas and upon the Great Lakes (Locklin, 1972, p. 746), but not jurisdiction over inland waterways. The Act legalized shipping liner conference agreements by granting them immunity from anti-trust legislation.

5. Discussion of the Shipping Act of 1984 is found in Frankel (1986), Chadwin, Pope and Talley (1990), and Cassavant and Wilson (1991).

6. Liner conferences are shipping line cartels that provide scheduled vessel service over specific trade routes and collectively discuss and set rates, usually only port-to-port rates. Liner conferences have immunity from anti-trust legislation in most OECD (Organization for Economic Cooperation and Development) countries.

7. The "independent rate action" and the "intermodal rate-making" provisions of the Shipping Act of 1984 reduced the ability of U.S. liner conferences to set rates. The Ocean Shipping Reform Act of 1998 (which amended the 1984 Act and took effect May 1, 1999) reduced this ability even further and contributed to the further decline of conferences. Its "confidential contract" provision allows, for the first time, confidential one-on-one contracts by shipping lines, but not conferences, with their customers. Other major provisions of the Act include: (a) shippers remain subject to standard U.S. antitrust law and ocean carriers are still subject to Federal Maritime Commission (FMC) regulation; (b) individual carrier tariff-filing requirements with the FMC have been eliminated, but carriers are required to publish rates via the Internet or other media; (c) contracts must be filed with the FMC for agency oversight; and (d) ocean carriers engaged in confidential arrangements with big shippers must disclose contractual information regarding specific dock and port movements to longshore unions. Between May 1, 1999 and May 31, 2000, 46,035 new service contracts and 95,627 contract amendments were filed with the FMC. During 1999 the number of active conference agreements on file at the FMC dropped from 33 to 22.

8. Improved service quality was a direct result of quality demands included in service contracts.

9. For the ten year period 1986–1996, world containerized seaborne trade increased 158%, from 61.0 million TEUs in 1986 to 157.6 million TEUs in 1996 (Ocean Shipping Consultants, 1997). The demand for dockworkers increased, reducing dockworker surpluses, followed by a shortage of dockworkers at some ports; the growth of international trade over the Pacific Coast supported employment, security and compensation increases for longshore labor (Prince, 1998, p. 7A).

10. This reluctance is also attributed to increased port competition; ports fear that strikes may result in cargo shifting to a competitor.

11. Regulated truck carriers were restricted to hauling only those commodities for which they had the authority to do so which often resulted in their trucks running empty on return trips. The routes of regular route carriers were often not direct but circuitous, resulting in wasted fuel and operating inefficiencies. Although there were approximately 18,000 truck carriers under ICC regulation, there were generally only a few carriers serving particular city pairs. Rates were based on value of service and not necessarily on the costs incurred in providing the service.

12. Nebesky, McMullen and Lee (1995) conclude that, given the prevalence of competitive pricing behavior, increased industry concentration in the LTL market in the post-deregulation period does not imply anti-competitive performance. "The substantial reduction in the number of LTL carriers following regulatory reform in 1980 may reflect superior efficiency of surviving firms" Nebesky, McMullen and Lee (1995, p. 571).

13. In 1963 general freight truck carriers created the Trucking Employers Incorporated (TEI) to bargain with the Teamsters in negotiating the first NMFA. At its height TEI represented between 800 and 1,000 carriers; by the time of the 1994 NMFA negotiations, it represented only 23 carriers.

14. Unlike the 1994 NMFA, the tentative 1998 NMFA between the Teamsters union and management negotiators for LTL carriers was reached several weeks before the expiration of the current NMFA. The 1998 NMFA provided for an immediate $750 signing bonus for LTL Teamster workers, no wage increases in the first year, but wage increases of 35 cents per hour in each of the final four years of the contract, topping out at $19.86 an hour in 2003.

15. It should be noted that the MSA-FIPS code is not reported for all individuals in the survey. This sampling problem results in a substantial reduction of the sample population

of owner-operator drivers. The owner-operator sample size is 2,952 when the sample is not restricted to drivers reporting their msafips code. In addition to containers the fifty busiest U.S. ports may handle break-bulk and bulk-commodity cargoes.

16. The CPS does not report information on the salaries of the self-employed.

17. Except for the exclusion of the transport of a few agricultural commodities, owner-operators were restricted to servicing the for-hire sector of the truck carrier industry.

18. Court approval of the leasing of owner-operator service to private carriage carriers occurred the same year that maritime shipping faced deregulation.

19. Past research by Rose (1987) and Hirsch (1988) indicate a non-trivial erosion of for-hire premiums for truck drivers following regulatory reform in the truck carrier industry.

20. The substantially larger percentage of owner-operators residing in busy port-cities for the 1979–1983 might be due in part to sampling bias associated with restricting the sample to drivers who report their residency location.

21. Traditionally a semilogarithmic specification is used to specify earnings equations such that the dependent variable is the log of earnings. The use of self-employed drivers' annual profits as the measure of owner-operator earnings precludes taking the log of this annual earnings measure because owner-operators report annual losses and gains. Losses are reported as negative numbers.

22. Information on national unemployment rates and motor fuel prices are taken from the U.S. Economic Report to the President.

23. Estimates of a more restrictive specification of the earnings equation that pools data for the entire sample population were also derived to examine owner-operator earnings patterns over regulatory regimes. The results from these estimates, though, do differ slightly from the findings presented in Table 2. Chow-test results indicate that the estimated coefficients are not homogeneous over regimes. This lack of homogeneity helps to explain why the earnings results differ by earnings specification. For this reason the results from the less restrictive specifications are presented in Table 2.

24. The t-statistic calculated to test the hypothesis of significant earnings change for port-city owner-operators following shipping deregulation is 0.0607.

25. The t-statistic calculated to test the hypothesis of significant post deregulation earnings differentials between port-city and owner-operators in other locations is 2.648.

26. The t-statistic calculated to test the hypothesis of a significant increase in increase in real annual earnings of port-city owner-operators following shipping deregulation is 2.08.

27. Residency in the western U.S. is the benchmark comparison region. Hence, compared to company drivers, owner-operators are significantly more likely to live in the southern U.S. than in the western quadrant of the U.S. The estimated coefficient on the southern residency dummy is also larger than the estimated coefficient on the North East and North Central dummies, which suggests that compared to company drivers, owner-operators are more likely to reside in the southern U.S. than in other U.S. regions.

ACKNOWLEDGMENTS

The authors thank Hosne Mridha for her valuable research assistance. We are also grateful for the comments and suggestions of Martin Dresner.

REFERENCES

Belzer, M. H. (1995). Collective bargaining after deregulation: Do the teamsters still count. *Industrial and Labor Relations Review*, *48*, 636–655.

Cassavant, K. L., & Wilson, W. W. (1991). Shipper perspectives of the shipping act of 1984. *Transportation Quarterly*, *45*, 109–120.

Chadwin, M. L., Pope, J. A., & Talley, W. K. (1990). *Ocean container transportation: An operational perspective*. New York: Taylor and Francis.

Frankel, E. G. (1986). Economic and commercial implications of the U.S. shipping act of 1984. *Logistics and Transportation Review*, *22*, 99–114.

Hirsch, B. T. (1988). Trucking regulation, unionization, and labor earnings: 1973–1985. *Journal of Human Resources*, *23*, 296–319.

Hirsch, B. T., & Macpherson, D. A. (1998). Earnings and employment in trucking: Deregulating a naturally competitive industry. In: J. Peoples (Ed.), *Regulatory Reform and Labor Markets* (pp. 61–112). Boston, MA: Kluwer Academic Publishers.

Locklin, D. P. (1972). *Economics of transportation*. Homewood, IL: Richard D. Irwin.

Mongelluzzo, B. (2001, December). Teamsters target port drayage. *JOC WEEK*, *2*, 17–23, 31–32.

Nebesky, W., McMullen, B. S., & Lee, M.-K. (1995). Testing for market power in the U.S. motor carrier industry. *Review of Industrial Organization*, *10*, 559–576.

Ocean Shipping Consultants (1997). *Global container port demand and prospects*. Surrey, UK: Ocean Shipping Consultants.

Peoples, J. (1998). Deregulation and the labor market. *Journal of Economic Perspectives*, *12*, 111–130.

Peoples, J., & Peteraf, M. (1999). The effects of regulatory reform on company drivers and owner-operators in the for-hire and private sectors. *Transportation Journal*, *33*, 5–17.

Prince, T. (1998, August). The last labor giant. *Journal of Commerce*, *7A*.

Rose, N. L. (1987). Labor rent sharing and regulation: Evidence from the trucking industry. *Journal of Political Economy*, *95*, 1146–1178.

Staff (2000, May). Lesson for shipping. *Journal of Commerce*, *6*.

Talley, W. K. (2000). Ocean container shipping: Impacts of a technological improvement. *Journal of Economic Issues*, *34*, 933–948.

Talley, W. K. (2001). Wage differentials of transportation industries: Deregulation vs. Regulation. *Economic Inquiry*, *39*, 406–429.

Talley, W. K. (2002). Dockworker earnings, containerization and shipping deregulation. *Journal of Transport Economics and Policy*, *36*, 447–467.

Zarocostas, J. (1996, May). Port industry jobs worldwide continue to decline, study says. *Journal of Commerce*, *8B*.

APPENDIX

50 Busiest U.S. Ports: Ranked by Cargo Volume

South Louisiana, Louisiana
Houston, Texas
New York/New Jersey
New Orleans, Louisiana
Corpis Christi, Texas
Baton Rouge, Louisiana
Hampton Roads, Virginia
Plaqumines, Louisiana
Valdez, Alaska
Beaumount, Texas
Long Beach, California
Lake Charles, Louisiana
Tampa, Florida
Pittsburgh, Pennsylvania
Texas City, Texas
Mobile, Alabama
Philadelphia, Pennsylvania
Los Angeles, California
Duluth/Superior, Minnesota
Baltimore, Maryland
Saint Louis, Missouri
Portland, Oregon
Port Arthur, Texas
Freeport, Texas
Pascagoula, Mississippi
Chicago, Illinois
Huntington, West Virginia
Paulsboro, New Jersey
Marcus Hook, New Jersey
Seattle, Washington
Port Everglades, Florida
Boston, Massachusetts
Jacksonville, Florida
Detroit, Michigan
Richmond, California
Charleston, South Carolina
Cleveland, Ohio
Savannah, Georgia
Tacoma, Washington
Memphis, Tennessee
Ashtabula, Ohio
San Juan, Puerto Rico
Portland, Maine
Indiana Harbor, Indiana
Lorain, Ohio
Honolulu, Hawaii
Toledo, Ohio
Two Harbors, Minnesota
Cincinnati, Ohio
Anacorres, Washington

Source: U.S. Army Corps of Engineers, Navigation Data Center, 2000.

AUTHOR INDEX

SUBJECT INDEX